D0501522

FAMOUS CRIMES REVISITED

FAMOUS CRIMES REVISITED

FROM SACCO-VANZETTI TO O.J. SIMPSON

Including:
Lindbergh Kidnapping
Sam Sheppard
John F. Kennedy
Vincent Foster
JonBenet Ramsey

BY
DR. HENRY LEE
AND
DR. JERRY LABRIOLA

STRONG BOOKS

First printing

ISBN 1-928782-14-0

Library of Congress Card Number: 00-106181

Published in the United States by Strong Books, an imprint of Publishing Directions, LLC

The character, Sam Constant, is wholly fictional and any apparent resemblance to any person, alive or dead, is entirely coincidental.

Printed in the United States of America

CONTENTS

Editor's Notes

1. Dr. Henry Lee's participation throughout the book—whether through his thoughts, description of events, analysis of evidence or conversations with Sam Constant—is presented in **bold typeface**. All other text is presented in this typeface.

2. Sam Constant is a mythical character. He represents the sentiment of the times and appears throughout the book.

3. Source material in the public domain is listed in the bibliography but not necessarily in the Chapter Notes. This material includes testimony obtained from the official transcripts of court trials and from any official and semi-official documents or personal communications relating to the cases.

Acknowledgments

The authors extend heartfelt thanks to the
following people and organizations for their roles
in the production of this book.

To our publisher Brian Jud, editor Roberta Buland, the entire staff at Strong Books, especially Ellen Gregory and Nicki Hartonavich, and to Mike Valentino of Cambridge Literary Associates, for their expertise, understanding and cooperation.

To the Howard Whittemore Library, especially Laurie Bleickardt, and to the Rare Books and Manuscripts Department of the Boston City Library, for their research assistance.

To Anthony Paul, Marshall Robinson, George Wilson, Robert Hathaway and the staff of the Massachusetts State Police Firearms Laboratory for serving with Dr. Lee on the Select Committee on Sacco and Vanzetti.

To Lt. Nicholas Theodos and other members of the New Jersey State Police for providing information and photographs regarding the Lindbergh segment.

To Dr. Cyril Wecht and Dr. Gary Aguilar for providing information and photographs regarding the Kennedy assassination, and Dr. Vincent DiMaio for his assistance to Dr. Lee in the reexamination of evidence related to the case.

To Jim Clemente from the FBI and Elaine Pagliaro, Robert Mills, Michael Bourke, Edward Jachimowicz, Fung Cho Kwok, Carl Ladd, Virginia Maxwell, Deborah Messina, Robert O'Brien, Kiti Settachatgul, Carol Scherczinger, James Streeter, Kenneth Zercie and the other scientists at the Connecticut State Police Forensic Science Laboratory for their assistance in the Vincent Foster research.

To District Attorney Alex Hunter and Attorney Michael Kane of the Boulder County (CO) District Attorney's Office, as well as the Boulder Police Department for their assistance in the JonBenet Ramsey segment.

To Dr. Michael Baden, Dr. Barbara Wolfe, Dr. Jacob Loke,

Dr. Effie Chang and Margaret Lee for their help in the examination of evidence in the Simpson case. And to attorneys Barry Scheck, Peter Neufeld, Johnnie Cochran, Robert Shapiro, Gerald Uelmen, F. Lee Bailey and many others for their support and help during the investigation and trial.

To Major Timothy Palmbach and Sergeant Joseph Sudol of the Connecticut Division of Scientific Services; Dr.Howard Harris, Dean Tom Johnson, President Larry DeNardis and the faculty members and students of the University of New Haven; Sherry Lee, Dr. Stanley Lee, Lois Labriola, Attorney David Labriola, Al Grella, Dr. Mary Tse and Attorney Linda Kenney for their encouragement and guidance.

And to veteran publisher, Kent Carroll, for his valuable insights and advice.

To our wives, Margaret and Lois,
and to all law enforcement personnel
around the world.

Prologue

Long ago I had a vague inkling of a machine...
that shall travel indifferently in any direction of
Space and Time, as the driver determines.

The Time Machine by H. G. Wells
Robert Bentley, Inc.

What if the world's foremost forensic scientist could be transported back and forth in time at will, observing crime scene searches, examining crucial physical evidence, bearing witness to famous trials in American history and offering commentary on the proceedings as they occurred? Such a possibility would offer an immediacy to his thoughts on evidence gathering and analysis, and on whether or not justice had been fairly served.

By allowing Dr. Henry Lee to be an eyewitness to famous crimes—from Sacco-Vanzetti in the early twentieth century to O. J. Simpson near its end—the reader will witness the drama up close. Onstage, so to speak. Thus, the narrative is presented in the third person with analysis in the first person—through Dr. Lee's eyes. And although the time machine device is make-believe, as is the role of Sam Constant who represents the public opinion of the time, the facts of each case have not been changed

Some authors have approached these cases from either a political or sociological perspective. Our approach emphasizes another dimension, one tailored to the expertise of Dr. Lee: forensic science. Therefore, not only may our odysseys enlighten the readers, but also these forays into investigative criminology may serve as resource material for students of forensic science, aspiring and licensed attorneys and law enforcement personnel at all levels. Also included is an Appendix entitled, *Forensic Science: Past, Present and Future.*

No matter the perspective, however, why add yet another commentary to the generous collection of both learned and popular accounts of these crimes and trials? The answer lies in our belief that from Sacco-Vanzetti and its primitive investigative techniques to the O. J. Simpson saga with all its sophisticated forensic support, the same technical and judgmental errors have persisted: crime scene contamination, less-than-adequate evidence recognition and collection, suppression of evidence. And there is the lingering perception that mistakes of a different nature have shaded the outcome in each case, allowing external factors such as political beliefs or social issues to influence the legal debate. The danger to society rests in part with the question of miscarriage of justice and—of equal importance—with the legitimate questions any reader might ask, "Could this happen to me or my loved ones? Could we be found guilty of a crime based on our beliefs or on an imperfect system?"

Yet, if our presentation appears to be an indictment of the criminal justice system, it is unintentional. Nor is it just another book arguing the guilt or innocence of accused killers or the legacy of their cases. It is, rather, an attempt to show that the same forensic errors committed during a celebrated investigation and trial 80 years ago are still occurring today. It is likely that similar flaws have spanned the entire twentieth century. This book is thus offered as a cautionary story to current and future generations.

Jerry Labriola, M.D.

Section One
Sacco-Vanzetti

Players

Defendants. At the Plymouth trial: Bartolomeo Vanzetti, a fish
peddler
At the Dedham trial: Nicola Sacco, a shoe edger,
and Vanzetti

Presiding Judge. At both trials: Webster Thayer

Defense attorneys: At the Plymouth trial: John P. Vahey and
James M. Graham
At the Dedham trial: For Sacco, Fred H. Moore
For Vanzetti, Jeremiah McAnarney

Major players for the prosecution:
Michael E. Stewart, Police Chief of Bridgewater,
Massachusetts
A. Mitchell Palmer, Attorney General of the
United States
Frederick Katzmann, District Attorney
Alvan T. Fuller, Governor of Massachusetts
Abbott Lawrence Lowell, President of Harvard
University

Chronology

1919   Spring: Sacco and Vanzetti move to Mexico to avoid military draft. Sacco returns in three months, Vanzetti in a year.

June: Widespread outbreak of bombings across country. U.S. Attorney General Palmer's house damaged.

November 22: Buick stolen in Needham, Massachusetts.

December 22: Theft of license plates used in Bridgewater, Massachusetts, crime.

December 24: Bungled holdup in Bridgewater.

1920   January: Theft of license plates used in South Braintree, Massachusetts, crime.

April 15: Murders and robbery in South Braintree.

April 17: Buick found in Manley Woods, West Bridgewater.

April 20: Michael Boda, an alien anarchist, interviewed by police.

May 3: Death of Andrea Salsedo in New York City.

May 5: Sacco, Vanzetti, Boda and Ricardo Orciani visit Johnson garage and house.

June 11: Vanzetti indicted for Bridgewater holdup.

June 22 to July 1: Vanzetti trial at Plymouth, Massachusetts. Verdict of guilty.

August 16: Vanzetti sentenced to 12 to 15 years in prison.

September 11: Sacco and Vanzetti indicted for South Braintree murders.

1921   May 31 to July 14: Trial of Sacco and Vanzetti at Dedham, Massachusetts. Verdict of guilty.

1924   October 1: Judge Thayer denies all five motions for new trial.

1927   April 9: Judge Thayer imposes sentences of death by electrocution.

August 23: Sacco and Vanzetti executed.

Key Locations in Massachusetts

Bridgewater
12/24/1919   Holdup attempt

Plymouth
6/22 to 7/1/1920   Vanzetti trial

South Braintree
4/15/1920   Armed robbery and double murder

Dedham
5/31 to 7/14/1921   Sacco and Vanzetti trial

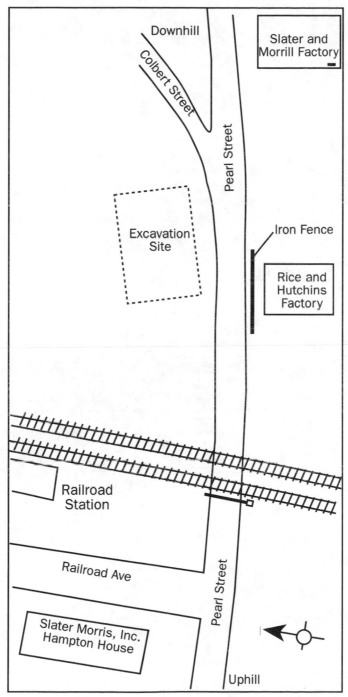

Map of crime scene area in South Braintree.

Chapter 1

<u>Historical Summary</u>

Most people have never heard of Nicola Sacco and Bartolomeo Vanzetti. They were Italian anarchists charged with the 1920 killing of a shoe factory paymaster and his guard in South Braintree, Massachusetts. Their controversial trial is universally included among America's most famous not only because of issues of ethnicity, draft evasion, radicalism and an arguably bigoted judicial system, but also because of the passion of the times. In the eyes of many, never in American legal history has public apprehension so shaped the outcome of a trial; never has one been conducted under such a shadow of ethnic hatred and political panic. And thrust in the middle of this landscape were two admitted radicals who embodied the twin threats of an unwelcome foreign element preaching a foreign political view.

World War I had just ended and political change was rampant abroad. The Bolsheviks had finally gained a foothold in Russia, a man named Hitler was advocating an anti-Semitic policy in Germany, the Austro-Hungarian Empire had been decimated, and the entire world appeared engulfed in a surging sea of socialism.

At home in America, an ailing Woodrow Wilson was president but would soon be succeeded by Warren Harding. Prohibition was in full force, sparking the boom of speakeasies, and F. Scott Fitzgerald wrote, "The uncertainties of 1919 were over. America was going on the greatest, gaudiest spree in history."[1] Outwardly, there was little doubt that the country's mood and its aspirations were changing. The start of the decade found its youth turning into social desperadoes: daring, hard drinking and cynical. Men mocked authority and flaunted their recklessness. Women's skirts were shorter while silk stockings and bobbed hair replaced hobble skirts and flowing tresses. Those were the days of "giggle water" and "the cat's meow," when a loaf of bread cost a dime and a pound of flour sold for less. People were caught up in Al Jolson, the Charleston and jazz, and they cheered wildly over Jack Dempsey in the boxing ring and Babe Ruth in the ballpark. All this was the veneer.

For in the face of the *Red Scare* or the rise of communism, the inner mood of the country was decidedly fearful. Unlike the Vietnam war nearly a half-century later, World War I was a popular conflict as Americans had rallied around Wilson's declaration that, "The world must be made safe for democracy."[2] Almost anyone who opposed the war, therefore, was looked upon with contempt.

Despite the finality of execution, this case has never achieved closure for it was cast from the beginning into a smoldering cauldron of judicial, scientific, political and social dispute. To this day, some people believe the trial and its aftermath—six years of legal wrangling—was a travesty of judicial procedure. They feel the defendants were framed, that forensic evidence may have been tampered with and that the police investigation was slipshod at best.

It is principally for this last contention that we begin our book with Sacco-Vanzetti, a four-generation-old case that in many ways might be considered a prototype—the forerunner of other cases in the twentieth century whose conduct merits the slipshod label.

The clock registered two-twenty and it was dark outside the window of my den. I leaned back in an easy chair, books and assorted papers about Sacco and Vanzetti strewn about the floor. The public wanted to reexamine the case and my consultation had been requested.

Eyelids weighted, I made a last conscious effort to keep from drifting off to sleep whereupon I discovered myself on a park bench in Dedham, Massachusetts, on May 30, 1920, the day before the trial was to begin. Was it a dream that whisked me back in time and space or a mechanism based on an

Einstein theory? I was as certain of the outcome of the case as other celebrated cases that followed for I had journeyed there in the year 2000 and had already witnessed the march of history. Yet, there was this nagging feeling that the Sacco-Vanzetti case might not turn out as history had recorded it, and I was anxious to observe the events firsthand.

The park, wedged between a granite courthouse and a white wood-framed church, appeared small beneath a thick fog, the kind you can touch. I could make out faint outlines of empty benches around me and could hear pigeons, their feeble cries drowned out by flutter.

Without warning, without even the slightest hint of footsteps, I felt the bench move at my right and, first shifting my eyes, then my head, beheld a man sitting an arm's length away. He looked to be a foot taller than I, angular, fair-skinned and smiling. He appeared about my age—in his sixties anyway— and wore a silk shirt with vertical blue and white stripes. In the several seconds our eyes met, his broad smile never left

"Hello," I said, extending my hand, "I'm Henry Lee, and you are?"

"How do you do?" he answered in a basso voice that belied his frame. "My name is Sam Constant." His handshake was firmer than most.

I studied his face. He appeared unreal and I almost told him so. Instead I settled for, "Where do you live?"

"Here and there—in and out," he replied.

"You live in and out?"

"Certainly. In and out of people's minds. Toss in hearts and souls, if you like." Sam locked his hands behind his head. "And I suppose you've come for the trial? For those ... radical immigrants."

I was hesitant in responding defensively: "I'm an immigrant myself, you know."

"I can see that. So you're on their side?"

"Neither side, my friend. I'm just here to observe."

For a moment I looked down at the packed gravel beneath my shoes, considering whether I'd possibly learn something tomorrow. I heard a clicking sound and looked back up. Sam had vanished.

Now what was that all about? He's in people's minds? Or just mine? It wasn't easy but I forced myself to dismiss Sam and to sit there for awhile to ponder the trial along with what I remembered of the accused and their lives on two continents.

Background and Bombings

In some fictional stories, *setting* is stressed more than in others. Its purpose is to set the stage for the drama to follow, to anchor it in time and place. But only infrequently will such a design drive the action or otherwise influence it. Not so in the nonfictional saga of Sacco-Vanzetti. Rarely has a confluence of events—the Russian Revolution, the armistice, Red hysteria, patriotism, journalism's focus on gangsterism—played on the emotions of an era's average citizen and on its movers and shakers alike: politicians, educators, the clergy and all tiers of the criminal justice system. Like an unwanted foreign substance introduced into the bloodstream, Nicola Sacco and Bartolomeo Vanzetti happened upon the national scene at the wrong time.

The Attorney General of the United States, A. Mitchell Palmer, didn't help in this regard, issuing statements to a war-weary nation, warning it of the danger of communism, socialism and any radical movement in general. In late 1919, he referred to adherents of any radical movement as potential murderers, and to their cause as criminal. Nor did Webster Thayer, the presiding trial judge, help in his charge to prospective jurors when he likened their uncoming service to that of patriotic servicemen who had served abroad in the war.

Taken as free-standing sentiments, one cannot argue against the merits of the first with the exception of, perhaps, the link to murder. Or the call to patriotism in the second. Expressed at a time when foreign migration and radical thinking were looked upon with disdain, however, these men had reinforced prevalent attitudes and, in so doing, had reduced Sacco and Vanzetti to a level of murderous invaders even before the trial started. National chauvinism was at an inflammatory pitch as the trial date approached. Strangely, the day after Memorial Day!

I wonder whether words like these created an early bias against the defendants and whether such words, alone, would have rendered the case appealable by today's standards. But I do remember reading that Attorney General Palmer's house had been bombed, presumably by the types he was criticizing. Under these circumstances, wouldn't I have said the same things?

The Palmer bombing was only one in a string of violent acts committed against government officials in 1919 and 1920. They occurred singly and in clusters; locally, regionally and nationally. Bombs even arrived at homes through the mail. One might speculate whether these events would have happened had not Mitchell Palmer aspired to the presidency. As President Wilson's attorney general, Palmer chose to use the "Red Menace" to make a mark for himself. The war against Germany had been won and Palmer decided pro-Germans were no longer dangerous, so he turned to socialist sympathizers as his new target, whipping up a "hundred per cent Americanism" frenzy coast to coast. Even as early as 1918, he had begun his campaign as thousands of arrests and hundreds of deportations took place.

Later, once the Sacco-Vanzetti case began to make news, Palmer concentrated his efforts on New England. In April 1920, at about the time of the Massachusetts murders, Wilson urged his attorney general not to burden the country with talk and action centered about the *Red Scare*. But it was already too late. Since the turn of the decade, Palmer had engineered raids on homes and union headquarters. On a single night in January 1920, he had 4,000 alleged communists arrested in 33 cities, the majority of whom had no connection to radicalism of any kind. Hundreds were seized on trumped-up charges, detained in jails and not fed, later to be found innocent of illegal plots.

All this fueled the activities of peddlers of hate, of those advocating anti-Semitism and anti-Catholicism such as the Ku Klux Klan. The result was that hatemonger and pro-American fever combined to produce increasingly more nasty groups who gained influence beneath a cloud of national distrust.

But not only were communists and socialists targeted; avowed anarchists and those leaning toward anarchy were included as well. At the time, the popular image of an anarchist was a bomb-throwing Italian who was hellbent on overthrowing the government. In reality, anarchists favored self-government of small social units, and many Italian immigrants—because of the political conditions in their homeland—were drawn to this concept. The leading figure in the anarchist movement in the United States was Luigi Galleani, a dynamic speaker who commanded the respect of thousands of followers including Sacco and Vanzetti.

The times shook with anti-this and anti-that. Some things never change. Where did Sam go, anyway? I would have liked to hear his opinion.

Sacco and Vanzetti emigrated to the United States in 1908 but did not meet until 1917, the year the country entered the Great War and, from that point on, they would forge an alliance that would carry them to their graves.

Their roots were at opposite ends of Italy: Sacco's in the south, Vanzetti's in the north. Both came from farming families and grew up in comfortable circumstances, but they left to seek opportunity and adventure in a democratic republic, far from the feudal society of their homeland.

Although Sacco had dropped out of school after the third grade, he was literate in Italian when he arrived in America. As a youngster, he enjoyed helping in his father's vineyard, orchard and vegetable gardens. He was a hard worker and considered cheerful, even jovial. His mother once said that hard work would always bring a smile to his face.

His father was a republican, his older brother a socialist, but neither appeared to have stirred any serious political thinking in the boy. However, after early experiences and associations in America, a hard left philosophy was to take form. This included changing views about religion as, over the years, he passed from a belief in God, through mounting skepticism and finally to atheism. The same was true of Vanzetti.

Some of Vanzetti's writings depict a deep respect for God especially during his early teens, a time when two circumstances shaped his thought. One was brought about by his father who stated unequivocally that formal education would be a waste of time for his son. He insisted on a trade. Over a six-year span, therefore, he apprenticed the boy to several owners of pastry and bakery shops located far from home. Vanzetti worked 15 to 18 hours a day and hated every minute of it. The other circumstance was a prolonged bout with pleurisy. Bedridden, Vanzetti began to read as never before, especially the works of St. Augustine. One line would become his favorite: "The blood of martyrs is the seed of liberty."[3]

Seeds had been planted. Those half-dozen years were spent journeying alone, and they afforded little shelter to a steady onslaught of ideas from casual acquaintances who called themselves socialists. Vanzetti appeared fascinated by their doctrines which were later to structure his life and prove to be incendiary in the United States.

It was as if an austere father plus Vanzetti's illness drove him to the extremes of bitterness and intellectual rebellion. He'd been deprived, after all, of friends, schooling and his mother's tangible love. This at a time when he was tired, depressed and subjected to a new philosophy that appeared to offer hope.

As for Sacco, his upbringing was more stable, but I can see that his future radicalism, though having a later onset, was just as intense.

When Sacco departed for the United States in 1908, he was 17, three years younger than Vanzetti who sailed two months later. They were short, dark men, one clean-shaven (Sacco), the other sporting a large, bushy mustache. Sacco lived in Milford, Massachusetts. He eventually married, had two children and worked as a shoe edger. He read little and, though quiet and polite, was considered excitable. Vanzetti, on the other hand, was calm and thoughtful. He was a voracious reader and often wrote flowery, idyllic passages about nature, human frailties and philosophy.[4] A bachelor, he at first moved around a great deal in New York, Connecticut and Massachusetts, working as an unskilled laborer. He finally settled in Plymouth, Massachusetts, as a fish peddler.

Later that morning, I headed for my flat two blocks away. A flat! That I would have one was as mysterious as the supplies and changes of clothes I knew awaited me there. And even my knowledge of its address—a mere block behind the courthouse—was amazing. I hadn't arrived there yet but, in my mind's eye, could picture it as a one-story structure whose red brick matched that of the adjacent public library. Its location, shielded on one side by the library and, on the other, by an enclave of simple homes, would be a virtual sanctuary for rest, study and meditation near the heart of downtown.

The fog had burned off, lifting the filter for rays of sun more common to August than April. I took off my light windbreaker and shielded my eyes in the direction of a voice bellowing from the street corner ahead.

"Dr. Lee. I thought you'd come here sooner or later." Sam stood leaning against a lamppost, a toothpick in his mouth. As I approached, he looked reedier and taller than before—his legs seemed to shoot out from his chest. He wore the same striped shirt, and shiny black pants enclosed his lower body.

"You know my address?" I asked

"Certainly."

Sam flicked the toothpick to the pavement and straight-

ened. "I'd guess you've been thinking about tomorrow and the days after that," he said, "and about what's in store for those aliens to the States." The angles of his mouth had drooped, his face now a dark, fierce mask.

I regarded him sternly before saying, "Sam, look, with all due respect—and I'm not implying either guilt or innocence, believe me—but how can they possibly receive a fair trial?"

No hesitation. "Are you kidding? Are they foreigners?"

I answered as quickly. "Yes."

"Are they radicals?"

"Yes."

"And they'd just as soon replace *my* government with one of their own?"

"I don't know. Maybe."

"Then where's the doubt? Why even have a trial?"

"Because that's the American way."

"So am I."

His stare stunned me into a momentary silence before I reverted back to a subject that had bothered me since morning.

"Look," I said, "can anybody else see you?"

Sam's face softened and he paused before answering. "I was waiting for you to ask me that. The answer is anybody and everybody, if they want to. Only one person at a time, though—I hate crowds. But I can spread myself around a pretty good size population in a few days, sometimes quicker— you know, like wildfire. Depends on my mood, or on what I hope to accomplish."

I was beginning to get the picture. Public opinion incarnate.

I gave Sam a dose of my own stare, one that begged the question of his remarkable admission. Then with a smug lifting of his chin, he clicked out of sight like a television picture gone dead. As I caught my breath, I imagined there would be many more disappearing acts in the weeks ahead.

I reached my brick "home" and, as if expecting me, an elderly woman, bent over in a black shawl, greeted me at a side door. She identified herself as the landlady. The rest of her words were indistinct, but she uttered them pleasantly as she led me down a hall where she unlocked the last door and handed me the key. She turned and shuffled away.

Inside, the one-room flat was furnished with a basic desk, dresser, cot, table, chairs and lamps, much like my apartment in midtown New York when I first arrived in the United States in 1965. In a single closet, I discovered clothes from my Connecticut home and on the desk were my briefcase along with some of my books and papers. Even my big magnifying glass! Someone had thought of everything. Next to it was a sheet of music penned by Irving Berlin and dated 1917. The title was *God Bless America*. Scrawled in the margin were the words, "Welcome to Dedham, Dr. Lee." It was signed, "Sam Constant."

I sat heavily on the edge of the cot thinking about Mr. Public Opinion and his points of view and whether or not he'd be at the trial the following day. I rationalized that if I could participate in a regression in actual time, then anything else was possible. Therefore, in my own mind (Was it totally mine any more?), I accepted the fact that Sam went with the territory—with the whole time defying experience. So I shifted my attention to my readings about Sacco and Vanzetti after they arrived on American soil: the marriage of their rebellious leanings and the forces that played upon them for a decade or more.

Politically, neither man was a radical when he left Italy, but over the next several years each was sharply influenced by what he heard and observed. Poverty, squalor and prejudice swayed them both, Sacco lamenting social injustice toward foreigners in general and Italians in particular.

What other factors spawned their attraction to an anarchistic philosophy? The friendships they forged among like-minded immigrants gave them solidarity in the face of taunts and rejection. Recent arrivals fed off each other and, in the process, repudiated anything that resembled the "American Way," especially business, government and the military. This new segment of the population drifted farther and farther away from mainstream political and economic thinking and was left vulnerable to any strong alternative voice. Such a voice belonged to Luigi Galleani who, with his passion, eloquence and charisma, was the champion of the anarchist cause in the United States. Thousands flocked to his lectures and read his paper, *Cronaca Sovversiva* (Subversive Chronicle), Sacco and Vanzetti among them, and for most, it didn't take long for a metamorphosis to occur—from uneducated greenhorns to philosophical anarchists.

Both followed the teachings of their new leader with fundamentalist reverence. They attended meetings, distributed literature, participated in strikes and helped raise funds for the strikers' families. As an itinerant fish peddler, Vanzetti circulated leaflets fomenting an idealistic revolution which scholars have called "noble nonsense." At the same time, Sacco was quick to inform any willing listener that all big governments should be overthrown by the force of ideas, not bombings. It was in the course of such activity that Sacco and Vanzetti first met on a picket line in 1917.

When World War I broke out, both men fled to Mexico along with some of their friends. They had often spoken openly about their opposition to all wars. The flight from the United States was an incompletely understood chapter in their story, yet was one of the compelling issues of the trial. They mistakenly feared the draft because as aliens, they were not subject to it. Of even more significance, however, was their fear of deportation for they knew that under the Immigration Act of 1917, they could be deported for their anarchist activities.

Homesick, Sacco returned to the United States within a few months. Vanzetti stayed behind until the armistice. The question of deportation was not mentioned at the trial or the appeals in order to protect their friends and the escape route via Mexico. Such a route allowed them to return to Italy, if they desired, rather than to exile.

Publicly, Sacco and Vanzetti maintained their flight was made not to avoid military service per se but to support Galleani's claim that wars enhance the fortune of capitalists at the expense of the working class.

Up to this point, my impression was that their experiences had shaped their beliefs, and certain questions should be asked. Would they have become radicals had they remained in Italy? In the United States, had they truly become hardened subversives or merely idealistic rebels, groping through webs spun by Galleani and other authoritative figures? Many radicals of that period adopted labels interchangeably because they didn't know what they meant—anarchist, Bolshevik, Red, socialist, Industrial Workers of the World. Nonetheless, this phase of the story was less clear in my mind than the one about to unfold, a drama whose outcome hinged on the veracity of certain details submitted in the subsequent trial. Truths? Distortions? Lies? And I remember chewing on each of those items when I was called into the case decades later, having gathered most of my information from books, newpaper accounts, conversations with colleagues and a careful review of evidence and the official transcript. One thing is certain: I'm first and foremost a scientist and it was in that capacity that I was consulted and that I offered my interpretation of the body of evidence that was presented to me. I was not a member of the jury so I did not then, nor do I now, render a verdict of guilt or innocence.

Chapter 2

The Crimes and Arrests

Although a botched robbery in a small New England town on the day before Christmas would ordinarily have been classified as a run-of-the-mill holdup attempt, it was to assume greater significance in light of the celebrated murders four months later in a shoe manufacturing town 14 miles away.

Bridgewater, Massachusetts
December 24, 1919

It was a snowy, biting morning. A Ford truck inched along an ice-encrusted road from the Bridgewater Trust Company toward the main office of the L.Q. White Shoe Company. On board were its driver, Earl Graves; a paymaster, Alfred E. Cox, Jr.; a local constable, Benjamin F. Bowles; and a payroll of $33,000.

Three men leaped from a parked car, screaming for the truck to come to a stop. When it didn't, they opened fire. One man, a heavily mustached individual, brandished a shotgun; the other two, pistols. The constable returned fire and in the brief but frenzied exchange, the driver lost control of the truck which skidded into a telephone pole. Evidently, the bandits became distracted by this and an oncoming streetcar, lost their nerve and scampered back into the car which sped away. An eyewitness, Dr. J.M. Murphy, picked up a spent shotgun shell at the scene and put it in his pocket. For the moment, the crime was not considered particularly noteworthy and therefore was filed.

Then four months later a more dramatic, deadly crime was to take place.

<u>South Braintree, Massachusetts</u>
<u>April 15, 1920</u>

At 3 p.m., on a cold, damp Thursday, Frederick A. Parmenter, the fortyish paymaster for the Slater and Morrill Shoe Factories, and his guard, Alessandro Berardelli, emerged from the company's administration building at the upper end of Pearl Street and headed down the incline toward its three-story plant some 200 yards away. They carried two steel boxes containing that week's payroll of $15,773. Berardelli, 28, also carried a .38 Harrington & Richardson revolver.

Parmenter nodded toward gate tender Michael Levangie as the pair neared his shanty at a railroad crossing. They stepped over the tracks which split the road, passed a water tower and an excavation site and, 50 yards into their journey, drew abreast of two men leaning against a metal fence in front of the Rice and Hutchins Factory. One wore a felt hat, the other a cap. The man in the felt hat spoke briefly to Berardelli, then grabbed at his shoulder. Shots rang out, the stench of gunpowder saturating the air. It was uncertain how many shots were fired but, by most accounts, Berardelli was hit by the initial shot, dropped to his knees, then took two more rounds. One of the attackers bent over the dying guard and snatched his revolver. Parmenter, hanging onto his box, tried to flee but was shot twice and died 14 hours later. During the melee, a cap had fallen to the ground.

A signal shot was fired and a seven-seater Buick—its driver, described as a pale and sickly man and a front-seat passenger, characterized as dark and foreign-looking—pulled up from the vicinity of the lower factory. Scrambling toward the car, the two assailants turned momentarily to scatter several shots at workers peering from the factory windows. Some 30 workers at the excavation site dove for cover as lead whined off a nearby brick pile. The two men gathered up the payroll boxes and piled into the Buick as did a third who had been hiding behind the bricks. Meanwhile, Berardelli had managed to lift himself to his knees only to be shot again by one of the men who sprang from the car.

The shiny car sputtered up Pearl Street, its front-seat

passenger firing at random out the windows. At the railroad crossing, the tender lowered the gates but one of the bandits, waving a pistol, shouted they would shoot if he didn't raise them. The tender obliged and the Buick sped away as one of its occupants tossed tacks onto the street to puncture the tires of any car that might try to follow.

Here's where it's important to keep the chronology straight because it's tricky.

Before the first crime, a Buick touring car had been reported stolen. It was later believed to be the same one used in that crime and in the South Braintree robbery and murders four months later. The thefts of two separate sets of license plates occurred on December 22, 1919, and on January 6, 1920. Was all this the work of political and social malcontents or of professional criminals?

The Bridgewater assault took place on December 24, 1919. The South Braintree robbery and murders occurred April 15, 1920 for which Sacco and Vanzetti were arrested on May 5. Then Vanzetti was indicted on June 11 for the attempted Bridgewater holdup *after* his and Sacco's arrest for the South Braintree murders. But to understand the circumstances surrounding the arrests, a sequence of events featuring three low-level but key anarchists must be examined.

Boda, Coacci and Salsedo

Michael Stewart, Bridgewater's police chief, determined that the bandits in his hometown were radicals seeking to replenish their coffers. Since they had been described as dark and foreign and had driven either a Buick or a Hudson Overland, he centered the investigation on one Michael Boda, an Italian who drove an Overland. Boda and Feruchio Coacci, both known anarchists, shared a house in nearby West Bridgewater.

On April 16, the day after the South Braintree murders, Stewart was asked by the Justice Department, then engaged in the wholesale rounding up of Reds, to check on Coacci who was supposed to have reported the day before for a deportation hearing. He had failed to appear, claiming his wife was ill.

When Stewart arrived at the Coacci house, Coacci was found anxiously packing a trunk. He was taken into custody and turned over to immigration officials.

Meanwhile, Boda's car was awaiting repairs in a garage owned by Simon Johnson. Chief Stewart who, up to this point had been focusing on the solution to the bungled Bridgewater crime, suddenly shifted gears and entertained the theory that both that crime and the one at South Braintree were the work of the same men. He reasoned that Coacci didn't show up for deportation proceedings on April 15 because he and his cronies were committing murder and robbery in South Braintree, and that whoever called for Boda's car at Johnson's garage would be suspect of the crimes at both locations. Stewart instructed Johnson to telephone the police if and when anybody called for the car.

After a two-week lull in the investigation, Andrea Salsedo, another one of Boda's radical friends, who was being held incommunicado on the fourteenth floor of the Department of Justice offices in New York City, fell to his death. Boda was convinced Salsedo was pushed out of a window by the investigators. Fearing for their own safety, Boda and his pals wanted to act swiftly to hide their anarchist literature and warn friends, and the car would be required for both purposes.

Thus on May 5, four Italians appeared at Johnson's garage: Boda and a friend, Ricardo Orciani, on a motorcycle with a sidecar, and Sacco and Vanzetti on foot. Johnson stalled while his wife stole next door to notify the police. The men became suspicious and left in a hurry but, within an hour, Sacco and Vanzetti were arrested on a trolley. Both men packed fully loaded guns. Sacco had a .32 Colt automatic with eight cartridges in the clip and one in the barrel. He also had 23 loose cartridges in his pocket. Vanzetti carried a .38 Harrington and Richardson revolver while in his pocket were four 12-gauge shotgun shells. Police Chief Stewart didn't realize it at the time but the arrest he'd planned—

the "trap" at the garage—helped solve the crimes at *both* Bridgewater and South Braintree. Or at least helped produce its defendants.

The two prisoners were taken off the trolley car at Brockton and brought to its police station. Stewart was summoned and questioned the men separately. It was 11 p.m.

The interrogation of Sacco proceeded along the following lines:

> Q. Are you a citizen?
> A. No.
> Q. Do you belong to any clubs or societies? (No answer was recorded. Judge Thayer excluded the answer at both trials.)
> Q. Are you an Anarchist?
> A. No.
> Q. Are you a Communist?
> A. No.
> Q. Do you believe in this government of ours?
> A. Yes, some things I like different.
> Q. Do you believe in changing the government by force, if necessary?
> A. No.

Vanzetti was asked the following questions and gave the following answers:

> Q. Are you a citizen?
> A. No.
> Q. Do you belong to any clubs or organizations? (No answer recorded.)
> Q. Are you an Anarchist?
> A. Well, I don't know what you call him. I am a little different.
> Q. Do you like this government?
> A. Well, I like things a little different.
> Q. Do you believe in changing the government by force, if necessary?
> A. No.

> Q. Do you subscribe for literature or papers of the Anarchistic Party?
>
> A. Sometimes I read them.
>
> Q. How do you get them, through the mail?
>
> A. A man gave me one in Boston.
>
> Q. Who was the man?
>
> A. I don't know him.
>
> Q. Did he know you?
>
> A. I don't think so.
>
> Q. Why do you think he gave you the paper?
>
> A. Well, he was an Italian man and maybe he know I am.

Both denied knowing Boda and Coacci or seeing Mrs. Johnson earlier. They also gave false accounts of their recent whereabouts and of how they had come into possession of their guns. One theory holds that they believed the arrests were based on their anarchist beliefs and their draft dodging since neither the Braintree nor Bridgewater crime was brought up. As Sacco subsequently put it, he was arrested because he wasn't registered and was working for the movement of the laboring class.

They were put in jail for the night and denied blankets. Vanzetti claimed the night officer loaded his revolver in front of them and pointed it through the bars. Then he allegedly spat at them.

The following day, District Attorney Frederick Katzmann arrived and grilled them about April 15, the day of the armed robbery and killings. Sacco said he thought he was working at the shoe factory while Vanzetti stated he was peddling fish. They again protested they had never heard of Boda, Coacci or Mrs. Johnson.

After it was established that Coacci was at work all day on April 15, he was deported. Three days later, Boda voluntarily sailed for Italy, never to return. It was also established that Sacco was at work the day of the Bridgewater holdup while Vanzetti said he was peddling fish. Finally, Sacco stated he was away from work on the day of the killings in South Braintree while, once again, Vanzetti said he was peddling fish.

The official charge by the Commonwealth of Massachusetts against Vanzetti was: "Assault with intent to murder" at Bridgewater. Its charge against both Sacco and Vanzetti was: "Armed robbery at South Braintree and the murders of Alessandro Berardelli and Frederick Parmeter."

The DA arranged for Vanzetti to stand trial in Plymouth *before* the joint trial in Dedham. Judge Webster Thayer would preside at both trials.

I jumped upon hearing the landlady's voice at the door: "Telephone. On the wall. Other end." By the time I'd opened the door, she was gone. I could see the wooden wall phone down the hall and on my way there, checked my watch. It was 8 o'clock.

"Just wondering whether you've settled in," Sam Constant said, his voice raised as though he were not comfortable with telephones.

"Yes, I have and thanks for your concern." He even knows my phone number.

"You'll be there tomorrow for the start of the trial?"

"Absolutely. That's why I'm here. And you?"

"I usually go to all of them."

"All of them? There are that many in Dedham?"

"Wherever I'm needed." Sam paused before delivering a full-throated, "Sure hope they get what's coming to them."

"Excuse me?"

"You know. What they deserve."

"But how do we know? Shouldn't the trial be based on the facts and not on fear and hatred?"

"Look, anyone like them can commit brutal crimes." Sam then enunciated each word with a flair: "And they deserve to *fry.*"

I was flabbergasted by his choice of words. "But don't you see," I countered, "you're prejudging them."

"So are you," he snapped. "Wait a minute! What are you anyway, some kind of commie?" I could hear his breathing. Then a click.

Back in my room, I sat on the cot, head cradled firmly in my hands. Too firmly. I relaxed them and told my body to do the same.

My fatigue and hunger had been swept away by the phone conversation and by my desire to complete the review of events leading up to the following day's trial here in Dedham, including the past year's trial in Plymouth. But in the morning, I would witness events firsthand. No more recollections.

Chapter 3

The Plymouth Trial. Dress Rehearsal?

In what some scholars consider was a matter that would presage the conduct and outcome of the joint trial of Sacco and Vanzetti, the earlier Vanzetti trial for the Bridgewater holdup was held from June 22 to July 1, 1920. Others contend that holding a trial for a lesser crime prior to a trial for a major crime was highly unusual and, at the time, was a maneuver without precedent.

Judge Webster Thayer was 63, a dapper individual who bore a striking resemblance to the actor, Boris Karloff. A member of Worcester, Massachusetts' social elite, he made no secret of his hatred of foreigners. Two months before, he had gained widespread attention when he presided over the trial of Sergis Zakoff, who was charged with advocating the overthrow of the government by force. After a not guilty verdict was announced, an enraged Judge Thayer chided the jury: "How did you arrive at such a verdict? Did you consider the information that the defendant gave ... when he admitted ... there should be a revolution in this country? ... he said to the police officers ... he believed in Bolshevism and that our government should be overthrown."[5] The press had a field day as they sided with the judge who, in the following year, would also preside over the joint trial.

Vanzetti was defended by J. P. Vahey, a prominent Plymouth attorney and political activist, and by J. M. Graham. The prosecutor was District Attorney Frederick G. Katzmann. One of the jurors, Arthur Nickerson, was a foreman at the Plymouth Cordage Company which had blacklisted Vanzetti for his participation in a strike.

The Case for the State: Suspect Identification

The linchpin of the prosecution's case was identification of the suspects. On the day of the crime, an operative of the Pinkerton detective agency interviewed witnesses to the holdup attempt, but this information was never brought up during the trial. Those interrogated were the three occupants of the truck: paymaster Alfred Cox, driver Earl Graves, and police officer Benjamin Bowles. A fourth person questioned was Frank Harding who saw the incident as he walked to work.

The answers listed in the Pinkerton report are at marked variance with those given at the trial itself. Furthermore, one of the eyewitnesses, driver Earl Graves, died before the trial began. Some of the initial descriptions of the bandits' car and the man who fired the shotgun at the payroll truck include the following summaries:

>Cox: 5' 8", 150 pounds, dark complexion, 40 years old, closely cropped mustache which might have been slightly grey. Didn't identify the car.

>Graves: dark complexion, black mustache and looked like a Greek. Believed the car was a Hudson.

>Bowles: black closely cropped mustache, red cheeks, slim face, black hair and was either Italian or Portuguese. Offered no description of the car.

>Harding: 5' 10" and thin. Did not get good look at his face but thought he was a Pole. He identified the car as a black Hudson # 6 auto.

Incredibly, the Pinkerton reports were not made known to the defense until June 1927, two months prior to the execution of Sacco and Vanzetti.

Five months after the crime, Cox, Bowles and Harding testified at a preliminary hearing in the Brockton Police Court. Cox, the paymaster, again stated the bandit had a short croppy mustache. Assistant District Attorney William Kane questioned him about the bandit's identity.

    Cox: I can identify the man with the shotgun.

    Kane: Where is he now?

    Cox: The man might look different today.

    Kane: Can you tell where that man is now?

    The Court: Answer to the best of your knowledge and belief.

    Cox: That's where it hinges on being positive.

    Kanc: To the best of your knowledge and belief where is that man now?

    Cox: I think there is a doubt.

    The Court: You can testify either positively or to the best of your knowledge and belief.

    Cox: I feel—

    The Court: Not what you feel. If you think you know the man say so. What judgment do you form to the best of your ability considering all the circumstances?

    Cox: How do you want it worded?

    The Court: The say (sic) you remember it.

    Cox: I think it is this man behind the rail, the man with the mustache.

    Kane: To the best of your judgement and belief, is that the man?

    Cox: I think he looks enough like the man to be the man.

Bowles reaffirmed that the bandit had a short croppy mustache, yet, pointing to the heavily mustachioed Vanzetti, fingered him as the shotgun bandit.

Harding, a garageman, changed his description of the car from a # 6 Hudson to a Buick. Back in December, he asserted he could hardly see the bandit but at this hearing he was "a man of medium height, dark complected ... hair cut close in back. Mustache, dark ... it seemed to be croppy. Not little and small, but one trimmed up ... high cheekbones ... swarthy, dark complected." He added there was "no question in my mind" that Vanzetti was the one.

Can you believe this? I'm talking to myself, but who's to know? It gets even worse.

At the trial, Cox gave a much more elaborate description: "That man was five feet eight, of slight build, that is, not a heavy man ... of medium complexion, with prominent cheekbones, rather high; he had a short, well-trimmed mustache ... The appearance of his forehead was long, that is, it had the appearance of a high forehead to me at the time, a long forehead. His hair was not especially thick. What there was of it as I could see him, stood up."

Bowles, who had never before described the car, now called it "a dark colored Buick car" similar to the car reported stolen and, after the crime, found abandoned in Manley Woods, West Bridgewater. He also stated he was "positive" the bandit and Vanzetti were one and the same. His previous descriptions of the mustache were "closely cropped" and "a short croppy mustache" but on the witness stand, it became "very dark, trimmed at the edges, and bushy."

At the trial, Harding expanded on his original identification of the car. It was, he now said, "A large car, dark car either blue or black, I should say, a seven passenger Buick." This was again, similar to the one believed stolen and later found in Manley Woods. And, staring at Vanzetti, he described the bandit as having "a round head, bullet shaped, I should call it."

Thus, it appeared to be more than coincidence that both Bowles' and Harding's testimony had been changed in a coordinated fashion. The jury was oblivious to the situation because it had never been made aware of either the Pinkerton reports or the testimony given at the preliminary hearing.

Strange how memories can improve and many things can be made to fit.

Two other prosecution witnesses worthy of mention were 14-year-old Maynard F. Shaw, a high school student who witnessed the incident while delivering newspapers, and Dr. John M. Murphy who lived near the crime scene. Should any trial testimony be considered comical, if not ludicrous, it was that given by Shaw:

> Shaw: No hat on and I was just getting a fleeting glance at his face, but the way he ran I could tell he was a foreigner, I could tell by the way he ran.
>
> Vahey (Defense Attorney): You could tell he was a foreigner by the way he ran?
>
> Shaw: Yes.
>
> Vahey: What sort of a foreigner was he?
>
> Shaw: Nation?
>
> Vahey: Yes.
>
> Shaw: Why, European.
>
> Vahey: What?
>
> Shaw: Either Italy or Russia.
>
> Vahey: Which was it, Russia or Italy?
>
> Shaw: There I can't say exactly.
>
> Vahey: Does an Italian or Russian run differently from a Swede or Norwegian?
>
> Shaw: Yes.
>
> Vahey: What is the difference?
>
> Shaw: Unsteady.
>
> Vahey: Both the Italians and the Russians run unsteadily?
>
> Shaw: As far as that goes I don't know.
>
> Vahey: You don't know how a Swede runs, do you?
>
> Shaw: No.
>
> Vahey: Does a Swede run cross-legged?

Shaw: No.

Vahey: You don't want to have this jury think, do you, that you can tell what the nationality of this man was by the way he ran? Do you want them to believe that?

Shaw: Yes, I do.

Vahey: Now what nationality did he belong to?

Shaw: Let me say that I believe—well, the first thing that came into my mind was that he was an Italian or a Russian. I would not say—he might be a Mexican for what I know. I would not say he was an Alaskan or an African.

Vahey: You mean by that he was not a colored man?

Shaw: No.

Vahey: You eliminate the African, do you, from your consideration?

Shaw: Yes.

Vahey: He was either a Russian or an Italian or a Greek or a Brazilian or a Mexican—either one of these?

Shaw: Yes.

Vahey: Or a Jap?

Shaw: Might be.

Vahey: Would you say he might be a Jap?

Shaw: No.

Vahey: You would not say that he was a Jap or a Chinaman or an African—those three are eliminated absolutely, are they?

Shaw: Yes, nor an American.

The judge allowed such testimony? In all my years in criminal investigation and forensic science, I'd never experienced the likes of this. The prosecution got away with it, and it stressed the prejudicial issue of foreigners.

Tampering with Evidence

Meanwhile, Dr. John Murphy who gave distorted and damaging information, and the jury itself, which tampered with physical evidence, teamed to seal Vanzetti's fate. The State attempted to link an empty shotgun shell which Dr. Murphy picked up at the crime scene to four shells reportedly found on Vanzetti at the time of his arrest. The physician, an avid hunter, had also found some shot near the exploded shell.

Pinkerton reports of December 1919 and January 1920 failed to mention either the shell or the shots, but a May 1920 report by one of the agency's operatives indicated that Dr. Murphy found the shell at the scene of the attempted holdup and identified it as a # 12-gauge Winchester Repeater shell, and the nearby shot as # 10. The operative claimed he gave the shell along with a report to Captain Proctor.

Whether or not Dr. Murphy presented the shell directly to the operative is unknown, while another mystery is why such crucial physical evidence remained in the possession of the Pinkerton Agency for five months. Furthermore, the report allegedly given to Captain Proctor had disappeared.

The prosecution faced a dilemma: The shot originally described by Dr. Murphy was # 10, a tiny shot used for hunting birds and ordinarily not fatal to human bodies. But the shells reportedly found on Vanzetti contained the much more deadly buckshot. What would be done? At the trial, prosecution witness Murphy stated simply that he had found a shell in a gutter near the crime scene. He didn't mention its weight.

Defense attorney Vahey's insipid cross-examination followed:

Vahey: Do you do any hunting, Doctor?
Murphy: I do.
Vahay: It is the ordinary bird shell, is it not?
Murphy: No, I don't know what shot it is.
Vahey: Such a shell as you use in hunting for birds,
      isn't it?
Murphy: Use it for anything.

Vahey: Small birds?
Murphy: Sure.
Vahey: Is it the ordinary gauge?
Murphy: Yes.

Some cross-examination. Whose side was Vahey on, anyway? There was no challenge of the witness' earlier statements, and what about the chain of custody issue? I couldn't believe this was the same John Vahey who had such an outstanding reputation.

Another uncertainty tainted the case. Some observers raised doubts about whether the shells introduced at the Plymouth trial (and even later in Dedham) were actually the ones taken from Vanzetti at the time of his arrest. They were not labeled as evidence.

Although a key phase of the trial occurred near its conclusion, it should be considered at this point because of its relevance to the shells. It hinged on an illegal act by the jury itself. After a few hours of deliberation, it asked Judge Thayer for an exact definition of "assault with intent to commit murder." His reply dealt with the defendant's firing a weapon capable of causing death or great bodily harm. The jury returned to the jury room and opened the shells introduced as having been found on Vanzetti to determine what they contained. They found buckshot and immediately concluded the bandit had also fired buckshot! After the trial, a juror swore that prosecutor Katzmann had said he "did not want it [the tampering with the shells] known." But the defense, learning of the tampering, found its hands tied because Judge Thayer had "placed on file" the conviction, thus making any appeal impossible.

The Case for the Defense: Alibi of Eels

If the heart of the prosecution's case were eyewitnesses, Vanzetti's defense rested primarily on a stream of people to confirm an alibi. Also, some time was spent on the appearance of

Vanzetti's mustache, several witnesses describing it as bushy or droopy and long and certainly not trimmed or cropped. John Vernazano, his barber of six years, was particularly convincing:

> Graham (Defense Attorney): Have you ever trimmed or cut his mustache?
>
> Vernazano: No, sir; sometimes I did trim a little round on the bottom.
>
> Graham: Point to where you mean on your own mustache.
>
> Vernazano: Just two or three hairs cut off there, right on the top of his lip.
>
> Graham: Did you ever cut the ends of it or trim the ends of it?
>
> Vernazano: No, no, no.
>
> Graham: Did you ever see it trimmed?
>
> Vernazano: No.
>
> Graham: Did you ever see it any different from what it is today?
>
> Vernazano: Never; always he had a long mustache.

But two police officers, offering defense testimony along similar lines, were torn apart by Katzmann.

The bulk of the defense hinged on the custom of many Italians who eat eels on Christmas Eve, and Vanzetti was their fish peddler. Fourteen Italians corroborated Vanzetti's alibi, that on the morning of the crime, he was making eel deliveries to his customers. The attempted holdup occurred about 7:30 a.m., and 14-year-old Beltrando Brini stated he saw Vanzetti delivering eels at that time and, half an hour later, began helping him and continued until 2 p.m.

Some years later, Brini said he believed that someone wanted to find a scapegoat for the crimes; that Italians felt unimportant and impotent in society; and that many were terrified of taking the witness stand. No wonder: They would have to endure Katzmann's excoriating style. The cross-examination of Vanzetti's landlady, Mary Fortini—through an interpreter—is a case in point:

Katzmann: What day was Vanzetti arrested?

Fortini: I think on Wednesday.

Katzmann: What Wednesday?

Fortini: I don't know.

Katzmann: Two months ago, was it not?

Fortini: I don't know.

Katzmann: Three months ago, wasn't it?

Fortini: I don't know.

Katzmann: A week ago, was it not?

Fortini: I don't know.

Katzmann: Yesterday, was it not?

Fortini: I don't know.

Katzmann: What time did Vanzetti get up on the day after Christmas?

Fortini: I don't remember.

Katzmann: What time did Vanzetti get up on the first day of this year?

Fortini: I don't know.

Katzmann: What time did Vanzetti get up on Washington's birthday of this year?

Fortini: No, I don't know.

Katzmann: What time did he go to bed the Saturday night before Easter morning of this year?

Fortini: I don't know, no, sir.

Then, Judge Thayer granted Katzmann permission to question her without an interpreter.

Katzmann: Do you know what language I talk? Do you know my language?

Fortini: No.

Katzmann: What is a horse—do you know?

Fortini: I don't understand nothing.

Katzmann: Do you know what a horse is?

Fortini: No, sir.

Katzmann: Do you know what a Brini is?

Fortini: No, sir.

Katzmann: Do you know what a Balboni is? That

is something you hang out on the line
washday, isn't it?

Fortini: Me don't understand you. You come in
my country and you don't understand nothing, and me just the same.

Neither Judge Thayer nor the defense attorneys came to Mrs.
Fortini's rescue and Katzmann bullied virtually all Vanzetti's Italian witnesses.

Two sidebars to this trial must be noted: (1) Vanzetti never
took the stand in his own defense and, if the members of the jury
were unbiased, this may have hurt his case. If they were biased, it
probably would not have made a difference anyway, although
consensus holds that, had he testified, the issue of radicalism could
not be prevented from being raised. (2) Two days after the verdict, District Attorney Katzmann relieved Captain William H.
Proctor, head of the Massachusetts State Police, from the responsibility of directing the South Braintree crime. True, he had given
innocuous testimony about the shotgun shells allegedly taken from
Vanzetti's pocket, but, by all accounts, the more concrete reason
for his dismissal was that he believed Sacco and Vanzetti were
innocent. After his later testimony at the joint trial in Dedham, he
was overheard in the corridor saying to Attorney Thomas
McAnarney that the Commonwealth had gotten the wrong men.[6]

On July 1, 1920, the jury, after five hours of deliberation,
found Bartolomeo Vanzetti guilty of assault with intent to rob
and assault with intent to murder. He and his closest friends were
stunned. One, Beltrando Brini, the youngster who testified he
had been with the defendant the entire morning of the attempted
holdup, later said he hadn't realized it at the time, but the verdict
was probably intended to influence the outcome of the joint trial
that lay ahead.

On its own merit, the Plymouth affair might have been
considered merely another garden variety trial, albeit one with
questionably orchestrated evidence and testimony. In this connection, it certainly left deep doubts about proper crime scene

investigation, the integrity of scientific evidence, the integrity of expert witnesses and the ethical behavior of the legal professionals involved. These doubts will again be brought into question during the consideration of the joint trial at Dedham.

Despite its imperfections, however, if taken in conjunction with the high drama that was to come—drama on a grander scale and with an international audience—then it must be assigned a more significant location in the sweep of jurisprudence.

No matter how one comes down on the various ethical and procedural issues of the trial at Plymouth, a convicted felon emerged, one who would be serving a 15-year prison term at the time of the cause célèbre in Dedham the following year. Whether the subsequent jury could possibly have been unmoved by the Plymouth verdict is a debate that continues to rage alongside the larger question of innocence or guilt.

Additionally, there are those who insist that if a verdict of not guilty had been returned in that small New England town, the joint trial might have never taken place.

It was after 10 p.m. and I shook my damp shirt loose from my shoulders. I'd had enough for that day, having played out the entire Sacco-Vanzetti story up to the cusp of the joint trial—the pièce de résistance. I suggested to myself that I attend only its pivotal moments—which will no doubt fill the sessions—and cover the gaps with what I remember reading before. Before? No, 80 years after!

Sleep I knew would not come easy, given the charged circuitry of my mind. Perhaps a snack would help after all. And a walk.

Outside, the soundless night was darker than most, the sky sooty, the air thin and crisp: an October evening in April. Hunched, I quickened an easy pace and headed straight for Martha's Home Cooking three blocks off, positive of its location, strangely familiar with the crude signs marking Norfolk, High and Pearl.

It looked like a converted burnt-red barn, out of place

amidst the white, green-shuttered homes lining the roads. Inside, a single room hummed with the chatter of late diners and I announced to an approaching waitress, "I'll come back another time."

"No, no," she said, "there are a couple openings at that two-seater behind the pillar over there."

Head bowed for no particular reason, I hobbled among the tables and, reaching the one which the waitress had pointed to, settled into it, at the same time casting a startled gaze at the rangy figure of Sam Constant seated across from me. But she said a *couple* empty chairs, I thought.

"You're eating rather late, aren't you, Dr. Lee?" The question fit the smirk on his face.

"I was reviewing some papers and lost track of time."

"I know."

"That I lost track of time?"

"No, that you were reviewing papers."

I felt a surge of annoyance at my collar and said, "What do you do, go around reading people's minds?"

"Just a cross section." Then came the click and he was gone.

After admonishing myself in nearly audible terms not to be sidetracked by the evanescent and mercurial Mr. Constant, I ordered a sandwich and a cup of hot tea. Tomorrow would be another long day.

Chapter 4

The Dedham Trial

I had calculated at least eight hours of available sleep but had taken up only five when I awoke on the other side of dawn. A recently scarce sun poured through the windows of my flat, its warmth on my body, now unblanketed and propped against the wall behind the cot.

Although I knew how the joint trial had turned out, I was determined to keep an open mind and, with several hours to kill, took a reluctant peek back at the highlights including a flood of posttrial commentaries which were overwhelmingly critical.

Once again, I aligned the chronology and relevant locations: Vanzetti's trial for the Bridgewater crime had been held in Plymouth; one year later, the trial of both Vanzetti and Sacco for the South Braintree crimes was held in Dedham, 10 miles south of Boston.

When Vanzetti was tried and convicted in that red-brick courthouse in Plymouth, not far from the rock embellished with the numerals 1620, he was under indictment for the South Braintree crime as well, a fact that undoubtedly played a role in the Plymouth outcome. And now, at the start of the Dedham trial, another aggravating factor hung over him: He had already served one year of a 15-year prison term for the earlier crime. As for Sacco, linkage to a branded highwayman undoubtedly worked to his disadvantage in the joint trial.

Another salient but curious factor was that the presiding judge at the first trial, Webster Thayer, also presided over the second one—and even over the six years of appeals that followed. He had written to his fellow Dartmouth College alumnus, Chief

Justice John Aiken, specifically requesting that he be given the appointment. Aiken complied, indicating that he was assigning Thayer to hear perhaps the most important murder case ever tried in Massachusetts. In a similar vein, Frederick Katzmann was the prosecutor at both trials. Sacco was represented by Fred H. Moore, a California attorney noted for his defense of radicals. Considered an outsider, the chemistry between Moore and the judge was less than ideal. Jeremiah McAnarney, an associate of Moore, defended Vanzetti.

The Twin Damnations of Radicalism
and Consciousness of Guilt

In the August 1960 edition of the *American Bar Association Journal*, Barry C. Reed, a South Braintree lawyer, anchored the setting for the trial with the following words:

> On Memorial Day, May 30, 1921, proud warriors of the Grand Old Army, the last remnants of the 2nd and 20th Massachusetts Infantry, who had fought at Fair Oaks and Malvern Hill, stormed Mayre's Heights and held the line at Resaca, stood at attention with veterans of recent wars as Taps drifted over Hyde Park cemetery, the final muster for those who died at Lexington, the Wilderness, Santiago and the Argonne. It was an era of patriotism and chauvinism that this country has never seen since and perhaps will never see again. The day following, within the dying echo of the bugle, two men, aliens, anarchists and draft dodgers, were to be tried for murder.[7]

Am I getting ahead of myself? But how do I block out all that I learned when called to review the case years later? How do I separate evaluations of the trial from testimony itself? The answer is that I don't. I'll be there, and once engrossed, will allow the flow to take over. Which doesn't mean my refraining from comments based on today's standards.

The milieu in Massachusetts at that time has been compared to the mood during the witch-hunt prosecutions of the seventeeth century. Hysteria was rampant. Boston newspapers ran banner headlines and articles about massive security measures against Reds and warned of a Bolshevik plan for the conquest of America. The massive raids of the previous year were fresh in people's minds, and many wondered why Sacco and Vanzetti had not been deported prior to their alleged crimes. Still others—students of the case—held that while the accused were on trial for murder, they were also on trial for radicalism.

One of the reasons why they had not been deported pertained to insufficient evidence of self-incrimination required under law. As a consequence, U. S. Department of Justice officials worked closely with state authorities, believing they could obtain damning testimony even if Sacco and Vanzetti were acquitted of murder. In addition, they wanted to obtain information that might implicate the pair in the rash of bombings throughout the country, especially those on Wall Street and at Attorney General Palmer's home in Washington.

Even before the trial, federal agents and District Attorney Katzmann conspired with one John Ruzzamenti to be either an informant in a cell next to Sacco's or as a lodger at his home where he might obtain useful information from Mrs. Rosina Sacco. Both ploys fell through. Subsequently, another informant, Antonio Carbone, spent several days in jail near Sacco but learned nothing new.

Soon afterward, federal agent Fred Weyand deposed:

From my investigation, combined with the investigation made by the other agents of the Department in Boston, I am convinced not only that these men had violated the Selective Service rules and evaded the draft, but that they were anarchists and that they ought to be deported. By calling these men anarchists, I do not mean necessarily that they were inclined to violence, nor do I understand all the different meanings that different people would attach to the word, anarchist. What I mean is that I think they did not believe in organized government or in private property. But I am also thoroughly convinced, and always have been, and I believe that it is and has always been the opinion of such Boston agents of the Department of Justice, as had my knowledge on the subject, that these men had nothing whatever to do with the South Braintree murders and that their conviction was the result of cooperation between the Boston agents of the Department of Justice and the District Attorney. It was the general opinion of the Boston agents of the Department of Justice, having knowledge of the affair, that the South Braintree crime was committed by a gang of professional highwaymen.

The concept of "consciousness of guilt" was especially critical: Sacco and Vanzetti behaved like guilty men. This related to their need for a car to warn radical friends and dispose of subversive literature; the fact that they carried guns when arrested; the fact that their weapons and bullets appeared consistent with those used in the shootings of the paymaster and his guard; and, upon their arrest, lying about the source of their guns and about where they had spent the previous few hours. Later, these issues will be examined in depth, but they are introduced here merely to connect them to radicalism. Consciousness of guilt and radicalism were closely intertwined for two reasons. First, the defendants' false statements to the police and their need for a car and, second, the defense had no choice but to introduce the issue of anarchism at the trial in order to explain away these elements.

The Jurors

There are those who state unequivocally that the most important component of any trial by jury is the jury itself. At Dedham, 700 people were summoned to serve as jurors and after more than a month, only seven of the 12 required had been selected. Many had feared retaliation by the Reds or the Black Hand, as the Mafia was then known. The judge, therefore, instructed a sheriff to round up more candidates posthaste. Deputies scoured adjoining towns and also raided a nearby Masonic Lodge, picking persons they deemed representative citizens. The jury had its complement of 12. No Italians were among them.

One of the questions each juror was asked was, "Are your opinions of such a character as to preclude you from finding a defendant guilty of a crime punishable by death?"[8] Commenting on that issue, Judge Thayer emphasized that if a juror had a conviction that he would not, no matter how convincing the evidence, return a verdict that might result in the death penalty, such a juror would be absolutely disqualified.

Since a jury should represent a cross-section of the community, was not the selection procedure in Dedham prejudicial to begin with, at least with regard to capital punishment? Does the exclusion from juries of those individuals opposed to the death penalty produce juries more likely to execute a defendant?

The DeFalco Affair

Instances of corruption or attempted corruption plagued the case. In January 1921, four months before the trial, an example of this unfolded. It was a major contributing factor in the hostility of Massachusetts officials toward Sacco and Vanzetti's plight.

A scheme was devised to replace Sacco's attorney, Fred Moore, with local influential lawyers and, at the same time, to pay off authorities to ensure Sacco's and Vanzetti's freedom. Pivotal characters in the operation were Angelina DeFalco, a court stenographer; Aldino Felicani, treasurer of the Sacco-Vanzetti Defense Committee; and Benjamin Cicchetti, a "fixer" from nearby Providence, Rhode Island.

Thirty-four years later, Felicani related the sequence of events to Dean Albertson of Columbia University. The story revealed that Cicchetti, through Felicani, contacted DeFalco who claimed that the defense attorneys in the earlier Plymouth trial were unfit, that the defense committee could obtain an acquittal by retaining Francis J. Squires, an experienced trial lawyer, and Percy Katzmann, brother of District Attorney Frederick Katzmann. The plan called for Moore to defer to Squires and Katzmann during the proceedings, and for Frederick Katzmann to retire as prosecutor in favor of one of his associates. What would be the price for this shake-up with its attendant verdict of not guilty? Fifty thousand dollars to be paid in installments.

Moore, when informed of the deal, labeled it a trap. A meeting was arranged to take place at DeFalco's home where, without her knowledge, a microphone and stenographer would be concealed in the cellar. At the designated time, Felicani, having been cautioned by Moore earlier in the week, circled the house in his car and recorded the license plate numbers of two upscale cars parked in front. He never entered the house. The next morning, a check of the numbers revealed the automobiles were registered to Francis Squires and Frederick Katzmann, the district attorney.

Felicani and his committee still wanted to pay the money but Moore was opposed, citing potential discovery and a charge of bribing public officials. Instead, he had DeFalco and Cicchetti arrested and the entire plot became front-page news. After favorable court testimony by the Katzmann brothers and Squires, DeFalco and Cicchetti were acquitted in a brief trial. But damage to Sacco and Vanzetti's fortunes had been done.

As for the effect upon Judge Thayer and the district attorney, Thayer interpreted the event as an indictment of the Massachusetts court system and never forgave the participants. Furthermore, the episode increased the district attorney's resolve to convict Sacco and Vanzetti because if they were acquitted, society might believe he had thrown the case. But if they were convicted, he would have demonstrated his incorruptibility.

One of the most important aspects of the affair was its impact on court authorities toward Moore. Already an outsider, he now became distrusted. In addition, DeFalco had many friends in the courthouse circle who were convinced Moore had set her up and had also leaked information about corruption to the media concerning powerful county officials.

All of this hurt the cause of Sacco and Vanzetti. The repercussions from this episode, coupled with the country's fear of radicalism and its hatred of foreigners, compromised Sacco and Vanzetti's presumption of innocence.

As It Happened

I tried to prolong a breakfast provided by the landlady, yet was still too early for the trial and, exiting the flat, could see that others were, too. I could tell a newsman when I saw one, and there were plenty sprinkled among the people who jostled for position in front of the courthouse doors. They blocked High Street as a solid human barricade running alongside the granite two-story structure. There was no choice but to circle around to my left and come onto the front through the park, the point of my advent the day before.

The morning was damp but clear. A mass of pigeons staked its claim there, perhaps discouraging the crowd of onlookers and hopeful attendees, their numbers thinner than on the other side. Ahead, two pin oaks straddled a bronze plaque. I assumed the inscription referred to the church at the far end of the park (or the square which I then believed to be a more appropriate designation). From that vantage point, as far as I could see in every direction, cleared squares, rectangles and triangles of spring grass separated roads or inns, taverns and shops with multicolored awnings. And everywhere there were benches and flagpoles.

At the plaque, I had to squint to decipher the chiseled words: "Unitarian Church gathering, 1638." I wasn't certain what prompted me to some rapid arithmetic which led to an irony that probably meant little, but the birth date of the United States lay roughly equidistant between the "gathering" and the start of the Sacco-Vanzetti trial.

I drifted toward the front entrance with a few others who had chanced such a direction and there I met the second irony of the day. According to a corner signpost, the Norfolk County Courthouse at Dedham fronted on Pearl Street. Nine miles away in South Braintree, the murders had been committed on . . . Pearl Street!

The courthouse, its majesty certified by four Roman Tuscan columns, was ringed by two levels of barred windows and, below, by armed guards at attention—a virtual fortress under siege. The crowd had reached and occupied the front steps clear across but, inexplicably, a narrow corridor opened to the side and, after squeezing up and in, I looked back to behold policemen searching people before their entrance was allowed. I had received a simple nod but had not been searched, as if some prearrangement had been made on my behalf.

One of the earliest to reach the second floor courtroom, I paused at the door and the first thing that caught my eye was a metal cage before the elevated judge's bench at the far wall. Stark against the oak of tables and chairs and wainscoting, the cage added yet another point to the odds against the defendants, odds already lengthened by anarchism and foreign heritage. I was aware that, in those days, all defendants in murder trials sat in cages. Still, I couldn't help but feel that each day Sacco and Vanzetti would be removed from incarceration in prison and taken to incarceration in that hall of Justice and that such a procedure spoke graphically against the dictum, "Innocent until proven guilty."

A police lieutenant waved me to a back row and I sat adjacent to the middle aisle.

The principals—judge, jury, prosecution, defense, the accused—had not arrived yet but, as spectators trickled in, I released the half-breaths I had been taking, a pattern of mine during strained and somber times. Soon, I would rediscover firsthand those other disturbing features of the trial I had read and heard about: the seven weeks of constant gaveling by Judge Thayer; the daily marches of Sacco and Vanzetti through the streets of Dedham between the jail and courthouse, handcuffed to each other, surrounded by a convoy of guards.

I noted the jury box at the right back corner and, beneath it, the witness stand with its gooseneck microphone and absent chair. Before me, the rows filled rapidly and then (Why hadn't I expected it?), Sam Constant slid in next to me, his face determined, his outfit resembling a bandsman in a "Yankee Doodle" parade: white shirt, open red vest, blue trousers tucked into golden leather leggings. No one else looked at him.

"Good morning," I said, "you made it." Obviously, I thought.

"I always make these things. What's the delay?"

Ignoring his question, I tried to atone for my comment. "I would have thought someone like you—you know, familiar with these parts—might want to sit up closer."

"Can't. They never let me."

I felt my eyebrows elevate. "Why not?"

"Too tall. Guess I interfere with some people's point of view—I mean, with some people's view."

Fifty-nine witnesses testified for the Commonwealth and 99 for the defendants. The prosecutors developed their case along three principal lines: identification witnesses, physical and circumstantial evidence and consciousness of guilt. But before embarking on a review of these facets, the subjects of anarchy and draft evasion were raised, the prosecution claiming it was the defendants who did so, defense counsel maintaining they were forced to in order to explain their actions. In any event, the incorporation of these emotional topics in testimony set an undercurrent in motion, one which the prosecutors no doubt considered a bonus. Representative of this was the defense's direct examination of Vanzetti deep into the trial. It referred to his visit to the Johnson garage along with Sacco, Boda and Orciani.

> MacAnarney (Defense Attorney): What were you
> going to get the automobile for?
> Vanzetti: We were going to get the automobile for

to carry books and newspapers.

MacAnarney said he didn't understand the answer.

MacAnarney: What were you going to get the automobile for?

Vanzetti: For to take out literature, books and newspapers, from the house and the homes.

McAnarney: What house and homes did you want to take the books and literature from?

Vanzetti: From any house and from any house in five or six places, five or six towns. Three, five or six people have plenty of literature, and we want, we intend to take that out and put that in the proper place.

McAnarncy: What do you mean by a "proper place"?

Vanzetti: By a proper place I mean in a place not subject to policemen go in and call for, see the literature, see the papers, see the books, as in that time they went through in the house of many men who were active in the radical movement and socialist and labor movement, and go there and take letters and take books and take newspapers, and put men in jail and deported many. And deported many, many; many have been misused in jail, and so on.

The defense attorney next asked Vanzetti about the details of his arrest and whether he had informed his interrogators about the motive for picking up the car.

Vanzetti: No, I don't tell them that thing.

McAnarney: You withheld that from him. You never told that to them before?

Vanzetti: No.

McAnarney: Why not?

Vanzetti: Because in that time there, there was the deportation and the reaction was more vivid than now and more mad than now.

McAnarney: The action?

Vanzetti: The reaction. What you call "reaction."
It mean the authority of this country and
every country in the world was more
against the socialist element in that time
than before the war and after the war. There
were exceptional times.

**Strangely, McAnarney didn't pursue this line of ques-
tioning in order to bring out what Sacco and Vanzetti feared.
He chose, instead, to switch to Vanzetti's flight to Mexico to
avoid the draft.**

McAnarney: Did you at one time go away from
Plymouth?

Vanzetti: Yes, sir.

McAnarney: And when was that, please?

Vanzetti: I should say it was in the year 1917, before the registration.

McAnarney: Why did you go away?

Vanzetti: I go away for not to be a soldier.

Once again, defense counsel switched the subject, preferring at this point not to raise two key points: that many U.S. citizens also ran from the draft and that, as an alien, Vanzetti was not
even subject to the draft. McAnarney's disjointed questioning
continued when he asked the defendant whether he drove a car.

Vanzetti: No.

McAnarney: Did you ever drive one?

Vanzetti: No, sir, I am not able.

Then, after further inquiries including one in which
McAnarney confused an important date, it was back to the night
of the arrest.

McAnarney: Why did you not tell Mr. Stewart the
truth that night when he arrested you and
talked with you at the station?

Vanzetti: I was scared to give the names and the addresses of my friends as I know that almost all of them have some books and some newspapers in their house by which the authority take a reason for arresting them and deport them.

McAnarney: Tell us all you recall that Stewart, the chief, asked of you.

Vanzetti: He asked me why we were in Bridgewater, how long I know Sacco, if I am a radical, if I am an anarchist or communist, and he asked if I believe in the government of the United States.

McAnarney: Yes.

Vanzetti: If I believe in the violence, if I believe in the use of violence against the government of the United States.

McAnarney left the question unanswered and Vanzetti hanging by turning to different topics in rapid succession—all of them trivial.

The defense attorney's conduct accomplished little in Vanzetti's favor. The presentation of his case seemed flawed not only in his lines of questioning but also in terms of understanding his client—and the jury. When Prosecutor Katzmann got his chance, however, he took immediate advantage of the jury, particularly its foreman who had saluted the flag each morning upon entering the courtroom:

Katzmann: So you left Plymouth, Mr. Vanzetti, in May, 1917, to dodge the draft, did you?

Vanzetti: Yes, sir.

The first five days of the trial dealt with several preliminary requirements including the selection of a jury and a visit to the scene of the crime and surrounding relevant territories by the jurors and representatives of both the prosecution and the defense. On their journey, they examined the Slater and Morrill Shoe Factories and other adjacent buildings and physical objects; the route the bandits' automobile allegedly traveled; the Manley Woods where it had been abandoned; the shed in which Michael Boda had kept his Overland car; Simon Johnson's garage where the car had been taken for repairs; and Johnson's house in front of which the defendants, Boda and Ricardo Orciani, had met on May 5, 1920, the night Sacco and Vanzetti were later arrested.

To that point, I'd attended all morning and afternoon sessions and had lunch at Martha's where I exchanged small talk with other spectators. Sam was never among them, having clicked off during the lunch break. At first, I felt uneasy sitting next to him each day, but later grew accustomed to his presence and looked forward to some blistering remark or two upon his arrival.

On the morning of day six, he announced, "I was on the trip to the crime scene, you know."

"They let you go there?"

"They had no choice in the matter."

Hmm, I thought, it wasn't a matter of choice; it was a matter of their noticing him. And how can you not notice a red, white and blue dude who towers over you?

"Did you learn anything?" I asked, just to keep the conversation going while I mulled over a different question I was eager to pose.

"Of course not. It was exactly as I thought—a complete waste of time. Besides, they don't need all that foolishness to convict."

Okay, now's the time. "Look," I said, "straighten this out for me once and for all. Can anybody else see you or only those you want to?"

"Can you?" he replied, smiling.

"Yes."

"Then that's all that counts, right?"

I was about to discount the last question and ask why he

had gone to South Braintree in the first place, but the taking of testimony had begun.

Chapter 5

<u>Witnesses and Evidence</u>

<u>Eyewitnesses Used Against Sacco</u>

Three eyewitnesses testified about events before the shootings and eight testified they witnessed the actual shootings.

Late on the morning of the crime, Lola Andrews was seeking employment in the vicinity of the shoe factories. She walked by a car parked near Slater and Morrill and noticed a "sickly-looking, fair-haired" man sitting in the back seat and a darker one bending over the hood. After her 15-minute visit to the factory, she swore the lighter man stood near the rear of the car while the darker one lay head first under the car, apparently repairing something. Andrews claimed she asked the darker man for directions to the Rice and Hutchins Factory and she stated the man was Sacco. But on cross-examination, she admitted her earlier failure to identify a photograph of Sacco, and five witnesses testified she had lied. One, her companion that morning, flatly contradicted her story.

William S. Tracy stated that just before noon, he saw two men leaning against a building he owned on Pearl Street. He recognized one as Sacco. "While I wouldn't be positive, I would say to the best of my recollection that was the man . . . to the best of my opinion, he is the man."

William J. Heron said he saw two men who spoke Italian in the South Braintree railroad station early on the afternoon of April 15. He was "pretty sure" one was Sacco but denied any knowledge of Italian and could not distinguish among Italian, French or Spanish.

The eight other individuals claimed they saw the shootings but none could offer an identification of Sacco that was solid and beyond a reasonable doubt. Much of this phase of the case contains references to sworn statements differing from those given at the inquest and during a preliminary hearing at Quincy.

One prosecution witness had not seen the shootings but presented testimony replete with inconsistencies and also with an improbable observation. Mary E. Splaine, a bookkeeper, claimed she saw the bandits' car from a second-story window of Slater and Morrill's western building. She said she was 60 feet from the street and the vehicle was departing at 18 miles an hour while in her view, a distance of 35 to 60 feet. A man stood behind the front seat leaning out of the car, his left hand draped over the seat about one-third of the way across. Ms. Splaine gave a detailed description of the man: no overcoat or hat, weight of 140 to 145 pounds, muscular, high forehead, dark eyebrows, greenish-white complexion, long hair which was brushed back, gray shirt. Staring at the cage before her, she made a positive face-to-face identification of Sacco as that man and added, "I noticed particularly the left hand was a good-sized hand, a hand that denoted strength."

Was the jury to believe such a precise description of a man with a strong-looking hand in a moving car she could only briefly observe for a time of less than four seconds? And from a distance of 60 feet?

On cross-examination, Splaine admitted she was unable to pick out Sacco in a police lineup at the Quincy Court. At that same hearing, she also said, "I don't think my opportunity afforded me the right to say he is the man." But then at the trial a full year later, she changed her tune: "From the observation I had of him in the Quincy Court and the comparison of the man I saw in the machine, on reflection I was sure he was the man." Of this and conflicting statements made by other witnesses, Jeremiah Gallivan, Braintree's Chief of Police commented, "I couldn't understand it, how they (the witnesses) got stronger in Dedham than they was (sic) in Quincy." He had been present at both the hearing and the trial.

The defense countered with its own eyewitnesses, 17 in all, none of whom could positively identify Sacco as being at the scene. One, Barbara Liscomb, was particularly emphatic. From a window of the Rice and Hutchins Factory, she observed Parmenter and Berardelli on the ground and "a short dark man standing on the ground facing me, with his head up holding a revolver in his hands." She added, "I will never forget that face. He, Sacco, is not the man. I am positive."

Eyewitnesses Used Against Vanzetti

Eyewitnesses numbered only four; two are worthy of mention. Michael Levangie, the railway crossing tender near the crime scene at South Braintree, testified that he was forced to raise the gates by bandits who pointed a revolver at him. The reason given for the gate's position was at variance with the one given at the inquest. Levangie swore that Vanzetti was the driver. This, too, was at odds—this time, with the prosecution itself which admitted Vanzetti was not the driver. Initially, in its opening remarks to the jury, it had described the driver as, "this light-haired man with an emaciated face," and put Vanzetti next to him as a passenger. But later in his summation, Katzmann moved Vanzetti into the driver's seat after all.

The question of a mustache involved gate tender Levangie also. It should be recalled that an inquest had been conducted on April 17, 1920, two days after the crimes, and that the minutes were not released to the defense until 1927, late in the appeal process. At the inquest, Levangie had described the driver as having a dark complexion and a dark moustache. But on the afternoon of the shootings and again on April 18, he called the man smooth-shaven. If the inquest statement had been known at the time of the trial, his testimony there would have constituted perjury.

Plus, during all of this, I thought, why didn't an important point come out? Neither Sacco nor Vanzetti owned a car or knew how to drive.

I decided to pique my bench mate, stretching up to whisper, "How come you don't wear a mustache?"

His response took longer than I'd expected. "Why should I?"

"Because so many men do nowadays."

Sam flashed a wicked smile. "But, you see, I'm not 'so many.'"

"You're not?"

He turned and fixed a level stare straight ahead, his chin sticking out defiantly. I believed he was getting the picture: not only that mustaches were popular, but also that I finally understood his points of view were just as popular, if not more so.

The other key witness insisting Vanzetti was in the fleeing automobile was Austin T. Reed, a gate tender at Matfield, 20 miles from South Braintree. He said Vanzetti called out to him, "What the hell I was holding him up for?" Cross-examination by Defense Counsel Moore was persuasive:

Moore: And his salutation to you was in a loud, bold voice, in the English phraseology that you saw fit to give, something I believe to the effect, "What in hell did you stop us for?"

Reed: Yes, sir.

Moore: And the voice was loud and full and strong back forty feet. Is that right?

Reed: Yes, sir.

Moore: What?

Reed: Yes, sir.

Moore: With a running motor?

Reed: Yes, sir.

Moore: And a train passing—approaching?

Reed: Yes, sir.

Moore: The quality of the English was unmistakable and clear?

Reed: Why—
Moore: Is that right? Answer yes or no. What?
Reed: Yes.

Vanzetti's English was halting and broken at that time and everyone connected with the case, including the jury, was aware of it. And another thing: The police knew the car was heading south toward Matfield. Why wasn't a roadblock set up? They could have phoned ahead. There was plenty of time—the town was 20 miles away.

Before moving on to the physical and circumstantial evidence introduced by the Commonwealth, the identification phase of its case can best be defined by the consensus of legal scholars who held that the evidence of identity had not been convincing and by the comments of Judge Thayer, himself: "These verdicts did not rest, in my judgment, upon the testimony of the eyewitnesses, for the defendants, as it was, called more witnesses than the Commonwealth who testified that neither of the defendants were (sic) in the bandit car."

<u>Physical and Circumstantial Evidence</u>
The following will be explored:
      1— Sacco's cap: tampering, misconduct and humor.
      2— Sacco's pistol at arrest and Fatal Bullet # III.
      Expert opinions
      Bullet evidence in victim
      Casing evidence at murder scene
      3— Berardelli's gun.
      4— Consciousness of guilt.
As related by the State, the tale of Sacco's cap was riddled with inaccuracies, and just as the prosecution attempted to show that a cap allegedly found at the crime scene did fit Sacco, so too did it try to fit this piece of evidence into its arsenal of attack. But as will be shown, size, timing, lies, tampering and suppression of evidence—all combined to provide a grave falsification of the

facts as they became known years after the verdict. In fact, it wasn't until 1927 when the case was reviewed by Governor Fuller and his advisory committee that many of the distortions were righted and that revelations were made about key information being withheld from the defense. And from members of the jury, because the size of the cap allegedly found at the crime scene had never been revealed to them. For the prosecution, the importance of a cap reportedly found either in the gutter near Berardelli's body or in the middle of the street rested with establishing that it belonged to Sacco, and it therefore placed him at the scene of the murders.

The adventure of the cap must begin with the fact that no witness at the inquest on April 17 testified finding one on the day of the murders two days earlier. The first mention of a cap, rather, was made in the same day's edition of the *Boston Herald*, which stated an "employee of Slater and Morrill found a cap in the middle of the road last night near the factory as he left the building."[9] According to the article, then, the cap was discovered 30 hours after the crimes were committed.

Certain characters had a hand in the cap's disposition, namely: Fred Loring, an employee of the Slater and Morrill Factory; Thomas Fraher, Loring's boss; Jeremiah Gallivan, Braintree police chief; John Scott, a state police officer; and George Kelley, Sacco's boss.

The sequence presented to the jury was that Loring found a cap at the scene and kept it for an hour. Then he gave it to Fraher who delivered it to Gallivan who showed it to a Pinkerton man. For reasons unknown, Chief Gallivan carried the cap around in his car for 10 days before turning it over to Scott. The Pinkerton man stated it was a heavy winter cap, size 6-7/8. The police went to Sacco's home and, without a warrant, seized one of his caps. It was size 7-1/8.

Eventually the cap was presented as evidence against Sacco but, early on, was simply marked for identification. The introduction of the cap into the case was initiated by Loring in testimony given to Assistant District Attorney Harold Williams—

testimony that was contrary to facts later proven:

> Williams: Where was the body of Berardelli lying with reference to the sidewalk, or the street, on that side of the street?
>
> Loring: Right in the gutter, but on the sidewalk.
>
> Williams: Now, when you arrived on the scene, was there anything which you noticed on the street near the body of Berardelli?
>
> Loring: A cap.
>
> Williams: Where was the cap?
>
> Loring: It was about 18 inches from Berardelli's body, towards the street.
>
> Williams: Did you do anything in regard to the cap?
>
> Loring: Yes, I picked it up.
>
> Williams: What did you do with it?
>
> Loring: Carried it down to the shop, kept it about an hour, looked it over, and finally carried it in the office and gave it to Mr. Fraher.
>
> Williams: Is that F-r-a-h-e-r?
>
> Loring: Fraher.
>
> (Mr. Williams hands a bundle to the witness.)
>
> Williams: Will you open that bundle, and see if you can tell the jury what it is?
>
> Loring: That is the cap.
>
> Williams: Do you mean the cap you found there that day?
>
> Loring: Found beside the body.
>
> Williams: And gave it to Mr. Fraher?
>
> Loring: Yes, sir.
>
> Williams: Can you tell whether it is in the same condition now as when you found it?
>
> Loring: Just the same.

Stark discrepancies in the above testimony are that the cap was found on the night of April 16, not in the afternoon of April

15, and, when found, it was not lying 18 inches from Berardelli's body but in the middle of the street. There were, in fact, no bodies there at all; they had already been removed. In addition, the cap was not in the same condition as when Loring reportedly found it because, by the time the trial started, it had a torn lining. Chief Gallivan had later torn it allegedly to see if it bore any identification markings. The State was to take advantage of the tear by claiming it was indeed the hole made by Sacco's routine of hanging it on a nail before starting work each day.

Chain of custody, alteration of evidence, false statements—if even there was a cap lying there in the first place. If not, it was found over a day later and could have belonged to any employee going in and out of work. And why wasn't Loring ever found guilty of perjury? I wanted to expound these thoughts to Sam but decided to wait until another time.

Later in the trial, Williams summoned George Kelley to the stand who said that he sometimes saw Sacco wearing a dark cap which he hung on a nail while at work. When asked if the cap found on the street bore any resemblance to Sacco's, Kelley replied, "The only thing I could say about that cap, Mr. Williams, from hanging up on a nail in the distance, it was similar in color. As far as details are concerned, I could not say it was."

In an extraordinary move, and damaging to Sacco, Williams, with help from Judge Thayer, succeeded in admitting into evidence a cap which many observers variously characterized as "stray" or "long-lost" or "suddenly turning up thirty hours after the robbery." The gambit is obvious in the following exchange, one in which the presiding judge muscles his way into the interrogation :

Judge Thayer: I would like to ask the witness one question: whether—I wish you would ask him, rather—according to your best judgment, is it your opinion that the cap which Mr. Williams now holds in his hand is like the one that was worn by the defendant Sacco?

Defense Counsel Moore: I object to that question, your Honor.

Thayer (to Williams): Did you put it? I would rather it come from Mr. Williams. Will you put that question?

Williams: Mr. Kelly, according to your best judgement, is the cap I show you alike in appearance to the one worn by Sacco?

Kelley: In color only.

Thayer: That is not responsive to the question. I wish you would answer it, if you can.

Kelley: I can't answer it when I don't know right down in my heart that that is the cap.

Thayer: I don't want you to. I want you should answer according to what is in your heart.

Kelley: General appearance. That is all I can say. I never saw that cap so close in my life as I do now.

Thayer: In its general appearance, is it the same?

Kelley: Yes, sir.

Moore: I object to that last question and answer.

Thayer: You may put the question so it comes from counsel rather than from the Court.

Williams: In its general appearance, is it the same?

Kelley: Yes.

Williams: I now offer the cap, if your Honor, please.

Thayer: Admitted.

It was during the cross-examination of Sacco that the cap taken from his home first made its appearance. It was also the first occasion of humor—unintended, but humor, nonetheless, as the interplay among the Court, prosecutor, defense counsel and defendant reveals. Exhibit 29 is the stray cap:

The Court: Will the defendant Sacco please return to the stand. I show you a cap. Will
you look it over, please, and tell me if you
know whose cap it is?

Moore: May—

(Mr. Moore confers with the Court.)

Katzmann: Don't answer for a minute.

The Court: You may answer the question.

Katzmann: It is all right now.

Sacco: It looks like my cap.

Katzmann: Yes. Did you have such a cap as that
in your house at the time of your arrest?

Sacco: Yes, sir, something like that.

Katzmann: You think it is. Did you speak, your
Honor?

The Court: No.

Katzmann: Oh, I thought you spoke.

Sacco: I said, "something like."

Katzmann: Isn't it your cap?

Sacco: I think it is my cap, yes.

Katzmann: Well, wait a minute, please. Look at it
carefully, will you?

Sacco: (Witness examines cap.) Yes.

Katzmann: There isn't any question but that is your
hat, is there?

The Court: "Cap," you mean.

Katzmann: Cap.

Sacco: No, I think it is my cap.

McAnarney (counsel for Vanzetti): I don't hear
you.

Katzmann: "No, I think it is my cap." Will you try
that cap on, please, and watch yourself
when you put it on, just how you put it on.
(Witness does so.)

Katzmann: The other side, this side. Is there anything you want to say? Did I catch you as

wanting to say something? I thought perhaps you did.

Sacco: I don't know. That cap looks too dirty to me because I never wear dirty cap. I think I always have fifty cents to buy a cap, and I don't work with a cap on my head when I work. I always keep cap clean. Right when I go to the factory, take all my clothes off and put overalls and jump. It look to me pretty dirty and too dark. Mine I think was little more light, little more gray.

Katzmann: Is that your hat?

The Court: Confine it to cap.

Katzmann: I beg your pardon. Is it your cap? I should not say "hat."

Sacco: I think it is. It looks like, but it is probably dirt—probably dirty after.

Katzmann: When you had it on, was that buttoned or unbuttoned when you just put it on?

Sacco: It was buttoned.

Katzmann: Put it on again and keep it buttoned, will you, please.

Sacco: Sure. (Doing so.)

Katzmann: On pretty hard?

Sacco: No, well, all right.

Katzmann: All right. Now, will you try—

Sacco: Not very loose.

Katzmann: Not very loose?

Sacco: No.

Katzmann: Will you try Exhibit 29 on, and use the same amount of force in putting it on that you used in putting that hat on?

Sacco: Yes. (Doing so.) Can't go in.

Katzmann: Can't go in?

Sacco: No.

Katzmann: Try and pull it down in back and see if

it can't go in.

Sacco: Oh, but it is too tight.

Katzmann: What is the difference in size between those two hats?

Sacco: I don't know, but it looks that is tight to me.

Katzmann: Is it any tighter than that hat?

Sacco: Yes, lots.

Katzmann: Lots tighter?

Sacco: Yes.

Katzmann: Is there any difference in the weight of material between the one that I now hold in my left hand and the one you have on your head?

Sacco: Lots of difference.

Katzmann: Yes. Now, assuming that they are the same head size, would one seem any tighter than the other because of the difference in the weight of materials?

Sacco: I don't say if it is material.

Katzmann: Look at the hats themselves. Any difference in head size between them?

Sacco: It has more material over there inside than this.

Katzmann: I will offer this hat. I can't offer it now, but I ask it to be marked for identification.

(Sacco's cap marked "Exhibit 27 for identification.")

Moore: (To the witness) Do you want an interpreter?

Sacco: All right. If you say so, all right.

Katzmann: I think it would be well to follow his suggestion.

(The testimony of the witness, however, is not given through an interpreter.)

Katzmann: I call your attention to Exhibit 27 for

identification, to that in the lining. What is
it?

Sacco: I never saw that before.

Katzmann: What is it?

Sacco: I don't know.

Katzmann: Don't know what that is?

Sacco: It is a hole.

Katzmann: It is a hole?

Sacco: Yes.

Katzmann: And you never saw that before?

Sacco: No.

Katzmann: Still you say that is your hat?

Sacco: Sure. Never saw that before.

Katzmann: Never saw that before. Was there any
hole in your hat when you last saw it?

Sacco: Hole, no

Katzmann: Sure of that?

Sacco: Pretty sure.

Katzmann: Where did you hang your hats up? If
this is your hat, did you ever wear it to
work?

Sacco: Yes.

Katzmann: What do you hang it on?

Sacco: On a wall.

Katzmann: On what on a wall.

Sacco: On the stake, on two stakes.

Katzmann: Two stakes?

Sacco: Yes, sticks.

Katzmann: Sticks of wood?

Sacco: One go across and put my jacket, my pants.

Katzmann: Is there a hook there?

Sacco: What do you mean, a hook?

Katzmann: A hat hook, or clothes hook?

Sacco: Yes, I made myself, for the purpose.

Katzmann: What is it made of?

Sacco: Sticks.

Katzmann: That is wood?
Sacco: Yes. Then there is a nail through.
Katzmann: Is it on the nail you hang your hat?
Sacco: Yes.
Katzmann: That is something you put up for your-
        self in the Kelley Shop, wasn't it?
Sacco: Yes.

Newspaper cartoonists had a field day with the testimony, one depicting the stray cap sitting on Sacco's head as a perched sparrow. Later, Mrs. Rosina Sacco testified she had never seen a hole in her husband's cap before.

What a bunch of hat experts, I thought. And of holes in hats.

I felt Sam's strong hand on my shoulder. "They never talked about hair," he said, his smile conspiritorial.

"What do you mean?" I decreased the decibel level a notch or two.

"I heard about two friends of the medical examiner— they got some hairs from the radical's cap and compared them to hairs from his comb—you know, under a microscope."

"And?"

"They matched, but Katzmann, he thought using it might backfire. The papers might say they tried to hang him by a hair." Sam let loose a laugh. No heads turned in our direction but I instinctively slid away.

I couldn't help but consider the many ways the caps could have been examined using the techniques of year 2000—for example, studying transfer evidence such as hair or sweat and utilizing DNA analysis in the process. Even now, I thought, their investigation is so superficial: Why not check things like possible manufacturer, style, additives, damages, wear patterns? But, after all, the cap could have been a plant, and the prosecution wouldn't have wanted the truth to come out. The defense would have, though. Seems to me the State got more

mileage out of a mysterious piece of clothing than it should have.

And in terms of size, I recalled the dramatic statement of O. J. Simpson's lawyer over 70 years later. The lawyer was Johnnie Cochran and he was referring to a glove that appeared too small for Simpson when he said, "If it doesn't fit, you must acquit." Strange that the same thing might have applied to Sacco and his hat, right?

Chapter 6

<u>Ballistics Magnified</u>

The major components of the ballistics evidence were Sacco's pistol at the time of his arrest, the so-called fatal bullet # III, the statements of expert witnesses, the bullets found in Berardelli and Parmenter, casings at the murder scene and Berardelli's gun.

Any serious observer of the Sacco-Vanzetti trial would agree that the most crucial and controversial issue involved Sacco's pistol, the fatal bullet removed from Berardelli's body by the medical examiner and the shell from which it was alleged to have been fired. Before scutinizing them, however (and then turning to the testimony of experts and the fate of Berardelli's gun), the probable sequence of events must be outlined as they pertained to each of these elements.

Of help in the understanding of this sequence is the definition of several technical terms used in the identification of handguns and bullets, terms such as "cartridge," "shell," "casing," "rifling," "land," "groove" and "twist." The cartridge used in a gun is composed of two main parts: a small tube called a shell or casing and a bullet (See Figure 1). The interior of a gun barrel has spiral grooves or rifling cut into it. If the grooves incline clockwise, the gun has a right twist; if counterclockwise, a left twist. Likewise, one may speak of a bullet with either a right or left twist, depending on the gun from which it was fired. Lands are raised portions between grooves.

The working particulars around the time of the trial were:
1. When he was arrested, Sacco had a fully loaded Colt .32-caliber automatic pistol tucked in the waistband of his trousers and 32 steel jacketed bullets in his coat pocket: 16 Peters, three Remington, six Winchester

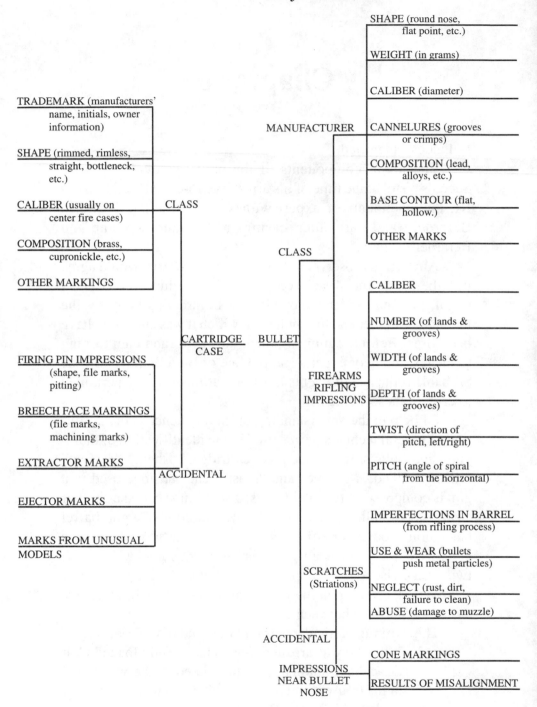

Figure 1.   Schematic Analysis of Firearms Identification

and seven U.S.

2. At the autopsies performed by Dr. George Magrath, the Medical Examiner of Suffolk County, Massachusetts, six bullets were taken from the two bodies: four from Berardelli, the guard, and two from Parmenter, the paymaster. Magrath used a needle to mark the base of each bullet with a separate roman numeral. The one he judged to have killed Berardelli by tearing through his aorta is known as fatal bullet # III.

3. Four .32-caliber cartridge shells were found at the murder scene: two Peters, one Remington U.M.C. and one Winchester.

4. It was alleged that fatal bullet #III had a left twist and the other five, right twists.

The differentiation of twists was clearly refuted 60 years later when testimony from a grand jury proceeding in September 1920 was first made public. At that proceeding, which had taken place before the trial, Dr. Magrath answered Katzmann's queries:

Katzmann: In plain English, he (Berardelli) was shot from behind?

Magrath: He was shot from behind, three of the wounds from his left side to his hip to a fourth from behind toward the middle of the body and backward. These four bullets I placed in the hands of Captain Proctor on August 3rd at his office in the State House. The bullets are all alike; they were jacketed and weighed 4 and 1/10 grammes; the dimensions and weight are consistent with what is known as a .32-caliber made to be used in an automatic pistol.

Katzmann: In your opinion, were those bullets fired by the same gun?

Magrath: I have an opinion that they all may have

been fired by the same gun, but I have no proof. The bullets were all of the same size and weight. A final determination I did not make, but I have a belief that they were fired from the same weapon and they very well could have been, judging from the size and weight.

Katzmann: They were the same type of bullet?

Magrath: *They looked exactly alike.* (emphasis added)

Katzmann: (After a discussion of Parmenter's wounds and the bullets removed from his body) What was the caliber of it (the Parmenter bullet)?

Magrath: It was a jacketed bullet 7 mm. in diameter—the same size and character as the bullets previously removed from the body of Baradelli (sic), .32, of the kind used in an automatic pistol.

Katzmann: You have personally been in consultation with me on experiments as to the type of gun from which the four bullets were discharged? You did not personally experiment to see?

Magrath: *No, I did not.* (emphasis added)[10]

Dr. Magrath's words speak for themselves. The conclusions to be drawn? That an experienced and respected medical examiner from the populous county which included Boston most certainly would have recognized a difference in rifling marks, and his sworn statements raised the question of a possible switch of the bullets. Indeed, the custody of all the bullets from autopsies to trial, a period of over a year, had never been traced. They passed willy-nilly among ballistics experts to law enforcement officials to clerks and possibly others, providing adequate time and opportunity to plant a bullet with a singular twist. Furthermore, each bullet had been placed in its own envelope and, at the trial, given exhibit numbers which were written on the envelopes, not on the bullets inside. Conceivably, a substitution could have occurred as late as the trial itself.

Prosecution witness James Bosteck declared he found three or four spent shells near Berardelli's body, but other accounts indicate a police officer picked up four and gave them to Thomas Fraher, the Slater and Morrill superintendent. Bosteck testified he left the shells in a desk at the factory, but Fraher stated he received them directly from Bosteck and kept them for one-and-a-half hours before turning them over to Captain Proctor. Proctor, in turn, retained them for an indefinite period of time and then, he asserted, gave them to the sheriff of the Dedham Court. The point is that the shells changed hands many times (as in the case of the bullets), allowing opportunities for an accidental or deliberate switch.

In this regard, if there *had* been a substitution, the prosecution must have desperately feared its discovery during Dr. Magrath's testimony, but Assistant District Attorney Williams managed to sidestep the danger with a lesson in chicanery.

> Williams: Let me show you these bullets, Doctor, and see if you can identify them as the bullets removed from the body of Berardelli (*handing bullets to the witness*). May we have a little light, Sheriff?
>
> Magrath: I identify that (*indicating*) as the bullet which I numbered "III" by placing three vertical marks upon it, on the left base.
>
> Williams: Is there any objection to me showing this bullet to the jury?
>
> Magrath: None whatever. I am not sure that the light in the jury box will show the light marks. If it doesn't, use the lens. (The bullet was offered and shown to the defense.)
>
> Williams: What kind of bullet is that?
>
> Magrath: It is a jacketed bullet, of the size

consistent with what is known as 32-caliber.

Williams: *Can you personally tell, Doctor, from what type of gun or shooting weapon that bullet was fired?* (emphasis added)

Magrath: *No.* (emphasis added)

Williams: (*to the jury*) Mr. Foreman, just look at that bullet and see if it is flattened in any way and look at the mark on the base. If you cannot see them with this reading glass very likely you can with the smaller glass. If any of you have any difficulty with it, I have a little more powerful glass. I will ask you, Doctor, *to save possibly a longer examination of other bullets* (emphasis added), if the other marks on the other bullets which you are about to examine are roman numerals similar in character to that No. III on the bottom of the bullet?

Magrath: They are; the number 4 being represented by four vertical lines and not by a "I" and a "V," but by four vertical lines.

Williams: Doctor, if you will replace that in the envelope marked "Bullet No. III." Now, if you will examine envelope marked "Bullet No. II" and tell us what you find there.

Magrath: This envelope contains a jacketed bullet bearing two marks which I placed upon its base, known as No. "II" of my record. (Bullet II becomes Exhibit 19.)

Williams: (*showing Exhibit 19 to the jury*). *Just pass it around to show its general appearance, gentlemen. That is all you need to do, I guess, unless you care to do otherwise.* (emphasis added) (The other bullets were then examined and admitted one by one.)

The thrust of this subterfuge was two-fold. First, Dr. Magrath was prevented from noticing the rifling marks and scratches by Williams' deft handling of the bullets: He showed Bullet III initially and then the rest, one at a time. And, two, Williams manipulated the jury itself so as not to allow the bullets to be examined closely.

If a switch *did* take place, then when? Most likely before February 1921. (Remember the crimes occurred in April 1920 and the trial began in May 1921.) Attorney Williams' notebook contains an entry dated February 1921 indicating that the four bullets removed from Berardelli include one fired from a Colt automatic.

The next question is, by whom? The possibilities are Captain Proctor or Charles Van Amburgh (a second prosecution expert), or Chief Stewart and State Police Officer Albert Brouillard. The latter two were the official investigators in the case. There is no record of the custody of the bullets between August 3, 1920, when Dr. Magrath gave them to Proctor, and the trial 10 months later. And, in his trial testimony, Proctor was never asked nor did he volunteer any information about the location of the bullets during that time frame. Some historians believe the perpetrators were Chief Stewart and Officer Brouillard, but they offer no specific motive other than to seal the case.

And the final question is, how? One theory is that the culprit or culprits may have test fired Sacco's pistol, substituted the resulting bullet for the original bullet III and then added the empty shell to the others. Ironically, the test-fired bullet became flattened during the firing and thus became the reason why—the theory goes—bullet number III was chosen—because it, too, had a flattened appearance.

In terms of either side's scoring points by the testimony of four expert witnesses (two introduced by the prosecution and two by the defense), the net result seemed to be a wash, at least on the surface. The experts were Captain William H. Proctor, head of the Massachusetts State Police; Charles Van Amburgh, an assistant in the ballistics department of the Remington Company;

James E. Burns, a ballistics engineer with 30 years of experience at the U.S. Cartridge Company; and J. H. Fitzgerald, in charge of testing at the Colt Factory in Hartford, Connecticut. The sworn statements of Proctor at both the trial and in an affidavit given later, in October 1923, carried the most weight.

My idealistic self wanted to believe that a switch had never occurred because such deception would tarnish the entire trial, but my realistic self warned that as long as human beings have the opportunity to effect outcomes, anything is possible.

Comprehension of the dynamics of this key phase of the case requires first skipping ahead to that affidavit, next returning to the trial and, finally, again moving forward to Proctor's affadavit. Sacco's and Vanzetti's defense team obtained the following statement from the State Police Captain over two years after the trial:

> During the preparation for the trial, my attention was repeatedly called by the district attorney and his assistants to the question: whether I could find any evidence which would justify the opinion that the particular bullet taken from the body of Berardelli, which came from a Colt automatic pistol, came from the particular Colt automatic pistol taken from Sacco. I used every means available to me for forming an opinion on this subject. ... At no time was I able to find any evidence whatever which tended to convince me that the particular model bullet ... came from Sacco's pistol and I so informed the district attorney and his assistant before the trial.

The passage clearly indicates that Proctor had informed the State he had found no evidence that fatal bullet # III was fired by Sacco's pistol. Even after consultation with another expert witness (Van Amburgh), Katzmann must have been convinced that

The defendants, Sacco (right) and Vanzetti (left). (Boston Public Library/ Rare Books Department. Courtesy of The Trustees.)

Crime scene of the double murder, South Braintree, Massachusetts. (Boston Public Library/Rare Books Department. Courtesy of The Trustees.)

All photographs, unless otherwise indicated, are from Dr. Lee's private collection.

The guns of Sacco (top) and Vanzetti (bottom).

Sacco and Vanzetti escorted to courthouse. (Boston Public Library/Rare Books Department. Courtesy of The Trustees.)

Sacco and Vanzetti boarding bus en route to learning verdict. (Boston Public Library/Rare Books Department. Courtesy of The Trustees.)

Presiding Judge Webster Thayer. (Boston Public Library/Rare Books Department. Courtesy of The Trustees.)

District Attorney Frederick G. Katzmann. (Boston Public Library/Rare Books Department. Courtesy of The Trustees.)

Exterior of Dedham courthouse.

Sacco and Vanzetti in courthouse cage.

*Dedham courtroom.
The jury box.*

*Dedham courtroom.
The witness stand.*

*Dedham courtroom,
full view.*

Four bullets removed from Berardelli. Note fatal bullet #III.

Dr. Lee examining Sacco-Vanzetti evidence in 1983.

Sacco-Vanzetti funeral. (Boston Public Library/Rare Books Department. Courtesy of The Trustees.)

Armband worn by Sacco-Vanzetti sympathizers. (Boston Public Library/Rare Books Department. Courtesy of The Trustees.)

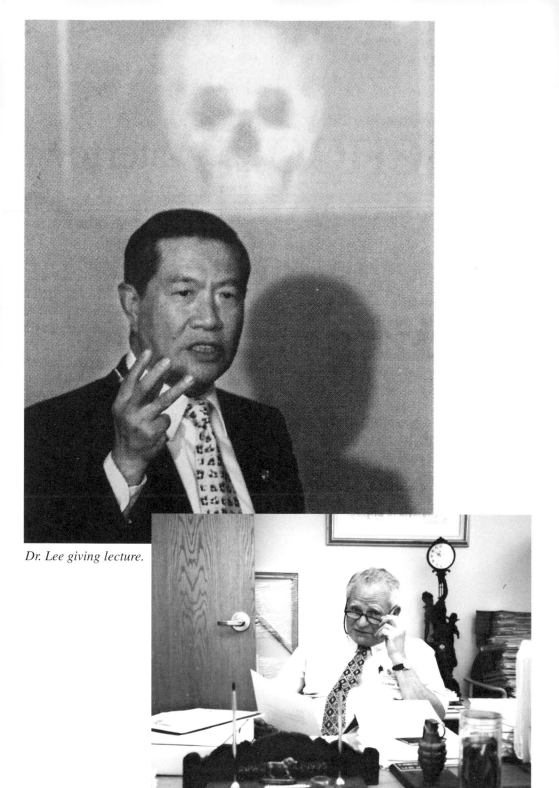

Dr. Lee giving lecture.

Dr. Labriola giving interview.

the introduction of ballistics evidence, as it then stood, would damage the State's case.

Surmising the prosecution's concerns, Defense Counsel Moore decided to act swiftly: He would arrange to have ballistics tests conducted if Sacco agreed to the experiment. Sacco told them to "experiment all they wished," a comment many believed was proof of his innocence.

Judge Thayer granted permission for the testing to be done on June 18, 1921, by Proctor, Van Amburgh and Burns. When testing was concluded, the experts gave three different opinions: Proctor declared there was no proof Sacco's weapon had fired the fatal bullet, Van Amburgh said it might have, and Burns said it definitely did not. When pressed, Proctor insisted that if he were to be asked at the trial whether bullet III was fired from Sacco's pistol, his reply would be that he would answer in the negative. Therefore, at the trial, Williams phrased his questions with deliberate care (and duplicity):

Williams: Have you an opinion as to whether bullet 3 was fired from the Colt automatic which is in evidence?

Proctor: I have.

Williams: And what is your opinion?

Proctor: *My opinion is that it is consistent with being fired by that pistol.* (emphasis added)

Williams: Is there anything different in the appearance of the other five bullets—

Proctor: Yes.

Williams: Just a minute, I had not completed— the other five bullets to which I have just referred, which would indicate to you that they were fired from more than one weapon?

Proctor: There is not.

Williams: Are the appearance of those bullets *consistent* with being fired from the same weapon?

Proctor: *As far as I can see.* (emphasis added)

Williams: *Captain, did you understand my question when I asked you if you had an opinion as to whether the five bullets which you say were fired from an automatic type of pistol were fired from the same gun?* (emphasis added)

Proctor: *I would not say positively.* (emphasis added)

Williams: Well, have you an opinion?

Proctor: *I have.* (emphasis added)

Williams: Well, that is what I asked you before. *I thought possibly you didn't understand. What is your opinion as to the gun from which those four (five?) were fired?* (emphasis added)

Proctor: *My opinion is, all five were fired from the same pistol.* (emphasis added)

In the foregoing exchange, Captain Proctor twice balked at answering as if he meant the word "consistent" definitely implied a positive response. Williams' persistence, moreover, bordered on coercion, but he succeeded in duping the jury into defining the word "consistent" exactly as the prosecution had intended.

Then, in an astonishing error of omission, the defense team did not ask for clarification in the cross-examination, nor did it emphasize Sacco's sincere willingness to have the test firing go forward, painting such cooperation as the supreme gesture of an innocent man. Instead, what follows is the sum total of Moore's words to the jury:

Gentlemen, if the time has come when a microscope must be used to determine whether a human life is going to continue to function or not and when the users of a microscope themselves can't agree, when experts called by the Commonwealth and experts called by the defense are sharply defined in their disagreements, then I take it that ordinary men such as you and I should well hesitate to take a human life.

Proctor's statement stood as presented, no less powerful than it would have been without the word "consistent." Parenthetically, it should be noted that District Attorney Katzmann, in his subsequent discussion of the ballistics evidence, never once mentioned Proctor's opinion—or even his name.

The captain defended his testimony in the affidavit two years later, a part of which has already been referred to. His additional remarks were:

> At the trial, the District Attorney did not ask me whether I had found any evidence that the so-called mortal bullet which I have referred to as number III passed through Sacco's pistol, nor was I asked the question on cross-examination. The District Attorney desired to ask me that question, but I had repeatedly told him that if he did I should be obliged to answer in the negative; consequently, he put to me this question. Q. Have you any opinion as to whether bullet III was fired from the Colt automatic which is in evidence? To which I answered, "I have." He then proceeded. Q. And what is your opinion? A. My opinion is that it is consistent with being fired from that pistol.

> That is still my opinion for the reason that bullet number III, in my judgment, passed through some Colt automatic pistol, but I do not intend by that answer to imply that I had found any evidence that the so-called mortal bullet had passed through this particular Colt automatic pistol, and the District Attorney well knew that I did not so intend and framed his question accordingly. Had I been asked the direct question: whether I had found any affirmative evidence whatever that this so-called mortal bullet had

passed through this particular Sacco's pistol, I should
have answered then, as I do now without hesitation,
in the negative.

In the firearms evidence testimony, there was much that
was primitive by the standards of year 2000, and I thought
about it during a lull in the proceedings. Sam was not there
that day and I thought about him, too, and especially about
his comments the day before. But first things first.

With respect to the bullets' evidence, four impressions:
In the twenties, the method of matching guns with suspect
bullets was fraught with error. For example, measuring the
distance between the marks of lands and grooves on a bullet,
or the exact location and size of firing pin indentations on
exploded shells—these approaches are now obsolete, having
been replaced with more sophisticated technologies. And not
only as they apply to ballistics but also as they assist us in the
whole spectrum of forensic evidence. Comparison microscopes, neutron activation analysis, scanning electron microscopes, computer imaging. It's a whole new ball game now
and, as I sat there giving myself a lecture in forensic science,
as it were, I thought the game could have been easily won if
those in authority had the tools of the twenty-first century at
their disposal. In other words, it would have been a solvable
case, even *before* the Vanzetti issue was debated.

I remember shifting in my seat upon realizing relevant
evidentiary questions would never be brought up—my second impression. And the reason was simple: Certain evidence
was never gathered and certain questions were never entertained. Things like, how many shots were definitely fired?
Was there any inventory or documentation of each shot? If a
bandit had sprayed bullets all over the place, where were the
bullets lodged? Where were the spent shells? And these basic
considerations were those applying to the firearms evidence
alone; I was certain there would be more dangling questions
to follow.

The third impression about the bullets? If a panel of so-called experts could not agree on what they measured in the exhibits or on what they deemed significant, how could an amateur jury make any sense out of it all? I wondered about the reliability of prosecution experts but also of defense experts who could have easily examined firearms in the courtroom, substituted a weapon and walked away with the real one. It was a distinct possibility that both sides had not been playing fair.

The fourth impression, related to the third and having to do with the professional integrity and ethical standards of attorneys and forensic experts, can be summed up by asking the question: In any criminal case, aren't two of the optimal goals of our justice system to discover truths and to establish the scientific facts?

Now turning to my friend, Sam Constant. In the courtroom, he was as mercurial as ever, present one day, absent the next—or even several in a row. Up to that point, I'd not missed a session and planned not to. He never joined us at noon down High Street at Gilbert's Lunch in Dedham Square. (I recall with great fondness some of the patrons I befriended there and the sobriquet we attached to our daily visit: "Sandwiches and Scuttlebutt.") It may have had something to do with his physicality, or lack of it. But wasn't he there that night, at Martha's Home Cooking? Even if the waitress didn't see him? In any event, as the days wore on, and as I became accustomed to the jolting sounds of the gavel and a century's worth of mustiness in the corridors, I also grew used to Mr. Yankee Doodle Dandy by my side and missed him when he stayed away.

But gradually he changed as the combatants bore into the case, and with every prosecution score, he would wink toward the jury while his full smile would turn into a purse of the lips, smug-like, with grey eyes constricting to BB shots.

On the previous morning, I had said, "Welcome back. You've lost interest?"

"On the contrary," he answered, "I come now only to check. See the way it goes. First, prime the pump of justice and, once in a while, check on the flow of truth. See if the flow continues."

The pump of justice? The flow of truth? The only words I could pluck from a frozen reservoir were, "And is the flow continuing?"

"Very nicely, to be sure. It often does in these things." And then the stunner: "You going to the Bruno Hauptmann trial?"

The Hauptmann trial! The Lindbergh baby! A dozen years away. He knows about that, too? Why not, don't I?

"Well," he said, "are you?"

I was only half there. "What? Oh, yes—uh—yes, of course."

I broke for lunch earlier than usual and on the way wondered why I was the only one who could visualize Sam. But then considering it in the context of my own presence there, the wondering eased. What's wrong with a phantom added to the whole surreal drama? I had finally come to grips with the notion that, in time and place, he was as unreal as I. Only thing was, I knew where I came from. Where did he?

I anticipated asking him that question and others during the afternoon session, but he was not there. And although the Vanzetti part of the trial lay ahead, I had a suspicion I was not to see anymore of Sam Constant in Dedham.

Chapter 7

<u>Verdict. Whose Victory?</u>

If fatal bullet # III doomed Sacco, then a .38-caliber Harrington and Richardson revolver doomed Vanzetti. An intriguing question was whether or not such a revolver belonged to him at all. That caliber and make was found on Vanzetti upon his arrest and—deceitfully or not—would provide the State with the only physical evidence linking him to the South Braintree robbery and murders.

At the trial, the prosecution asserted that the gun had, in fact, belonged to Berardelli and was snatched from the slain guard during the course of the crimes. Thus, if both Vanzetti's gun and the one habitually carried by Berardelli were of the same make and caliber, the State's case in the matter might have been validated. It further held that Berardelli's gun had recently been repaired and that the one in Vanzetti's possession had evidence of this. But conflicting records involving the Iver Johnson Company in Boston clouded the issue, especially with regard to a reception receipt listing the revolver as a .38-caliber while the repair record listed it as a .32-caliber. In fact, there was no proof, at the time of the crimes, that the weapon had actually been returned from the repair shop.

Through a February 18, 1921, memorandum (after the murders and before the trial), it was learned that Police Chief Stewart brought the Vanzetti gun to the shop and met with George Fitzmeyer who had worked on Berardelli's revolver. In the document, not released by the state police until 1977, Stewart described what took place:

> He (Fitzmeyer) was shown the gun and asked to take it apart. I then asked him if that was a new spring, pointing to the spring of the gun and he said, "No

that is not a new spring." I said, "What about the hammer?" Looked at the hammer and he said, "It is a new hammer." Asked him how he knew and he said that the notch on the back of the hammer which might be called the spring notch shows no sign of wear and the general appearance of the hammer itself would indicate that it was a new hammer. He further stated that the case hardening or finish on the hammer which is done with bone dust has only been used by the Harrington and Richardson Firearms Company for two or three years at the outside and the gun itself cylinder and barrel, showed that it was a much older gun than that. In answer to the question "Then in your opinion there is no question but what this is a new hammer?" said "There is no question at all about it."[11]

There is no doubt that today such tampering with physical evidence would constitute grounds for a mistrial, but of an even more egregious nature, Bartolomeo Vanzetti was later to be electrocuted on evidence the State knew to be false. The same Stewart memorandum reveals that the prosecution had the serial number of Berardelli's revolver all along, and it knew it was not Vanzetti's. It had previously been determined that paymaster Parmenter had bought the revolver for his guard, Berardelli. Stewart elaborated:

Thursday, February 16th, found on the revolver book of C.A. Noyes Hardware Company in Brockton a entry showing that on October 10, 1919 F.A. Parmenter purchased a Harrington and Richardson, 32-caliber, nickel finish revolver No. 394717.

This revolver was sold to Mr. Parmenter by Karl Tehurnert, a salesman in the employ of the above concern.

Went through all the books showing sale of revolvers at this concern, which dates from July 10, 1911 to the present day. Was told by Mr. Chandler that July 10, 1911 was the day on which they sold their first gun.[12]

The revolver purchased by Parmenter was therefore not Vanzetti's which had been established to be a .38-caliber with the serial number of G-82581, but Berardelli's, a .32-caliber with the serial number of 394717. And the date of the purchase coincided with the date Mrs. Berardelli stated her husband had been permanently hired by Slater and Morrill. These facts offer conclusive proof of the Commonwealth's distortion of the truth, and they fly in the face of the absurd postulation that during the swift and frenzied commission of a robbery and double murder, a bandit would have taken the time to steal Berardelli's revolver.

Consciousness of Guilt

Behavior that gives the appearance of guilt holds little sway in modern judicial circles, but in the early part of the last century, the concept of consciousness of guilt was regularly used against defendants.

After the verdict was returned and a motion was made for a new trial based on the defense's claim to have discovered a new eyewitness, Judge Thayer evoked such a concept when he stated, "The evidence that convicted these defendants was circumstantial and was evidence that is known in the law as 'consciousness of guilt.' This evidence, corroborated as it was by the eyewitnesses, was responsible for these verdicts of guilty."

There had been no challenge to the claim that both defendants had lied on several occasions, but it was just as indisputable that, in the early going, they were never informed they were suspected of the crimes. In lying to the police officers and to the prosecuting attorney, the defendants maintained they were trying to shield radicals and to conceal their own unpatriotic conduct. They maintained that even the trip in search of Boda's automobile and the flight from the Johnson garage were not related to the South Braintree incident but, rather, to their desire to dispose of radical literature and their fear of being exposed as anarchists.

At one point in the trial, in a pressing attack laden with sarcasm, prosecutor Katzmann asked Sacco why his memory was better there in Dedham than it had been at the time of his arrest:

Katzmann: Is your memory very good, Mr. Sacco? Good memory?

Sacco: Yes.

Katzmann: Working well?

Sacco: Not all the time.

Katzmann: How is it today?

Sacco: Pretty good.

Katzmann: How was it the night I talked to you?

Sacco: I was real disturbed.

Katzmann: Were you half as much disturbed when you were talking with me when you did not know what you were there for, as you say, as you are now when you are charged with murder?

Sacco: I would not say it is better than that time.

Katzmann: I am asking you to say which time were you better, now or that night?

Sacco: It looks to me now the charge is more bad.

Katzmann: Does that mean you were in better shape then as to memory than you are now?

Sacco: I did not know at that time they put in this murder ... I got to remember very particular things (now), because the charge is awful on my shoulders.

Katzmann: The worse the charge the better your memory?

Sacco: I suppose so. (Man) have to remember where he was.

Sarcasm is often used to intimidate and therefore to fluster. Katzmann's line of questioning was a perfect example.

For better or for worse, the whole issue of consciousness of guilt must have impacted decisively on every tier of the criminal justice system of the day. The defendants' conduct reflected the unmistakable depth of their emotions, especially the fear which stemmed from their evasion of the draft, their association with known anarchists, their own avowed political views, the loss of friends through deportation, and the anti-Italian atmosphere of that era.

Summations and Verdict

One hundred sixty-seven witnesses testified in 30 days of trial. After what has been universally regarded as pitiful addresses by defense counsel, characterized more by omissions, incoherences and repetitions than by substance, Prosecutor Katzmann followed with a skillfully crafted and spellbinding rebuttal. Perhaps the three most convincing kernels from his four-hour speech were:

This left-handed twist bullet, No. III, was fired by a Colt .32. Was it fired by this Colt .32? Some one of the learned counsel for the defense has said that it is coming to a pretty pass when the microscope is used to convict a man of murder. I say heaven speed the day when proof in any important case is dependent upon the magnifying glass and the scientist and is less dependent upon the untrained witness without the microscope. Those things can't be wrong in the hands of a skilled user of a microscope or a magnifying glass.

I say to you on this vital matter of the No. III bullet. ... Take the three Winchester bullets that were fired by Capt. Van Amburgh at Lowell and take the seven United States bullets that were fired by Mr. Burns at Lowell, and, lastly, take the barrel itself which we will unhitch for you, and determine the fact for yourself or yourselves.

Take the glass, gentlemen, and examine them for yourselves. If you choose, take the word of nobody in that regard. Take the exhibits themselves. Can there be a fairer test that I ask you to submit yourselves to?

The District Attorney's closing command was brilliant: "Gentlemen of the jury, do your duty. Do it like men. Stand together, you men of Norfolk!"

Katzmann's tour de force worked, for shortly after deliberations began, the jurors requested a magnifying glass. In essence, he had cleverly brushed aside the conflicting testimony of ballistics experts by allowing each of the jurors be his own expert. Based on the closing arguments alone, the defendants had little or no chance.

Then, on July 14, 1921, Judge Webster Thayer delivered his 24-page charge to the jury after arriving at his desk which was festooned with flowers placed there by admirers. The charge, recognized more for its appeal to patriotism than to eloquence, was simply an extension of Katzmann's effort. It contained these words:

The Commonwealth of Massachusetts called upon you to render a most important service. Although you knew that such service would be arduous, painful and tiresome, yet you, like the true soldier, responded to that call in the spirit of supreme American loyalty. There is no better word in the English language than "loyalty." For he who is loyal to God, to country, to his state and to his fellow man, represents the highest and noblest type of true American citizenship, than which there is none grander in the entire world.

When the judge left the courtroom, he addressed a reporter from the *Boston Globe*. "Did you see that jury when I finished my charge, three of them in tears?" Receiving no answer, he then said, "I think I am entitled to have a statement printed in the

newspapers that this trial was fairly and impartially conducted."
Again, there was no response but the judge persisted: "Don't you
think this trial was fairly and impartially conducted?"

The reporter answered, "We have talked it over, and I think
I can say, I have never seen anything like it."[13] Thayer stalked
away.

**Was this a variation of the theme, "Methinks you doth
protest too much"?**

That afternoon, the jury left to deliberate at 2:30 and re
turned five hours later.

> Thayer: Poll the jury, Mr. Clerk. (The jury was
> polled).
> Thayer: If the jury is agreed, you may please take
> the verdict.
> Clerk: Gentlemen of the jury, have you agreed
> upon your verdict?
> Ripley (Foreman): We have.
> Clerk: Nicola Sacco.
> Sacco: Present. (Sacco stood).
> Clerk: Hold up your right hand. Mr. Foreman, look
> upon the prisoner. Prisoner, look upon the
> Foreman. What say you, Mr. Foreman, is
> the prisoner at the bar guilty or not guilty?
> Ripley: Guilty.
> Clerk: Guilty of murder?
> Ripley: Murder.
> Clerk: In the first degree?
> Ripley: In the first degree.
> Clerk: Upon each indictment?
> Ripley: Yes, sir.
> Clerk: Bartolomeo Vanzetti. (Vanzetti stood).
> Clerk: Hold up your right hand. Look upon the
> Foreman. Mr. Foreman, look upon the
> prisoner. What say you, Mr. Foreman, is

Bartolomeo guilty or not guilty of murder?

Ripley: Guilty.

Clerk: In the first degree, upon each indictment?

Ripley: In the first degree.

Clerk: Harken to your verdicts as the Court has recorded them. You, gentlemen, upon your oath, say that Nicola Sacco and Bartolomeo Vanzetti is each guilty of murder in the first degree upon each indictment. So say you, Mr. Foreman. So, gentlemen, you all say.

Jury: We do, we do, we do.

Thayer: (To the jury.) I can add nothing to what I said this morning, gentlemen, except again to express to you the gratitude of the Commonwealth for the service that you have rendered. You may now go to your homes, from which you have been absent for nearly seven weeks. The Court will now adjourn.

Sacco: *They kill an innocent man! They kill two innocent men!*

The verdicts didn't shock me. And probably no one else. But, of course I knew the outcome. What did shock me, though, was the length to which the Commonwealth went to convict two men. This is not necessarily disputing the verdicts but, rather, inferring gross misconduct of the representatives of the Commonwealth, from the presiding judge on down.

I'd thought before of the fate of other bullets fired at the crime scene. To this I added other irregularities: tampering with evidence (taking the revolver apart); deceit and withholding of evidence (serial number of Berardelli's gun); possible switching of the gun barrel or of the bullet and shell; possible collusion involving Captain Proctor's sworn testimony. These are just for openers, as they say, because the list is much longer. I'd squirmed at least once a day, itching to jump up and scream, "Hold on, now! You can't *do* that. You can't *say* that. You can't *deduce* that." And how about a whole host of questions such as, "What became of the boxes containing $15,776? The money was never recovered. What happened to it? Did the cap fit or didn't it? What about the jury Foreman who died a few months after the trial? Could he have taken any pertinent secrets to the grave? Any record of that? How about fibers, hair, trace evidence or shoe prints in the car? At the crime scene? How many bullets were actually test fired? Any inventory of those bullets and their casings? What happened to the others in the getaway car? Any follow-up on them?"

I also had a problem justifying the time line in the case and believe that if such a crime had happened today in the year 2000, reconstruction of the crime scene would have clarified this and many other issues, or, at least, rendered a "probably" versus an "impossible" designation.

There were so many problems, but the one that distressed me the most (because I thought I knew the answer and felt it represented a flagrant violation of all that should have been right about Anglo-American justice), was the one dealing with fingerprint evidence. I don't remember the exact quote but I believe it was Justice Oliver Wendell Holmes who talked of a "magnetic point" and said that evidence can be attracted to it or repelled by it. The state police had taken prints from the defendants and compared them with those lifted from the abandoned car. They then met with the district attorney in his office but the subject never arose during the trial or later. Was this an instance when evidence was repelled from the magnetic point? An instance when the prints did not match? But why didn't the defense ever ask about it all?

I decided then and there not to hang around the Dedham area to witness seven years of fruitless appeals and to read original accounts of the international uproar over the verdicts. I was familiar with it all and, after the high pitch of the trial itself, had no stomach to go through more, especially knowing the men were headed for execution anyway.

But I wondered where Sam was and whether he'd broken open the champagne, yet. And whether he'd join me in New Jersey for another famous trial.

Section Two

Lindbergh Kidnapping
Sam Sheppard
John F. Kennedy
Vincent Foster
JonBenet Ramsey

Chapter 1:
Preamble

Chapter 2:
Lindbergh. The Murder of an American Hero's Baby

Chapter 3:
Sam Sheppard. The Case That Spawned *The Fugitive*

Chapter 4:
John F. Kennedy. Who Killed Our President?

Chapter 5:
Vincent Foster. Suicide or Murder in Washington?

Chapter 6:
JonBenet Ramsey. What Is Wrong with the Case?

Chapter 1

Preamble

It is safe to postulate that many of the crimes of past generations could have been solved with impunity if modern forensic tools had been available and used. From the pioneering work in France of Professor Edmond Locard in the early 1900s to Dr. Paul Kirk's contributions in the field of criminalistics in the mid-century, there has been an explosion of scientific techniques that have rendered the old methods obsolete. Many now have only historical value. From the 1920s through the 1960s, for example, the analysis of blood taken from a crime scene depended in large part on ABO blood grouping and hemoglobin subtypings. Some investigators would even attach meaning to bloodstains based on only presumptive and weakly positive test results. Today, one may turn to more sophisticated DNA typing techniques such as DQA1, polymarkers, STR, mt-DNA and any of a host of additional genetic markers.

In the area of trace evidence, there has been a similar leap. Locard, considered the father of criminalistics, developed the notion that whenever two objects come into contact with each other, traces are exchanged. Thus, hairs, fibers, skin cells, soil and other traces may be left behind at crime scenes or, conversely, picked up there by the perpetrator. And technology aimed at identifying such transfer evidence has dramatically changed from a simple magnifier to high resolution scanning electron microscopes.

In recent years, there have been many other important advances. DNA typing, image enhancement, computer mapping and artificial intelligence systems are now part of the forensics landscape, while modernization has kept pace in the important areas of latent fingerprints, toxicology and firearms identification.

Clearly, forensic science is on the move. In the context of

this book, moreover, if it had begun its move sooner, perhaps the cases discussed could have been labeled open-and-shut. And therein lies the purpose of this section: to demonstrate how modern technology might have helped solve past criminal cases and improved the conduct of jury trials, and to suggest that human error and/or misconduct might have tarnished the end results.

Everyone interested in the history of crime has his/her own choice for the crime or trial of the twentieth century. The cases included in this second section were not selected with such notoriety or lofty legal inquisitions in mind. They were chosen, rather, because of flaws in their criminal investigations and/or within the trials themselves and, therefore, they lend themselves as testimony to the worth of present-day forensic science. In all five instances, it will be shown how the application of modern technology and strict adherence to proper investigation protocol might have rendered decisions that are irrefutable. As of this reckoning, however, each in the group remains controversial; each continues to be fiercely debated; each continues to be investigated to some degree; and, in the case of some, there may never be a satisfactory resolution.

A glaring feature of this section—in case after case after case—is the remarkable presence of human fallibility and the effect of public opinion on either the outcome of the case or the nature of its aftermath. It is difficult to ignore the strength of these factors in shaping results in criminal cases but—as in the Sacco-Vanzetti era with its rampant emotions of fear and hatred—the human element does not lend itself to easy measurement. One of the theses of this section is that in many classic episodes, outside influences might have been compromised had modern forensic techniques been in place. Whether or not outcomes would have changed is a question that only history may answer.

The visit to the 1920s had been the first of my several journeys back in history and it gave me the experience needed to maneuver in the past while aware of the future—to be objective in the face of known subsequent events. The Sacco-

Vanzetti story was like an enormous dose of déjà vu, or like the reconstruction of a crime scene when all the pieces were numbered so you knew where they fit. And once home in 2000, I looked forward to more trips back, hopscotching among cases that had intrigued me, each with its own fascination, each branded with patterns of mishandling and misconduct. What an irony, I thought: looking forward to the past! A past whose criminal investigations and trials would have yielded so much more in the way of concrete results had the sophistication of today's forensic science been available. Based on what detectives and forensic scientists had at their disposal then, it's little wonder their results were often what I call "wobbly" for, in the resolution of some cases, there continues to be doubt. More or less than reasonable doubt? That's the overriding question.

I sat writing at my desk at the State Police Headquarters in Middletown, Connecticut. My office is twice as large as any I'd occupied before. Its walls are covered with plaques, medals and commendations; the corridors above and beyond are busy with police officers in pressed unforms and shiny shoes; and the nameplate on my door reads, *Commissioner*. A thought flashed through my mind like a ticker tape out of control: that one could hardly have predicted the rungs of a career ladder which included street cop in Taiwan at age 22, emigration to the United States in the mid-60s, advances through master's and doctoral degrees in biochemistry, tenured full professorship at the University of New Haven, founder of the Connecticut Institute of Forensic Science, and most importantly, the opportunity to work with tens of thousands of police officers, prosecutors and defense attorneys around the world, and to assist in the investigation of over 8,000 criminal cases. I felt both privileged and proud but needed this review in order to offset the mystical excursions of a time machine, a conscious yank back to reality.

I put aside a manuscript I was working on (this one, in fact) while my mind, alive and skittish, took another turn, wandering past thoughts of future trips, trying to will the right ones, and settling on one brief moment nearly two decades before. I had been asked to chair the Select Committee on Sacco and Vanzetti. Its charge was to reexamine firearm-related evidence and, late that evening in 1983, I pored over books and articles that dealt with the case. I recalled the cluttered table before me at the State Police Forensic Lab in a converted men's room of an old dormitory building and the article that lay separated from stacks of reports and bulletins and folders. It was written by a distinguished Harvard professor, Francis Russell, and entitled, "Sacco Guilty, Vanzetti, Innocent?" Always a question mark, I thought.

I retreated to the only easy chair in my office, anxious to read the professor's views and midway through the article, experienced that same drowsy sensation from my not-too-distant past, one that presaged retrograde travel, but I wasn't certain whether my departure was about to take place in the year 2000 or in 1983. It made little difference, however, because I was filled with the confidence to withstand any time warp, to slip among decades, witnessing their triumphs and their tragedies. Thus, despite heavy lids, the smile I felt on my face conveyed wonder and not confusion, and my mind was swept of past care and future worry. Except one: Would Sam Constant again be my companion, sharing his thoughts with me?

Within the time it takes to say, "Voilà," I awoke in daylight, strangely certain of my surroundings and perched on the steps of a veranda which wrapped around three sides of a grey wood frame house in New Jersey. I had received the first of my "willed" requests and felt confident that after returning home to Connecticut, two others would be fulfilled: that in due course, I'd be whisked to Ohio for the second Sam Sheppard trial and to Washington, D.C., for the investigation of President John F. Kennedy's assassination, both in the 1960s. Then home again for a brief stop, followed by an equally brief return to Washington to review the questionable suicide of Vincent Foster, a case that, along with JonBenet Ramsey and O. J. Simpson, was still fresh in my mind. I had, in fact, participated in the investigation of these three most ballyhooed crimes of the 1990s.

During the Sacco-Vanzetti saga, never had I been concerned about time away from my family and professional responsibilities, rationalizing that if time could be manipulated from one reference point, it could be condensed from another—and no one would know I was away at all. But this second trip back in time seemed far different, perhaps because the visits would span almost 30 years. I therefore vowed a time limit at each stop, gathering just enough firsthand information to make intelligent interpretations and commentaries for the "middle collection," as my writing collaborator and I call them: Lindbergh, Sheppard, JFK, Foster and Ramsey.

At about the same time, I had been preparing a special series of three, three-hour lectures for my winter semester, a graduate class in Advanced Forensic Science at the University of New Haven. My hope was that the journeys would provide new information which could be used for illustrative teaching purposes. Thus, elements in the Lindbergh case would serve as examples of individual principles in forensic science. The opposite approach would be equally valuable: that is, starting with the case in its entirety and then demonstrating where certain forensic techniques were applied, or were ignored, or might have helped had they been those currently available. I felt confident that both students and teacher could learn from the past in order to improve the future. All this would form the backbone of Lecture Number 1. Along the same lines, material for Lecture Number 2 would be enhanced by my trips to the Sheppard trial and the Warren Commission hearings on JFK in the 1960s. The third and final lecture? A combination of the features of both the Foster and Ramsey episodes.

While some cases within the center collection of the book

may be strong contenders for "Crimes of the Century," they are here presented as a bridge between two that have been classified for that distinction by the media and by the public.

Standing, I saw the sun plastered high on a slate background and felt a few snowflakes melt on my face. I headed toward the side stretch of the veranda, drawn to a door I had already imagined. It was open a crack and, lifting a folded newspaper from a wicker basket hung at its center, I marched through, positive the two visible rooms comprised the living space assigned to me.

Inside, the size, furnishings and lighting reminded me of the flat in Dedham, Massachusetts. Its smell alone—old but scrubbed—transported me back to the previous decade and, just as in that time and place, the same personal belongings were about me. I sat at a writing table in the corner of the front room and spread open the newspaper. It was dated December 31, 1934, and front-page headlines screamed of the Hauptmann murder trial that would begin on January 2 at the Hunterdon County Court House in Flemington, New Jersey. Two days away. Why had I arrived so early? I deduced that fate, destiny or whatever force had brought me here was allowing a needed escape from the rigors of work at home and around the world: solitude to concentrate on the new book and on material for my teaching, whether in the large lecture hall in New Haven or during special sessions at State Police headquarters or the forensic lab.

I cleared my head of extraneous thoughts and began writing the more didactic Appendix, sketching the essentials of Trace Analysis, Latent Fingerprints, Firearms Examination and Forensic Serology, but lingering on Crime Scene Investigation, Physical Evidence and DNA since these would figure most prominently in the consideration of all the cases in this section.

My wristwatch read four as I leaned back to stretch and allowed my mind to wander; specifically to query myself on whether fatigue is the same as energy depletion. Is going back in time a tiring process? Invoking Einstein again, I understood that part of his theory of relativity dealt with mass, time and energy. I felt playful in proposing that I was the mass which had just retreated over a vast amount of time and, according to his equation, if either mass or time increased, so did energy. But what if retreating in time gives a negative value? Is energy then lost? I answered in the affirmative, dismissed any further writing that day as counterproductive and cursed myself for being overly scientific and simplistic. Plus wrong. Why not just admit I was drained? But why hadn't I felt the same way when I was whisked back to the Sacco-Vanzetti era? Maybe there's more wear and tear the second time around, or maybe the pace of 20-hour working days had finally caught up with me.

I could picture my favorite winter jacket hanging in the near by closet and the county courthouse that was within walking distance. By then, I had stopped questioning my powers of intuition, for the overarching power was the one that had brought me here in the first place, and everything else mystical was to be expected. Would a leisurely stroll in the direction of the courthouse enliven me?

Two streets away, I pulled up the collar of my fleece-lined jacket as I gaped at the sight ahead, a near clone of the granite structure in Dedham, with expansive steps beneath four Tuscan columns. A gangling figure leaned against one of them, studying his fingernails. I knew it! I'd felt it! It was like an old friend resurrected.

I raced across the street and as I approached Sam Constant, he appeared startled. "Well, Dr. Lee," he blurted, "I'm so glad you came."

From what I could see beneath his long black overcoat, he wore a shirt striped in red, white and blue. He was hatless.

"Sam," I said, curbing my enthusiasm, "how's it going?"

He reached down to shake my outstretched hand. "We'll see," he answered. "By the way, Dr. Lee, you didn't stick around for the aftermath in Dedham, I noticed."

"No, I'd had enough. Plus, just like you, I have many other obligations."

"Enough? Obligations? You sure it wasn't because you didn't get your way?" Sam said, his lips curling with disgust.

I should have been offended but why spar with an apparition? Besides, I felt a mysterious connection to Sam, one born not of days of contact but of years, even though they, too, were apparitional. I responded, "No, it wasn't that at all—but simply a matter of a fair trial. So many unanswered questions, you know."

Moving closer, Sam shifted his eyes from side to side as if he were about to share a secret. I smelled bubblegum when he leaned over and whispered, "Do you believe heroes are important?"

"Heroes?" I knew what he was driving at, but I continued, "You mean like Michael Jordan or Larry Bird?"

Sam's jaw dropped. "Don't be silly," he said. "They aren't even around yet."

I knew, of course, that Sam was as preternatural as I had become—only more so— flitting around in time, clicking on and off at will. Yet somehow this recognition of future basketball heroes reinforced my conviction that Sam would be just as mercurial in Flemington as he was in Dedham. And that such clairvoyance signaled his presence in future cities.

"Not like *them*," he said. "I mean like Lucky Lindy." Sam smiled for the first time but only briefly. His words grew fiendish: "That Bruno bastard—he must *fry* for tampering with the life of an American hero."

I was determined to remain calm and said evenly, "But should Lindbergh's reputation be the issue at hand? Isn't Hauptmann's guilt or innocence in the taking of a child's life the more important question?"

Sam didn't respond but stared at the small pad I had

taken from my pocket. The pages were crammed with an amalgam of English scribbling and Chinese characters. I added a few more and put it away.

He creased his brow and said, "You're taking plenty of notes. How come?"

"Lectures back home."

"Hmm, maybe I'll attend a few myself," he said before clicking away.

Same old Sam, I thought. But what's he up to? There hadn't been a chance to ask if he'd be at the trial but I would have bet he would. Fine. This case has more discrepancies than he can handle. Let's see what he does with them. Which reminded me: Did Sam know all the outcomes as I did? Probably not. He gets too revved up to fake it.

The walk, the fresh air, the encounter with my unilateral friend did little to increase the energy level I'd been concerned about. I was flat-out tired and needed no scientific formula or equation to tell me so. On the way back to my rooms, I passed a few early New Year's Eve revelers and realized that the only kind of celebration I was in the mood for was to toast lady justice with a cup of tea. I'd find a diner for that plus something to eat, then head back for a full sleep before another day of writing.

Chapter 2

Lindbergh. The Murder of an American Hero's Baby

    I woke up at 9 a.m. on the first day of the New Year and couldn't recall having slept so late since my teenage years. No doubt the time warp had played havoc with my body and with my sleep. It had also curbed any appetite for food since the thought of breakfast or future meals struck me as repulsive. But I awoke refreshed, relieved of the malaise from the previous day and anxious to tackle the Appendix of our new book. And now, at dusk, having completed that assignment, I shifted my attention to the kidnapping and murder of Charles A. Lindbergh, Jr., revisiting what I had read and what I had heard in legal and scientific circles.

    My first thought was that some might ask: "How does the evolution and review of modern forensic science bear on that case and on a cursory glance at other famous crimes?" The answer stems from assertions made earlier but worthy of repetition: If contemporary forensics had been available *and* utilized, and if proper police protocol had been followed, such as securing the crime scene and recognizing crucial evidence, the outcome of all the following cases could have been different. "Could have been" is to be stressed because, as we shall see, even if the scientific and procedural operations had been ideal by today's standards, a pattern of human blunders and/or misconduct probably shaded the results. In this connection, the integrity of physical evidence and the interpretation of autopsy findings will be brought into question.

    Three months before the executions of Sacco and Vanzetti, twenty-five-year-old Charles A. Lindbergh flew a monoplane, the *Spirit of St. Louis*, from Roosevelt Field, Long Island, New

York, to the LeBourget Airdrome just outside Paris. He was the first person to fly the Atlantic Ocean alone, covering a distance of 3,735 miles in 33 hours, 39 minutes. The time was May 20-21, 1927. Lindbergh burst onto the international scene as a genuine hero, was made a Colonel by the United States Secretary of War and received the Congressional Medal of Honor and the Distinguished Flying Cross. At the request of the U.S. government, he traveled widely as a special goodwill ambassador and, on a trip to Mexico, he met Anne Spencer Morrow, the daughter of the American ambassador there. They married two years later. Subsequently he taught her to fly and, together, they embarked on numerous flying expeditions around the world, charting new travel routes for several airlines. But Anne's first love centered on writing, and in the following years, she received critical acclaim for her poetry, memoirs and novels.

To escape media attention, the Lindberghs built a home on a remote, 400-acre tract of land near Hopewell, New Jersey. There, on the rainy Tuesday night of March 1, 1932, their 20-month-old son was kidnapped from his nursery. Within hours, an unorganized horde of police and press personnel swarmed over the grounds and by morning scores of curious onlookers had joined them.

The child's disappearance was detected at 10 p.m., the police were called at 10:25 and at midnight, H. Norman Schwarzkopf, chief of the New Jersey State Police, arrived to take command. (He was the father of the 1991 Desert Storm commander.) Much of Schwarzkopf's authority was usurped by Lindbergh, since the hero in effect took charge of the investigation.

In the wet ground directly below a second-story window to the nursery, the police discovered shallow footprints but neglected to measure them, photograph their sole pattern or cast them with plaster. Sadly lacking also were measurements and photographs of apparent footprints found inside the nursery.

A homemade ladder lay flat on the ground, 70 feet from the house. It was built in three sections with the top section lying 10 feet away from the other two. A 3/4-inch chisel was also found nearby.

Two holes were located in the clay beneath the window, and one of the troopers immediately fit the ladder into these impressions without first checking for trace evidence at the leg ends of the ladder. Nor had the holes been examined, measured or cast for future comparisons.

Eventually, Lindbergh's attorney and family friend, Henry C. Breckinridge, arrived. They, along with Schwarzkopf and a "crime scene man" began a detailed examination of the nursery where, on the windowsill, they spotted an envelope which Lindbergh said he had seen earlier but had not touched. It was dusted for fingerprints as were other areas of the room. No prints were found anywhere. The envelope contained a single sheet of paper upon which the following message was written in blue ink:

Dear Sir!

Have 50.000$ redy 25.000$ in 20$ bills 15.000in
10$ bills and 10.000$ in 5$ bills. After 2-4 days we
will inform you were to deliver the Mony.

We warn you for making anyding public or for
notify the polise the child is in gute care.

Indication for all letters are singnature and 3 holes.

At the bottom of the paper was a drawing of two interlocking circles. The area within the overlap of the circles was solid red while the rest of the circles were outlined in blue. Three square holes pierced the crude symbol in a horizontal line.

Over the next few days, authorities theorized that the theft was the work of more than one person, possibly a gang, and three possibilities emerged:

1. Lindbergh believed the kidnappers were professional.
2. Schwarzkopf thought that the criminals were local and unprofessional because of their familiarity with the house, the location of the nursery window with its broken shutter latch and the modest ransom request.
3. Other investigators believed domestic employees were

involved because somehow the kidnappers knew that, because the child had a cold, the family decided against their custom of returning Monday mornings to Anne's parents' estate in Englewood, New Jersey.

More ransom notes were received, chiding Lindbergh for alerting the police and increasing the demand to $70,000. One week after the crime, Dr. John F. Condon of New York City, a retired physical education teacher, placed an ad in the *Bronx Home News* offering the kidnappers $1,000 and his services as a go-between. The next day, he received an acceptance letter which contained the intertwining circles with square holes and also a sketch of a box, 7 by 6 by 14 inches, in which the money was to be inserted. On the night of April 2, 1932, a month after the kidnapping, Lindbergh drove Condon to St. Raymond's Cemetery in the Bronx, the site prearranged for delivery of the ransom money in exchange for knowledge of the child's location. The money was all in gold certificates, making them easier to trace; in addition, their serial numbers had been recorded.

Lindbergh waited in the car outside the graveyard while Condon wandered about the tombstones expecting to encounter the person who had been dubbed "Cemetery John." Unsuccessful, Condon returned to the car whereupon a voice called out, "Hey, Doctor. Over here! Over here!" Condon slipped back to the graveyard and eventually confronted a shadowy figure with a German or Scandinavian accent. Condon handed over the bills and, in return, received a folded note which he was instructed not to open until six hours had passed, but a mile from the cemetery, Lindbergh stopped the car and read the following message:

The boy is on the Boad Nelly. It is a small boad 28 feet long. Two persons are on the boad. They are innosent. you will find the Boad between Horseneck Beach and gay Head near Elizabeth Island.

This area on Martha's Vineyard off the coast of Massachusetts was searched; neither the boat nor the child was found. On May 12, however, the child's badly decomposed body was discovered only four miles from the Hopewell mansion. He was face downward and covered by leaves and insects. Less than 24 hours later or 73 days after the kidnapping, the remains of Charles A. Lindbergh, Jr. were cremated.

Before that, what many called a "rinkydink" autopsy had been performed, because the county physician had suffered an arthritis flareup and delegated a funeral home director to make the actual dissections. Examination of the skull revealed four fracture lines and a decomposed blood clot. No photographs of this pathology were taken.

Other than the boy's remains prior to cremation, the principal pieces of evidence at that point in the investigation were the ladder, the chisel and a number of notes from the kidnapper(s). There were no fingerprints or useful footprints. The ladder would later prove to be crucial.

Early isolated spottings of the ransom bills were made in New York City but such detection escalated when, in the spring of 1933, President Franklin Roosevelt ordered all gold certificates to be exchanged at Federal Reserve Banks, thus taking the country off the gold standard. None of the sightings could be traced. And then, a major breakthrough occurred in September 1934, when a dark blue Dodge sedan appeared at a gas station in Manhattan and its driver paid for gas with a $10 gold certificate which was on the ransom list. The attendant wrote the license number of the car on the bill which was eventually traced to a Bronx resident, Bruno Richard Hauptmann. He was arrested the following morning.

Once the suspect was in custody, the task of matching some of the other clues to him was undertaken. Comparisons of the ransom notes to several documents written in Hauptmann's hand including insurance card and auto license applications showed some apparent but not definitive matches. The police searched his garage and apartment, stripping the latter to its laths. A blurred address and phone number found written on a piece of trim proved to refer to Dr. John Condon. Furthermore, several bundles of gold notes were found stashed within the walls of the suspect's garage.

Perhaps the most important offered evidence linking Hauptmann to the kidnapping was the ladder found at the scene of the crime. It was both professionally and crudely constructed; its rungs, for example, were placed six inches further apart than in an average ladder. Wood experts were consulted including one from the U.S. Forest Products Laboratory in Madison, Wisconsin. He determined the ladder was made of pine from North Carolina, Douglas fir from the West, birch and ponderosa pine. Some of the lumber was traced from a mill in South Carolina to a lumber dealer in the Bronx, New York. Subsequently, a part of the ladder's rails was found to match existing floorboards in Hauptmann's attic. One of the boards was missing and the rail section fit the space perfectly.

I had attended only a handful of the court sessions and on each occasion, the areas in and around the courthouse were swollen with spectators, reporters and police personnel—reminiscent of the Sacco-Vanzetti trial. The room resembled the one in Dedham except the witness stand wasn't a stand at all, but only a wooden chair. I had stuck to my resolve to limit my appearances there and at future sites and thus saw little of Sam at the trial, my recollection dominated by misty snapshots of a face in sync with the flow of events: now a joker's, now a devil's, but nothing in between. Most of my critical appraisals were made at my apartment: lists of notes about the case and of possible errors of omission, commission and misconduct, and instances where more modern forensic techniques might have been of assistance. I decided to incorporate a few of my notations into the body of my writing each night.

The prosecution was led by Attorney General David T. Wilentz of New Jersey, a fiery, cigar-smoking little man whose white fedora with a turned down brim reminded some observers of the gangster, Al Capone.

Hauptmann's chief counsel was a well-known Brooklyn defense attorney and boozer, Edward J. Reilly. Many believed he was "over the hill" and suffering from tertiary syphilis. He would become, within two years, an institutionalized psychotic.

Wilentz based the state's case solely on circumstantial evidence. First was the discovered $14,460 ransom money. Hauptmann testified that a friend, Isador Fisch, had left a shoebox with him before departing for Germany in December 1933. Fisch, he said, owed him $7,500 so he felt it was within his rights to spend some of the money he found in the box. Fisch died in Liepzig in March 1934.

They called it the "Fisch story" but, later on, reliable evidence surfaced that Fisch had been a buyer of "hot" money.[1] This tended to clarify some of the issues related to the "Fisch story."

Another piece of prosecution evidence, and possibly the most damaging, was the connection of the section of floorboard from Hauptmann's attic to the ladder used by the kidnapper(s). The defense argued that not only was the placement in the ladder's rail disputable but also that such evidence could have been planted.

The argument and the theory! Is history always repeating itself? Why wasn't the defense team ever allowed to inspect the attic?

Third was the issue of handwriting. The state's array of handwriting experts overwhelmed the defense's feeble two.

But more recently, document examiners for the U.S. Secret Service and for the U.S. Army concluded that Hauptmann did *not* write the ransom notes.[2]

Dr. John Condon figured prominently both before and after the trial. He testified in court that the defendant was definitely the person who took the ransom box in St. Raymond's Cemetery and later—too late, in fact—his name surfaced again in conjunction with his phone number written inside a closet at Hauptmann's house.

Two things were disturbing here. One, Condon was unable to identify Hauptmann in a police lineup after his arrest, yet fingered him in court as "Cemetery John." And two, after the trial, several newspaper reporters stated that a fellow journalist seeking an exclusive story had penciled Condon's number on the closet trim.

On the days Sam was in the courthouse, he varied where he sat and did more whispering to those near him than listening to the proceedings. (That settled the question of whether or not others could see him. Or could he control that at will, too?) But when it came time for Lindbergh himself to testify, Sam slid in next to me.

On the third day of the trial, the state resumed its examination of Lindbergh, focusing on the events at the cemetery where the ranson money was delivered.

Q. And then what happened, Colonel? Proceed with your story.

A. Doctor Condon, as I said, went to the corner of the cemetery; he stood there for a few minutes, then he turned around and started to walk back across Whittemore, which runs next to the cemetery. When he arrived at about the center of Whittemore, I heard very clearly a voice coming from the cemetery, to the best of my belief calling Doctor Condon.

Q. What were the words?

A. In a foreign accent: "Hey, Doctor."

Q. How many times?

A. I heard that voice once.

A few minutes later, the district attorney continued:

Q. Since that time have you heard the same voice?

A. Yes, I have.

Q. Whose voice was it, Colonel, that you heard in the vicinity of St. Raymond's Cemetery that night, saying, "Hey, Doctor"?

A. That was Hauptmann's voice.

Q. You heard it again the second time where?

A. At District Attorney Foley's office in New York, in the Bronx.

I whispered through the corner of my mouth, "That was more than two years ago and he was in a car 100 yards away. And did he hear the rest of it: 'Over here! Over here!'" Sam didn't respond.

Lindbergh was generally vague about his whereabouts on the day of the kidnapping but admitted he'd failed to keep a speaking engagement that evening. On cross-examination by the defense, the following exchange occurred:

Q. Now, will you give us an outline of your movement on Tuesday?

A. Tuesday I was in New York City during the day.

Q. Where?

A. I don't recall in vivid detail where I went. I think I went to the Pan-American Airways office, probably to the Trans-Continental Air Transport offices. I was at the Rockefeller Institute during part of the day and I believe that I stopped at my dentist's that afternoon late, to the best of my recollection.

I turned to Sam and said, "Don't you think he would have remembered every single thing about the day his son was murdered?"

"Nah, " he replied, "he's probably blocked out most of that day."

"But shouldn't detectives have checked and verified his activity as they did in the Sacco-Vanzetti case?"

"They ... ah ... probably were too busy conducting the investigation and search of the crime scene." Sam's lips quivered as he added, "Hey, wait a minute! You aren't suggesting that Lindy had anything to do with the killing, are you?" He seemed more surprised than angry.

"No, definitely not me—but maybe others might."

Sam flushed and appeared too flustered to speak further. Instead, he bolted from the room but returned while Lindbergh was still testifying. I looked at him quizzically.

"Had a gagging spell," he said.

I hesitated to bring up an old subject but proceeded with, "So you *do* have human traits?"

Unfazed, he nearly stepped on my words. "Feelings? Yes. Intellectual carelessness? No."

It was universally acknowledged that attorney Reilly's behavior was shameful, his defense of Hauptmann flimsy. His wardrobe was hardly endearing to a jury: a swallow-tailed coat and striped trousers. A known alcoholic, he spent each lunch break drinking and his lackluster afternoon performances reflected that habit. He alienated almost everyone associated with the trial by repeated bullying of prosecution witnesses, by his bombast and by the defiant flaunting of his chorus of beautiful "stenographers" who ended up in his quarters each evening. Reilly spent less than 40 minutes conferring with his client during the entire case.

On the other hand, a confident David Wilentz, trying his first criminal case as attorney general, parlayed a charming smile and dapper attire with impressive cross-examinations, particularly of Hauptmann who endured 11 hours of savage interrogation. His summation was devastating:

> Now, men and women, as I told you before, there are some cases in which a recommendation of mercy might do, but not this one, not this one. Either this man is the filthiest and vilest snake that ever crept through the grass, or he is entitled to an acquittal. And if you believe as we do, you have got to convict

him. If you bring a recommendation of mercy, a wishy-washy decision, yes, it is your province, I will not say a word about it. I will not say another word, once I sit down here in this case, so far as this jury and this verdict is concerned. But it seems to me that you have and you will have the courage if you are convinced, as all of us are—the federal authorities, the Bronx people who were here, the New Jersey State Police who were here, the lawyers who were here, Colonel Lindbergh who was here, everybody who has testified—if you believe with us, you have got to find him guilty of murder in the first degree.

Throughout the trial, an estimated 75,000 to 100,000 people filed into Flemington each day. After hearing 29 days of testimony, the jury retired for deliberations and returned 12 hours later with a verdict of guilty. Arguing his innocence to the end, Bruno Richard Hauptmann was electrocuted on April 3, 1936.

Sam was seated next to me at the time the verdict was announced, and one would have thought his audible sigh marked the fall of a weighty load from his shoulders. Once pandemonium had subsided in the courtroom, I said to him, "Are you satisfied now?"

"Damn right!" he shot back. He appeared to resist the temptation to hug me and then, tilting his head to the side, spoke in a mellow tone of mocked pity: "Aw, but Dr. Lee isn't happy, is he?"

"No, I'm afraid not. That man may be guilty of something, but there are just too many discrepancies and inconsistencies to say he was the only one to carry out the murder. Remember Sacco and Vanzetti? They may have been guilty of something, but history has proven they might not be the killers."

It was doubtful Sam had heard my answer as he jumped to his feet and sidestepped along the row of still clapping

spectators. At the aisle, he stopped short, turned and, leaning over a gentleman's shoulders, shouted, "I'm going out to join the crowd. See you next time."

Assuming "next time" referred to Cleveland, Ohio, at first I wasn't certain I could face more of Sam's exhilaration. But then again, I reminded myself, the next case had a different twist, one that in all likelihood would tug at my friend from different directions.

Meanwhile, I sat among a thinning collection of smug faces, more disturbed than I'd expected because, of course, I knew exactly what the outcome would be. That wasn't the point. The point was the kind of justice Hauptmann had been offered during a month-long process whose main characters were an international hero and an obscure carpenter, an immigrant—again, just like Sacco and Vanzetti a decade before. The defense was so tepid; there were so many gaps and miscues and bungled opportunities to discredit the forensic evidence as well as the witnesses. Anything holding to solid forensic science, even to those techniques available at the time, was sadly lacking. Suppression of evidence was there. Perjured testimony was there. Disregard for the laws of evidence was there. The possibility of tampering with evidence was there. Was there a frame-up, or did he really do it? I couldn't wait to get back to my apartment to create a litany of irregularities to present to my students back home.

It took over an hour to muscle my way through an ocean of celebrants and, once seated at the writing table back at the room, I jotted down my thoughts as if time—that perverted element in my life at the moment—might suddenly run out. I feared that all the nuances of the trial could elude me once I was transported to my next destination, so I listed two dozen questions and observations with a speed I never knew I had and without any order of importance.

After a protracted yawn, I examined what I had written and once again came to the conclusion that even if modern forensic technology had been available and the authorities had strictly enforced police crime scene protocols, there was still the ingredient of human integrity to contend with. Were personal motivations at work? Despite scientific refinements, would the same verdict of guilty have been returned? Would conclusions drawn by using modern forensic techniques have been too persuasive to ignore?

It was well past 2 a.m. and I was ready for my cot. In a small window of consciousness before drifting into sleep, I tried to slow down my mind and defer thoughts about the next case—Dr. Sam Sheppard's—because first I was heading home for the initial lecture to a new group of forensic science students, a lecture that would include the two dozen notations for sure. I believed the decision to return to Connecticut was a correct one, enabling me to ease into my new teaching approach rather than to become bogged down with the material of three landmark cases all at once.

Hauptmann's execution was preceded by a year of legal appeals, and late in that process, sentiment about Lindbergh began to change. Remarkably, as the public turned more and more against the one-time international hero, doubts about Hauptmann's guilt arose across the country. The positions of the two became reversed for reasons that involved, among others, the public's perception of the prosecution team and Lindbergh's decision to abandon his homeland. He sailed for England in late 1935 with his wife and second son and lived there and on an island off the coast of France for more than three years.

In the immediate posttrial months, those players important to the prosecution—Wilentz, Conlon and Schwarzkopf among them—became transformed into unattractive personalities in the eyes of the media, principally because they were suddenly viewed as persecutors and self-promoters. Lindbergh, meanwhile, operated from his base in Europe and entered into an intense and open relationship with Nazi Germany, this at a time when the Second World War was at hand and American sympathies were being scrutinized. He made frequent trips to Germany, announced his admiration for the German *Luftwaffe* and befriended its leader, Hermann Goering.

At home, many people labeled Lindbergh a dupe of German propaganda, a fascist, even a Nazi, and after the war had begun, he was considered an unpatriotic appeaser.

Through the years, Anna Hauptmann, Bruno's widow, initiated several attempts to clear her husband's name. All were unsuccessful. Meanwhile, a combination of newer evidence and a reinterpretation of the old have led many to believe that Bruno Richard Hauptmann could not have been the kidnapper and murderer.

If only I'd been around then and called to the scene shortly after the baby was found missing. I would have had the opportunity to conduct a detailed crime scene search and to examine all the physical evidence in its original state at the time of collection. The story might have had a different ending.

It was exciting to greet my incoming graduate class at the University of New Haven, probably the largest and best I'd ever had. All had degrees and many were seasoned detectives and attorneys. The class had been moved from the usual lecture hall to the central amphitheater, affectionately called the "pit," its tiers of seats tilting from the back down to a well where I stood. Student chatter stopped abruptly when I entered and placed my notes and slide transparencies on an elongated bench which stretched before me. An equally wide chalkboard dominated the wall behind me and several TV monitors hung suspended overhead. Every seat was occupied.

As I surveyed the surroundings, I couldn't help but dwell on the audiovisual materials scattered about: maps, flip charts, opaque and overhead projectors; and off to both sides, tables burdened with audiotape and compact disc recorders, VCRs and computer screens. I'd seen and worked such devices thousands of times before but for a moment they

served as reminders of how antiquated the equipment had been during the Lindbergh era.

I planned to show only two or three slides, preferring the spontaneity of writing on the board as I spoke, turning to notice the students' reactions, twirling a piece of chalk in my hand as I responded to their questions. To me, it was the equivalent of acting in the movies versus acting onstage. It was quite a different matter, however, in my talks to the general public or keynote addresses to large groups. In such instances, the presentations were built around several collections of slides I'd accumulated over time.

That first day, I spent the initial 45 minutes relating the Lindbergh story, most of which the students had some familiarity with. Then I plunged directly into the list I'd composed 65 years ago (but only a day ago, *our* time!). I wrote some of the points on the board in complete sentences; others were designated by fragmented sentences or several words, but each point was followed by a healthy give-and-take between the class and me, a process I'd always encouraged during my teaching years. The list began as follows:

1. Why didn't the family terrier, *Wahgoosh*, ever once bark on the evening of the kidnapping even though he was in the house? He was known to be a high-strung dog who barked loudly at strangers.

2. Crime scene was allowed to be trampled on by media, investigators and later by curious onlookers. Guess what happened to the integrity of the crime scene?

3. No latent fingerprints were found anywhere. Modern technology for developing latent prints with lasers and new chemicals might have helped.

4. No photographs, plaster casts or accurate measurements made of the shoe prints in the wet ground beneath the window of apparent entrance. No mention of whether or not the prints were similar to Hauptmann's.

5. Did ladder wood and floorboard wood come from the same tree? Could have been decided indisputably by twenty-first century plant DNA analysis.

6. How did kidnapper(s) know which second-story window had a broken latch, the only such malfunctioning one in the entire mansion?

7. How did kidnapper(s) know the height of the second-story window in order to construct a three-section ladder that reached the window perfectly? What was its total weight and can one person carry it?

8. Trace evidence on the end of the ladder was destroyed by a trooper when he inserted it into the two holes beneath the nursery window. That also changed the size, depth and shape of the holes during the insertion.

9. Before the trial, the defense was never given any investigative notes or otherwise apprised of the evidence it would have to face. Thus their own experts not given opportunity to inspect the evidence firsthand.

10. Once discovered, child's body was immediately cremated. There was no legitimate autopsy, no documentation of the injuries and no possibility for exhumation for later forensic testing.

11. Defense team never allowed to inspect Hauptmann's attic or to conduct its own investigation and documentations *before* the floorboard had been removed.

12. The defense initially had time sheets showing Hauptmann worked in New York until 5 p.m. on the day of the crime, making it virtually impossible for him to travel to central New Jersey.

I had just concluded writing the last sentence when a deep voice from the back resonated throughout the amphitheater: "But Dr. Lee, I beg to differ. That trip is possible if you hurry."

I turned and dropped my chalk. The voice belonged to Sam Constant! He stood against a corner wall in the aisle rimming the uppermost tier of seats and, flashing that half-circle smile, waved at me with two fingers. He sported a blue blazer, striped tie (red, white and blue) and tan slacks, and he appeared younger than I'd remembered. A pencil was wedged over his ear and he carried a clipboard. The tallest forensic science student ever?

The entire class had turned in unison toward Sam, then glanced quizzically at one another. The room filled with a buzz almost as loud as the chatter I'd encountered earlier. Finally, silence restored, 200 pairs of expectant eyes focused on me. I had deduced therefore that Sam was in his visible mode.

There was no way I would treat him other than as a student. Nonchalantly, I picked up the chalk while responding, "Good point, Mr. … ah … Mr. … "

"Constant, Samuel Constant."

"Okay, Mr. Constant. I agree it might have been possible, but not if you're carrying a ladder." The buzz recurred, only to dim when I added, "And those sheets disappeared, you know. Plus other time and pay sheets favoring Hauptmann were clearly altered."

Sam bowed his head toward me in surrender, then took his pencil, wet its tip with his tongue and made a notation on the clipboard.

Oh, brother, I thought. Having collected myself from an unexpected jolt and reasonably certain the students had decided Sam was not an intruder of sorts but rather "one of them," I proceeded with my list:

> 13. Why did Defense Counselor Reilly allow the identification of a corpse in the woods to stand without rebuttal, especially when the autopsy was not professionally performed and confusion reigned over the body's height and age? Hadn't Reilly ever heard

of planting a seed of doubt? He surprised and angered even his legal associate in this regard.

14. There were no photographs or enhancements of the footprints in the nursery. These could have been compared to those found on the ground outside.

15. Were any tool marks discovered at the scene and, if so, were they made by the chisel found there?

16. Only two holes were found in the clay beneath the window, which indicates the suspect(s) had definite knowledge of the window latch at the target area.

17. The origin of the envelope and sheet of paper found on the windowsill was never explained.

18. The ink (both blue and red) was never traced to its origin. Were any pens recovered from Hauptmann's house or, for that matter, from the Lindbergh estate?

19. Were the holes that had been punched into the crude design on the paper ever checked as to how and where they might have been made?

20. Was the broken shutter latch an old or new defect?

21. Had any new chemical procedures been employed to bring out latent fingerprints on the ladder, chisel, envelope and paper? In 1932, the Ninhydrin Procedure had been introduced in the field. Why wasn't it used?

22. Had any comparisons been made between the writing, paper and ink of the first ransom note and subsequent ones? Any tracing attempts for the subsequent paper and ink?

23. The body was wrapped in some clothing. Was any trace or transfer evidence recovered during the autopsy?

24. Were any fingerprints found on the shoebox containing the ransom money? Was any attempt made to trace the origin of the box?

Throughout this last sequence of a dozen comments, the

discussion was lively—so lively in fact, I wondered why my presentations were advertised as lectures. But, I would not have it any other way. With students eager to learn: face-to-face exchange, verbal combat if necessary. With all other audiences: a bona fide lecture.

After considerations of Imprint/Impression Evidence, Questioned Document Examination and Trace/Transfer Evidence, I indicated how important it is to secure and maintain the integrity of the crime scene; to identify, collect and preserve all the evidence; to utilize all available forensic techniques to assist in the investigation; and to follow all possible leads, however painstakingly (See Appendix). As suggested by the list we had covered, many of those fundamentals were violated in the Lindbergh case.

Sam stayed till the end, glued to the corner. He had made an occasional note but expressed no further opinions. I fully expected we'd chat after the room had emptied but, while assembling my papers, I heard the usual click and, without looking up, knew that he was gone. Although I was flattered Sam had attended my lecture, I dismissed a possibly deeper meaning with the supposition that public opinion is everywhere, even in the classroom.

Chapter 3

Sam Sheppard. The Case That Spawned *The Fugitive*

Once again, temporary quarters awaited me within walking distance of a courthouse, on this occasion a single room in a boardinghouse in Cleveland, Ohio. It was the year after I emigrated from Taiwan to the United States, 1966, the year of the retrial of Dr. Sam Sheppard who had been accused of murdering his wife.

I arrived in Cleveland a day early and found myself inserting a key into my door as if I had performed the task there thousands of times before. The room was ample but austere and had my usual complement of books, instruments, writing materials and personal effects scattered over a small desk.

I felt alert, not fatigued—as enlivened as I was after the trip home to Connecticut from the Sacco-Vanzetti case in the '20s. I entertained the notion that eventually I might unravel the secrets behind my time travel, from where the power originates to how I can "will" the destination, from the compression of time to the encounters with an apparition. But most of all: Why me?

I noticed a sheet of stationery pinned to the pillow of the bed along the far wall. A welcome message from the landlord, I figured. Why no chocolates? Or at least cookies. They should know I love cookies. Written in a firm hand was the following:

Flemington, N.J.
November 12, 1939

Dear Henry,
Sorry I couldn't stay long in Connecticut. I'm now back
in 1939, three years after you left here. A lot has happened
over that period including the start of a war with Germany.
I write to offer an apology (I make them occasionally).
When they convicted Hauptmann, they got the wrong man.
Everything points to it. As for the former hero, Lindbergh,
they ought to put that foreigner in solitary confinement somewhere. See you sooner or later.

Sam Constant
P.S. Nice class at the University of New Haven.

I was shocked to receive the note as well as its contents.
Predictable though, I thought: the pulse of the times once more
at work. And now I'm "Henry"?

The Sam Sheppard murder case which began in the mid-
'50s has been described as the case that will not die, the story
with nine lives. It spawned a popular television series, *The Fugitive*, and a motion picture of the same name which became a box-
office smash.
In the Bay Village section of Cleveland, Ohio, 31-year-old
Marilyn Sheppard, four months pregnant, was found bludgeoned
to death sometime during the early morning hours of July 4, 1954.
An attractive suburban housewife, she was discovered in her bed
in the second- story bedroom by her husband, Sam, a neurosurgeon who, even at age 30, was already prominent.
Dr. Sam's story remained consistent through the years. The
couple had entertained dinner guests at their lakefront home and
after their departure, Sam fell asleep on the couch in the first-
floor den while watching a TV movie. He awoke, believing he
heard his wife calling his name and dashed up the stairs and into
the bedroom where he saw a figure in a light garment and then

grappled with something or someone. He heard moaning before he was struck from behind and blacked out. When he regained consciousness, he was lying on the floor and, pulling himself up, saw his wife covered with blood. He felt for but could not obtain her pulse, then ran into the next room to check on their seven-year-old son, Chip. The boy slept soundly. Hearing a noise below, he ran to the first floor and saw a man running out the back door toward the lake. Dr. Sam stated that the man was about six-feet three inches, middle-aged, with dark bushy hair and wearing a white shirt. He reportedly chased him across the lawn and down the wooden steps leading to the beach. He caught up to him and grasped him from the back. They struggled before he felt himself choking and again lost consciousness. After an unspecified period of time, he returned to the blood-spattered bedroom and paced. He believed he was disoriented and the victim of a nightmare, yet may have reexamined his wife and accepted that she was dead. His next move, he said, was to call a neighbor, Bay Village Mayor Spencer Houk. The mayor and his wife, Esther, arrived quickly. It was 6 a.m. on the Fourth of July.

Following a brief hospital stay for shock and neck injuries, Sheppard was interrogated repeatedly by Bay Village authorities and by the Cleveland police who formally assumed responsibility for the investigation three weeks later. That interval was filled with massive media scrutiny and included a three-day inquest conducted by the coroner, Dr. Sam Gerber. Newspapers were emblazoned with challenging headlines:

"Why Don't Police Quiz Top Suspect?"

"Police Captain 'Urges Sheppard's Arrest.'"

"Why Isn't Sam Sheppard In Jail?"

Finally, the doctor was arrested on July 30, indicted on August 17 and brought to trial a month later.

Once again, a repeat of history? A rush to judgment just as in the Sacco-Vanzetti and Bruno Hauptmann cases? Or was it, in fact, the pressure of public opinion and the news

media on law enforcement authorities to solve the case.

The trial covered six weeks of testimony, the defendant was found guilty of murder in the second degree and was sentenced to life imprisonment. The prosecution had hammered away at allegations that Sheppard was unfaithful to his wife, that the injuries he sustained on July 4 were self-inflicted and superficial, and that it was his personal surgical instrument—the murder weapon—that had made the imprint on a bloody pillowcase, a contention advanced by Coroner Gerber. The defense introduced witnesses who told of seeing a cigarette floating in an upstairs toilet although the Sheppards were not smokers, others who testified they had seen a man with a white shirt and bushy hair near the Sheppard home, and still others who corroborated the seriousness of Dr. Sam's injuries.

That cigarette—it disappeared, you know. Poof! And, how could they have minimized the testimony of x-ray technicians; a neurosurgeon; a radiologist; an ear, nose and throat specialist; and a dentist—all of whom verified that Sheppard had suffered a fractured cervical vertebra, a swelling at the base of the skull, a spinal cord injury and chipped teeth? Self-inflicted? Or, he must have taken a pretty hard fall on concrete. Both hard to imagine.

Other glaring mistakes in that investigation? There were many, such as not analyzing Marilyn's stomach contents, not making a microscopic study of her wounds, not determining whether or not she had been raped. Plus they never searched for trace evidence like semen, hair, wood, or foreign material on the sheets—or fibers such as wool and cotton under Marilyn's fingernails. They also failed to analyze a broken tooth found under the bed. Later it could not be matched to either of the Sheppards. Today, DNA can be extracted from teeth. And how could they explain away the large amount of blood at the crime scene, yet the lack of any on the defendant's pants, shoes or socks? Lots of questions. There was no

analysis of blood spatter patterns, and a proper reconstruction of the crime was never conducted. Or even a complete identification of *all* the bloodstains. But I recall listening to a talk by Dr. Paul Kirk in which he presented his cogent findings during the second trial, and that three decades later, DNA testing conducted by my friend, Dr. Mohammed Tahir of the Indiana Crime Lab, would show that someone other than the Sheppards bled in the bedroom. Moreover, new questions would be raised based on recent autopsy interpretations by the world's leading forensic pathologist, Dr. Cyril Wecht.

Following Sheppard's incarceration, a series of occurrences altered the nature of the case and added to its litany of human and judicial twists. For example, within two weeks of the verdict, Dr. Sam's mother died from a self-inflicted gunshot wound and 10 days after that, his father died of a bleeding stomach ulcer. Some years later, the deceased Marilyn Sheppard's father committed suicide with a shotgun. The most important events, however, were the overturning of the 1954 trial by the U.S. Supreme Court and the ensuing second trial which exonerated the suspect in the eyes of the law, but not in the eyes of the public.

Several characters, either newly engaged or held over from the first trial years, would assume key roles in the second trial and beyond:

1. Dr. Paul Leland Kirk. Criminalist from the University of California at Berkeley.
2. F. Lee Bailey. Defense attorney from Boston.
3. Ethel Durkin. Elderly murder victim.
4. Richard Eberling. Window washer for Sheppard home.
5. Dr. Samuel Gerber. Coroner, 1936-86.
6. Mayor Spencer and Esther Houk. Sheppard neighbors and first on the scene.
7. Sam Reese Sheppard (Chip). Son of Dr. Sam and Marilyn Sheppard.

At one time or another, Eberling and the Houks were suspects in Marilyn's murder and, to this day, theories abound over the exact sequence of events on the night of her murder and who could possibly have been in her bedroom.

From the start, the first trial was a media "carnival," a not inappropriate term, for it was the basis for the dramatic Supreme Court decision after 12 years of continuous appeals. Speaking for the Court, Justice Tom Clark ruled in Sheppard's favor because, "The massive, pervasive and prejudicial publicity attending petitioner's prosecution prevented him from receiving a fair trial consistent with the Due Process Clause of the 14th Amendment." The Justice continued, "Despite his awareness of the excessive pretrial publicity, the trial judge failed to take effective measures against the massive publicity which continued throughout the trial or to take adequate steps to control the conduct of the trial."

Was this a repeat of Sacco-Vanzetti and Lindbergh?

Clark went on to say the judge should have postponed the trial or moved it to a county "not so permeated" with publicity. He elaborated on the impact of the media upon jury members, citing the pretrial publication of the names and their addresses of those called for duty. "As a consequence, anonymous letters and telephone calls, as well as calls from friends, were received by prospective jurors." They were "thrust into the role of celebrities."

In the courtroom, the press table had been placed inside the bar and less than three feet from the jury box. This, Clark stated, "precluded privacy" between the defendant and his attorneys.

The Justice also suggested a prejudicial court. The judge had said on the first day of the trial, "Mystery? It's an open and shut case ... He is guilty as hell. There is no question about it." And a prejudicial coroner who allegedly claimed at the crime scene, "Well, men, it is evident the doctor did this, so let's go get the confession out of him."

At the start of the second trial, Dr. Sam had been a free man for two years, ever since a surprising ruling by District Judge Carl Weinman in 1964. He ordered Sheppard's release from prison, stating, "If ever there was a trial by newspaper, this is a perfect example." The judge cited five separate violations of Sheppard's constitutional rights and wrote, "Each of the afore-mentioned errors is by itself sufficient to require a determination that petitioner was not offered a fair trial ... and when these errors are cumulated, the trial can only be viewed as a mockery of justice."

So chronologically what happened was that Dr. Sam spent 10 years in prison, then was released, and was retried two years after that. The key years were 1954-1964 and 1966. Tough to keep this straight. But let's complicate it a bit further: In 1959, a window washer named Richard Eberling was arrested for stealing valuables from his customers' homes. When grilled by the police, he admitted he had washed the Sheppards' windows shortly before the murder and explained that he cut his finger and dripped blood as he walked to the basement to cleanse the wound. This development received little attention until 30 years later when he was convicted of killing a wealthy Lakewood widow, Ethel May Durkin. During the investigation it was learned he had been associated with a number of women who had met violent death. Eberling thus became the leading suspect in the Sheppard case, but he was never convicted.

One other sidebar: Sheppard had been carrying on a "prison romance" with Ariene Tebbenjohanns, a dazzling blonde divorcee who wooed him by correspondence from her home in Dusseldorf, Germany. She eventually moved to the States and within a week of his release from prison married Dr. Sam. I mention this only as an item of unusual coincidence. Remember Charles Lindbergh's friendship with

Nazi Germany's Hermann Goering? Well, Ariene was the sister-in-law of Nazi Propaganda Minister Joseph Goebbels!

Judge Francis Talty was assigned to hear the second trial at the Cuyahoga County Courthouse: the State of Ohio vs. Sam Sheppard. That he adopted the Supreme Court's objections to the first trial was reflected in his decision to limit drastically the number of reporters and spectators allowed into his courtroom.

I made no effort to challenge the judge's directive but for reasons as murky as my presence itself, a bailiff waved me through the door and even said, "Good morning, Dr. Lee." And so it was on each succeeding day.

Sheppard was represented by defense attorney F. Lee Bailey who had entered the case five years earlier and was instrumental in securing Sheppard's release from prison. The prosecutor was John T. Corrigan (no relation to the defense lawyer in the first trial, William J. Corrigan).

The prosecution's tack was markedly different the second time around. There was no attempt to introduce evidence supporting the earlier claim of faked injuries or marital discord or a surgical instrument. In cross-examination, Bailey pressed Coroner Gerber to admit that in a countrywide search he was unable to locate any instrumant that would fit the impression on the bloody pillowcase.

Mary Cowen, Gerber's medical technologist, testified that blood on Sheppard's wristwatch came not from contact with a wound but from spattering blood. The defense countered with its star witness, Dr. Paul Kirk who contended that:

1. Blood patterns indicated Marilyn's slayer had to be left-handed (Dr. Sam was right-handed).
2. One bloodstain in the murder room was neither Marilyn's nor Sam's and thus must have been been the blood of a third person, who was the murderer.
3. The blood on Dr. Sam's wristwatch was the result of contact with Marilyn when he had examined her.

Dr. Kirk made his points convincingly over more than five hours of direct examination by Bailey, thus in effect nullifying Mary Cowen's performance. The doctor had investigated all the right open questions before the trial and, with Bailey's brilliant orchestration, had found the right combination for the trial. Kirk's turned out to be the last testimony of evidentiary importance in a trial that markedly contrasted with the first in terms of high drama and media frenzy. And while his testimony was crucial to the defense, it was not well-received by the law enforcement and forensic communities. Many likened his support for the defense to an act of treason, breaching a silent code among forensic scientists of the day.

Kirk's application for membership in the criminalistics section of the American Academy of Forensic Science (AAFS) was rejected. But standards have changed. Now, most experts in the field, in admiration of his courage and pioneering contributions, consider Professor Kirk the father of modern forensic science. And ironically, the AAFS's Distinguished Criminalist Award has been renamed the Kirk Award.

In 19 days of testimony and summation, Sam Constant was nowhere to be found. I was anxious to get his opinion and mildly annoyed when it dawned on me that I had no way to contact him. But who was I to argue? I'd been dealt a rare opportunity to witness past history firsthand and if my irrepressible friend went with the deal, so be it.

On the other hand, I hadn't missed a single day of testimony or summation and on the 20th day, I listened intently when Judge Talty delivered his charge to the jury. Its members then withdrew and deliberated into the early evening hours, time I spent uneasily reading and pacing outside in the crisp pre-Thanksgiving air.

At 9 p.m., I returned to my seat and there he was—Sam Constant—sitting in the next chair, beanpole straight, eyes forward, feet fastened to the floor as if he anticipated a frontal assault. He wore a navy blue toggle coat with a band

collar bearing twin pins of the American flag on either side. He remained motionless until I spoke and then, turning with recognition, met my words with an improvised smile.

"Sam," I said, "so happy you're back. Where have you been?" Dumb statement, I thought. Dumber question. What business is it of mine?

He answered with no hint of displeasure, and I felt certain his mind was on the verdict about to be delivered. As he replied, I went into one of my internal monologues: But he knows the result as well as I, doesn't he? Perhaps, but haven't I wondered before if things would come out the same, the second time around? If there are flukes of time and place, why not jury verdicts?

"Sorry," he said, "I popped in on the Kennedy thing in Dallas."

"But that was three years ago."

Sam glared at me as if I should have known better. "Does it make any difference?" he asked. He didn't wait for an answer. I had thought my initial greeting hadn't registered with him but he followed with, "I'm happy to be be back, too. By the way, did you pick the Sheppard case because of my first name?"

I decided to be as quick on the draw. "Sure, Sam, sure." Our full smiles matched.

At 9:20 the verdict buzzer pierced the nearly empty courtroom and within minutes, Judge Talty walked in, grim faced jury members filed in and the room filled to capacity.

The judge was handed the verdict and after perusing it impassively, read it aloud:

"We the jury empaneled in the above entitled case find the defendant not guilty."

Pandemonium erupted. It was mostly joyous and was led by Dr. Sam who appeared to release an aching energy lying dormant for 12 years.

Based on the evidence introduced, the insipid case presented by the prosecution and the skills of the defense's F.
Lee Bailey, I concurred with the outcome. I even sighed. Sam
Constant's reaction was not unexpected. Although he hadn't
flinched, his face took on that frozen appearance I had seen
before. And immediately after the verdict had been read, if
Sam Sheppard's body language was just this side of manic,
Sam Constant's was just the other side of marbleized. It was
a spell of sorts and I decided to break it.

"You okay?" I asked, trying to sound as blasé about the
verdict as I was concerned about his condition.

"What, what's that? Oh, yes ... yes, of course. It simply
threw me for a minute. Those things happen." Sam loosened
his collar while fidgeting in his seat. "Look, Henry," he continued, "I feel worthless here now. The world has changed.
I'll catch up to you one of these days. Bye." The click signal-
ing his disappearance came as expected.

I should have been used to his sudden departures but
this one rankled me nonetheless. It seemed to help when I
rationalized that whereas children pout for hours when they
don't get their way, good old Sam Constant beat a fast re-
treat. Which is what I too decided to do. Back in the '20s, I'd
opted to skip the interminable appeals in the Sacco-Vanzetti
case. Similarly, the aftermath of the Sam Sheppard case
seemed anticlimactic to my purposes. I had learned all I'd
wanted from a forensic scientist's viewpoint and felt it was
time to move forward ... uh ... backward to the assassination
of a United States president.

After the trial, Sheppard's life deteriorated. Severely im-
paired by alcohol and drugs, he encountered a series of setbacks:
a malpractice suit, divorce, insolvency and, in 1970, death.

In the following years, there were still many who doubted
his innocence and just as many who believed that justice had
been finally served. Among the latter was his son, Samuel Reese
Sheppard, the youngster "Chip" who, in 1954, lay sleeping while

his mother was slain. He took up the cause of validating the verdict in his father's retrial by attempting to establish the identity of the real killer. In the process, he became a staunch opponent of the death penalty and often spoke out against it in speeches throughout the country.

Nearly half a century later, Sam Reese conceded to the exhumation and DNA testing of the bodies of both of his parents in a quest to win a civil suit filed against the state of Ohio. It was reported that their DNA did not match the DNA of a blood spot that had been discovered at the crime scene.

The latest chapter in the Sam Sheppard saga occurred in early 2000 when the jury in the "third Sheppard trial" refused to find the doctor innocent. The county prosecutor stated, "I didn't think the DNA had anything to say because it was inconclusive. There was a lot of contamination."[3]

Chapter 4

John F. Kennedy. Who Killed Our President?

In the cases of Sacco-Vanzetti, Bruno Hauptmann and Sam Sheppard, the collection of evidence was incomplete, there were instances of probable misconduct within the criminal justice system and the resolution of each one remains clouded. The same can even be said about the case of a presidential assassination.

John Fitzgerald Kennedy, the 35th President of the United States, flew to Dallas, Texas, on November 22, 1963. He was scheduled to speak at a luncheon and try to heal some wounds among warring factions of the Democratic Party. At 12:30 p.m., he rode in the presidential limousine as part of a motorcade headed for the Dallas Trade Mart where he was supposed to deliver his speech. Because of pleasant weather and JFK's style, the plastic bubbletop of the dark-blue Lincoln had been removed, its bullet-proof side windows rolled down. Jacqueline Kennedy, the President's wife, sat to his left in the rear seat. In the jump seats were Texas Governor John B. Connally who was in front of the President, and Mrs. Connally at the Governor's left. Two Secret Service agents occupied the front seats, one of whom was the driver.

In the Dealey Plaza section of downtown Dallas, cheering crowds lined the streets and, when the motorcade reached a point to the left and just forward of a seven-story, orange-brick warehouse and office building, the Texas School Book Depository (TSBD), it began a gradual descent down Elm Street toward a freeway for the last leg of the trip. Suddenly, gunshots resounded in rapid succession (variously described as three or four in number) and the President slumped forward, hit in the neck and head. Connally received a bullet in the back. Mrs. Kennedy cradled her stricken husband's head while the limousine raced to nearby

Parkland Hospital where doctors worked desperately to save the President, but he was pronounced dead at 1 p.m.

Back at the scene of the shooting, an eyewitness stated he had seen a man take deliberate aim from the sixth-floor corner window of the TSBD and fire a rifle in the direction of the Presidential limousine. An employee of the building, later identified as Lee Harvey Oswald, was spotted passing through the second-floor offices. Forty-five minutes after the shooting, Patrolman J. D. Tippit of the Dallas police force was shot, allegedly by Oswald after he had resisted arrest. Oswald fled but was soon found and, after a struggle, was captured in a movie theater.

What followed in the next 24 hours was unique in the annals of Presidential, criminal and television history. The following day, Saturday, Oswald was officially charged with the President's assassination and on the next morning, arrangements were made for his transfer from the city jail to the Dallas county jail. After emerging from the basement jail office and before a nationwide television audience, he was shot by Dallas nightclub owner Jack Ruby who, after a lengthy interrogation, denied any connection with a conspiracy to kill the President, instead maintaining he had erupted in a fit of depression and rage over Kennedy's death. Oswald died 48 hours after the President was assassinated. Ruby was convicted in 1964, but two years later the conviction was reversed on a legal technicality. A new trial was ordered but Ruby died of cancer before a new trial could begin.

A week after Lyndon B. Johnson assumed the duties of President, he issued an Executive Order creating the Warren Commission to investigate the deaths of both Kennedy and Oswald. It consisted of seven members and a general counsel and was chaired by Earl Warren, Chief Justice of the United States. Over the next 10 months, the Commission received voluminous reports from the Secret Service, FBI, Dallas Police Department, several congressional committees and many government agencies. All of the witnesses—552 in total—testified before the Commission in closed sessions except one. It also took sworn depositions, statements and affidavits and in September 1964 handed over its final report to President Johnson, a report contained within 888 pages and accompanied by 26 volumes of supporting documents.

The Warren Commission concluded that Lee Harvey Oswald, acting alone, shot Kennedy from the sixth floor of the TSBD and that Jack Ruby acted alone in killing Oswald in the Dallas jail basement. It posited that three shots were fired—two hits, one miss. The first hit pierced the President's neck and continued on to strike Governor Connally. The second hit struck Kennedy in the head, killing him. The Commission was unable to determine which of the three shots went awry. It added that it had found no evidence of a conspiracy between Oswald and Ruby.

Critics disputed the findings and, in 1978, a special committee of the U.S. House of Representatives, the House Select Committee on Assassinations (HSCA), released a statement accepting the testimony of witnesses and acoustical experts who claimed that shots were fired from two locations along the motorcade route at the same time, one point from the rear and one from the right front. The committee concluded that the President "was probably assassinated as a result of a conspiracy." But four years later, yet another group, the National Research Council, disagreed with the House committee findings. Thus, the lone gunman versus the conspiracy theories evolved, and they continue to be debated today. These and other questions will soon be addressed:

1. How many shots were fired?
2. What were their trajectories?
3. What did witnesses see and hear?
4. What can be said about the crime scene, fingerprint evidence and the alleged murder rifle?
5. What did the doctors really find at the autopsy?

I felt my eyes open and scan incredulously across the semicircle of distinguished-looking men before me. Actually, they sat more in a reversed letter U, clustered at one end of two long oak tables juxtaposed for greater width. Behind them

and continuing around the small, narrow room were flags of all 50 states; on the back wall, photographs of President Lyndon Johnson and former President John F. Kennedy straddled the shoulders of the Honorable Earl Warren. I recognized the others from pictures I had seen and accounts I had read about the composition of the Warren Commission: senators Richard Russell and John Cooper; representatives Gerald Ford and Hale Boggs; former CIA director Allen Dulles; former Kennedy advisor, John McCloy. I didn't recognize one person at the table who I later learned was the Commission's General Counsel, J. Lee Rankin. On some days, his assistant, Arlen Specter, was at his side.

I sat in a chair at the near right corner of the room, perhaps 30 feet from the tables. It was one of those "student chairs," the kind with a surface that swings up and toward your body to form a desk top. It was already in place for writing and on its top were a yellow legal pad and several pencils. Again, someone or something had provided for me.

Within moments of my arrival, I was certain security officials, guns drawn, would approach and search me, escort me away in handcuffs or worse still, arrest me as a trespasser and haul me off to jail. But no one noticed me that day—or on any succeeding day. I showed up for every session from a modest apartment within walking distance of the nation's capitol. Moreover, during each of those days, I was never questioned—and, I'm sure, never even seen! I had become a phantom like Sam Constant; I had become a member of the Warren Commission, but without participation or visibility.

Speaking of Sam, in the corner opposite me and to my left, there was a chair like mine. It was empty on that first day.

The proliferation of material dealing with Kennedy's death has been staggering: books, magazine and newspaper articles, TV shows, motion pictures, documentaries, government archives, medical records, eyewitness accounts. Then there are the theories, speculation and hearsay evidence.

<u>Bullets</u>

A vast number of people—experts and average citizens alike—have taken exception to the findings of the Warren Commission. Its basic tenet embraces what has come to be known as the Single Bullet Theory (SBT), a theory likely devised to discount a conspiracy conclusion. In this connection, two major camps have evolved:

(a) SBT theorists; lone gunman; supporters of Warren Commission

(b) Conspiracy theorists; more than one gunman; supporters of the House Select Committee on Assassinations (HSCA)

What is the SBT? Does it support or discredit a conspiracy? The theory contends that a bullet, identified officially as CE399, struck Kennedy in the back, exited his neck without leaving any metal fragments behind, hit Governor Connally near his right axilla (armpit), coursed through his chest after smashing a rib, left the chest and then shattered his right radius bone at the wrist. From there it bounced to Connally's left thigh where it lodged superficially into the flesh. In this theoretical excursion, the bullet's nose, lands and grooves remained intact and less than four grains of its substance were lost.

The SBT must not confound the issue of how many bullets the Warren Commision believed were fired by a single gunman. The answer is three. SBT refers only to the bullet alleged to have passed through Kennedy and become imbedded in Connally's thigh, half in and half out. Supposedly, the slug which was non-fatal to either of the men was later found on the governor's stretcher at Parkland Hospital. Most critics believe four shots were fired although Connally, himself a staunch critic of the SBT right up to his death in 1993, maintained the number was three.

When Assistant Commission Counsel Arlen Specter questioned Connally about the SBT, the governor shook his head and said, "They talk about the 'one bullet' or 'two bullet theory,' but as far as I'm concerned, there is no 'theory.' There is my absolute knowledge ... that one bullet caused the President's first wound, and that an entirely separate shot struck me … It's a certainty. I'll never change my mind." [4]

Many are adamant in labeling the theory implausible and have dubbed CE399 the "magic bullet," stating it was hastily conceived to discredit a conspiracy, thus stabilizing the country at a time of crisis and potential panic. In the unsettled political times of the early 1960s, the Warren Commission was forced to address not only the facts of the case as it saw them but also the international ramifications as it perceived them. Whether or not some facts were distorted or suppressed because of a more global agenda, therefore, is a puzzle that may never be solved. Put more bluntly: Was there a cover-up? Who would have ever imagined that the number of shots fired in Dallas as announced by a blue-ribbon commission might have had a bearing on Cold War tensions and possible nuclear conflict? The gravity of establishing the exact number of shots rested with the Commission's dilemma of how to explain two sets of nonfatal wounds with one solitary shot. If that could not have been accomplished, that is, if Kennedy's and Connally's nonfatal injuries were not caused by the same bullet, then there must have been more than one assassin, and hence a conspiracy. Expert analysis of time intervals became the necessary process and, correct or not, the Single Bullet Theory became the answer.

With regard to timing, the most important piece of evidence examined was an eight-millimeter film taken by Abraham Zapruder, and members of the Warren Commision relied heavily on the film for its conclusions. As the Kennedy motorcade rounded 120 degrees from Houston onto Elm Street, Zapruder stood on a four-foot slab of concrete on a slope facing Elm Street. The TSBD building was to his left, a mere 200 feet away. To his right were a triple underpass and a grassy knoll, at the top of which stood a stockade fence, and over his right shoulder were a parking lot and railroad yard. The Presidential limousine passed directly in front of him and, traveling at 11 miles per hour, became the primary focus of the most famous 22-second film recording in American history.

The film was recently enhanced but, unfortunately, no new information was discovered.

Assuming two bullets accounted for nonfatal damage, the film footage showed that the maximum amount of time that could have elapsed between the firing of the bullet striking Kennedy and the one wounding Connally was 1.66 seconds. But FBI testing of the rifle found at the TSBD showed it would have been impossible to have fired the bolt action weapon that fast. Translation? Two rifles, two assassins, conspiracy. For the Commission's purposes, that was unsuitable. The assumption then *had* to be the "magic bullet."

Autopsy Findings and Trajectories

The FBI published a report that was inconsistent with the U.S. Navy's autopsy findings on the President.[5] The autopsy was performed by Commander James J. Humes at the Bethesda Naval Hospital on the evening of the assassination. Doubt exists even today as to whether or not he had ever before performed an autopsy on a gunshot victim. His report stated that the bullet which hit Kennedy in the upper back exited at the front of the neck, but the FBI account stated, "Medical examination of the President's body revealed that the bullet which entered his back had penetrated to a distance of less than a finger length."[6] Later, a panel of world-renowned forensic pathologists, including Dr. Michael Baden and Dr. Cyril Wecht, concurred with that account.

At the close of the autopsy, Humes asserted with confidence, "One bullet had entered the President's back and had worked its way out of the body during external cardiac massage, and a second high-velocity bullet had entered the rear of the skull and had fragmentized prior to exit through the top of the skull."[7] The official view announced was that the President had been shot from behind. The next morning, however, Dr. Malcolm Perry who had performed a tracheotomy (windpipe incision to aid breathing) on Kennedy, stated that his findings casted doubt on a back to front transit.[8] In addition, after time there was strong suspicion that some autopsy photographs were missing while others had been altered.

In similar fashion, there were discrepancies in the description of the President's fatal head wounds and, therefore, in whether the firing point was at the rear of the motorcade or also at the right front. Both the FBI report and, later, several legal scholars argued that by a careful interpretation of the head injuries and the Zapruder film, one should conclude that a second assassin had fired from in front of the Presidential limousine.[9]

The spot generally referred to as the "front" location of firing was a position on or near a grassy knoll, to the right of the motorcade as it drove west along Elm Street. Many witnesses in Dealey Plaza said they heard shots coming from the front—from either the stockade fence on the knoll or from the far west of the knoll, next to the triple underpass. The sworn affidavit of Presidential Assistant Dave Powers was typical. He rode behind the President in the Secret Service follow-up car and stated he had a fleeting impression that shots came from the front—in the area of the triple overpass.

Furthermore, there were numerous witnesses who testified before the Warren Commission that they had seen men milling around the back of the fence hours and even seconds before the killing.

Ballistics

The Warren Commission stated that President Kennedy was struck by a 6.5 mm full metal jacketed (FMJ) bullet fired from a medium velocity Mannlicher-Carcano rifle. Autopsy x-rays demonstrated over 40 tiny bullet fragments within the President's skull. Also, a sizable bullet fragment had sheared off and imbedded on the skull bone's outer table.

But many experts, including Dr. Cyril Wecht, former President of the Academy of Forensic Science, have said such findings were incompatible with those produced by an FMJ missile. Most assert that, because of the strength of the jacket, the bullet would not shear off a fragment upon entering the head and then deposit it on the outer table of the skull.

Even world authorities on gunshot wounds came forward to dispute the x-ray findings, noting that FMJ missiles are used by the military and stating categorically that such bullets tend to pass through the body undisturbed and do not discharge fragments in their paths.

Three 6.5 mm cartridge cases were found on the floor of the Texas School Book Depository shortly after the assassination, two abutting the window wall and a third some five feet away. A rifle (described below) was also discovered. Oswald's fingerprints were found on it, but no prints were lifted from any of the cases. Unfortunately, a police officer put all three spent cases into an envelope without marking their locations of discovery. Later, a police captain allegedly removed one bullet and kept it until the FBI demanded it five days later. Unlike the other two, it was found to have a substantial dent in its lip, three sets of marks on its base and an absence of chambering marks. Taken together, these findings suggested to many that two of the cases had been ejected from Oswald's rifle but the third, possibly the one separated from the other two on the floor, was most likely an extra— a deliberate plant. Today, many researchers continue to hold to such a "plant" theory. This would mesh with the belief that only two shots had been fired from the TSBD, and at least another from the grassy knoll area.

With respect to the rifle, here again there was some initial confusion as to whether or not the one found in the corner of the sixth floor was an Italian Carcano (Oswald's) or a German Mauser. Subsequently, Seymour Weitzman, the sheriff who found it, clarified the discrepancy by stating:

> To my sorrow, I looked at it and it looked like a Mauser, which I said it was. But I said the wrong one because … just at a glance I saw the Mauser action and, I don't know, it just came out as a German Mauser which it wasn't. It's an Italian type gun. But from a glance it's hard to describe it, that's all I saw, was at a glance. I was mistaken and it was proven that my

statement was a mistake but it was an honest mistake.

Perhaps the most controversial piece of physical evidence was CE399, the "magic bullet," or the "pristine bullet," or the "perfect bullet" that the Warren Commission claimed sped through the bodies of both the President and the Governor. The controversy hinges on the Commission's claim that "all the evidence indicated that the bullet found on the Governor's stretcher could have caused all his wounds." A major school of thought holds that the bullet was so "pristine" in appearance, its nose and mid-section perfectly preserved, that it could not have been the one that had shattered two bones and created seven separate wounds in two people. Moreover, the phrase "the bullet found on the Governor's stretcher" may be totally inaccurate, for considerable evidence exists that such a bullet was found on neither that stretcher nor the President's.

But back to the bullet, its human journey and, once more, the testimony of experts. Dr. Robert Shaw, Governor Connally's chest surgeon:

> I feel that there would be some difficulty explaining all of the wounds as being inflicted by bullet Exhibit 399 without causing more in the way of loss of substance to the bullet or deformation of the bullet.

Dr. Cyril Wecht:

> I do not think that it could have been possible for the bullet shown as CE399 to have been a bullet that traversed the bodies of both President Kennedy and Governor Connally. I think that it's something which I could not accept, that this bullet which is not fragmented, not deformed or mutilated, with just a slight defect at the tail could have inflicted this amount of damage. Particularly the damage I'm talking about to the bony structures, the rib and the right radius

(just above the junction of the wrist)—I doubt that this bullet could have done it. It just does not fit with any of the cases I've seen of what happens to bullets after they have struck bone.

Dr. Milton Helpern, Chief Medical Examiner of New York City and an internationally famed forensic pathologist:

This bullet wasn't distorted in any way. I cannot accept the premise that this bullet thrashed around in all that bony tissue and lost only 1.4 to 2.4 grains of its original weight. I cannot believe either that this bullet is going to emerge miraculously unscathed, without any deformity, and with its lands and grooves intact.

And what of the origin of the stretcher bullet? This of course refers to the same "pristine bullet" number 399. As previously noted, whether or not it had been found on a stretcher is unclear. But assuming it had, some of the same analysts who believe that such a bullet could not have caused all of Governor Connally's wounds also believe it could not have landed on the stretcher on its own.

Was it therefore another plant just like the cartridge case? If so, and if much of the evidence heretofore presented pointed to a conspiracy, then by or for whom? Anti-Castro Cubans, or Cuba, itself, because of the Bay of Pigs disaster? The Soviets because of their distrust of Kennedy's Cold War intentions? The Mafia because of its outrage over the Kennedy war on organized crime? Or perhaps because they were enlisted to assassinate the President by Cuban loyalists? The CIA because of Kennedy's reported intent to dismantle the organization?

The amount of testimony taken and evidence submitted was dizzying. But I attended each and every session in that Washington hearing room, which is more than I can say about

Sam Constant. There were many, many questions and inconsistencies which troubled me—too numerous to list here even though I'd made such a list later, in my room. I would add it to one I'd compiled from the Sheppard case and incorporate the sum total into my next lecture in Connecticut.

What information the Warren Commission had that wasn't in full view, including mine, may never be understood, and I'm not certain whether or not there was a cover-up. Some areas of the investigation lend themselves more to a "misconduct" tag than others, but if indeed there had been a massive cover-up by the Commission, it would have to be considered the ultimate conspiracy.

And the beat goes on. The similarities in the high-profile cases we've chosen thus far are remarkable, not in terms of the murders themselves but in terms of judgmental mistakes and possibly—quite possibly—any combination of matters affecting physical evidence: collection, suppression, tampering, planting, substitution.

Meanwhile, my pal, Sam, had skipped the whole 10 months of hearings, or so it seemed. Unless he could have been there and not there at the same time. Do you know what I mean? As I left the building for the last time, I happened by him as I returned to my apartment. He came at me slowly from a side street, his head down as if counting cracks. He wore a faded beige shirt and no jacket, meager attire for the breezy fall air.

"Sam!" I said, "So you *are* here."

"Oh, hi, Henry. Yeah, I've been here, but I made myself … you know." He looked pale and drawn. His handshake was limp.

"Why?"

"Didn't feel like talking. Can't sleep."

As we walked two abreast, I gave him a sidelong glance. "You having a problem, Sam?" I asked.

"Only when I'm disgusted."

It was an oblique answer but I followed along. "And

when's that?"

"When I'm indefinite about something." He said it apologetically, as if he wanted to get it off his chest, then added, "But maybe things will shape up better back here in ... let's see ... in 30 years or so. That's easy: a hop, skip and jump."

I turned to congratulate him on his quick arithmetic but the click beat me to it and he was gone.

My step had slowed as I realized how unfulfilled I was for, in my view, there had been no real closure in the JFK case in contrast to verdicts in an adjudicated murder trial. Nor was there in the subsequent two: a reported suicide which some believe had all the earmarks of murder and the slaying of a little girl in northern Colorado. But first I'd return home for the second lecture to my new class of students. Then, a revisit to those contemporary events of the 1990s which I had been officially consulted on—Vincent Foster and JonBenet Ramsey—roles that were more current than those I had in the Sacco-Vanzetti and JFK cases. My analysis of those historic cases had been requested years after the crimes were committed.

In most of my classes, I never dramatize or illustrate the elements of forensic evidence as I had during Lecture Number 1 in New Haven. Occasionally I'll refer to some obscure murder case to make a point, but never before had I resorted to such a high-profile case as the Lindbergh kidnapping and killing. And I chided myself for not doing so sooner because, from legal, forensic and educational perspectives, such a case is one of only a handful that provides many rich examples of essential forensic principles. They have been scrutinized by the best scientific minds, dissected and written about by scholars of divergent disciplines—the law, medicine, the criminal justice system, sociology, psychology—and most have been considered landmark cases within the annals of crime. I would use the same approach for my second lecture, building it around fresh observations made during my last two visits,

Sheppard in Ohio and JFK in Washington.

Thus, Lecture Number 2 would be modeled after the first one, with one exception—it would take place at the State Police Forensic Science Laboratory instead of at the University of New Haven. The reason was a matter of logistics: it could accommodate more people. On my return home, I had received word that students, laboratory scientists, police officers and college professors from surrounding states had called to inquire about possible attendance. They had heard about the previous presentation and wished to attend the upcoming ones. Upon my approval, our staff extended invitations.

The forensic lab is a spanking new building on the crest of a Meriden, Connecticut, hill, overlooking a modern hospital to the west and a shopping mall to the east. Its location seems symbolic to me: straddling life and death on one side and modernization and progress on the other. The inside is a labyrinth of rooms, some administrative but mostly functional laboratories stacked with state-of-the-art technology and highly specialized equipment to analyze anything analyzable.

A separate training wing houses a collection of classrooms whose walls radiate outward like the spokes of a wheel. At its hub is Center Hall, split down the middle by an adjustable partition. Each side seats approximately 150 people and normally only one side would be used. For Lecture Number 2, however, the partition had been rolled back. A total of 300 were expected, 200 of the enrolled students and half as many law enforcement officers and forensic scientists.

On the morning of the lecture (I had arrived from 1963 Washington two days before), many people had arrived early for a tour of the facility. At five minutes before the hour, I wended my way toward Center Hall, past a sprinkle of saluting, uniformed state troopers. An unoffensive chemical smell hung over the corridors. Marcella Drupeau, my deputy at the lab, was heading toward me, shaking her head.

"Morning, Dr. Lee. You won't believe this."

But I didn't wait for her to elaborate, for there was something else on my mind. I hadn't done this when I returned home from my previous trips but I should have: test the perceived duration of my absences. Were they indeed so contracted that no one was aware of them? My wife, Margaret, had assured me that my time away went unnoticed, but I had explained the preposterous voyages to her, both before and after they took place. You might ask, then: "If she didn't realize I was gone, did she really believe I *was* gone?"

My response is, "I'm not sure, but when the whole surreal adventure is over, she and I will talk further about it." The point to be made now is that I wanted to get someone else's opinion.

"Believe what?" I said, but quickly followed with, "Wait, don't answer that. First, did you miss me?" I'd often asked that of my staff, a stab at humor.

"I always miss you, even over the entire day since I saw you last."

"I was worried." I countered with a wink. She, I'm sure, believed I was making a stab at humor, but I'd found my answer without asking the direct question. I exhaled before adding, "Okay now, what shouldn't I believe?"

"Well, there's this guy who took the lab tour. You should see him—he looks seven-feet tall, skinny as a rail. And he's wearing a lab coat—the longest one I've ever seen."

Tall? Long coat? Sam! I struggled to maintain my composure but fell short. Marcella looked anxious.

"You alright, Dr. Lee?"

"Oh ... alright ... yes. I'm fine. A bit puzzled, but, yes, I'm fine. See you later." I hurried toward the lecture hall.

The response to my entrance was different from New Haven. There, deafening silence replaced chatter. Here, deafening applause greeted me. It was as if I had gone on safari and had returned safely with some booty. I simply smiled and nodded, more preoccupied with whether or not Sam was here.

I didn't have to look far, for he sat in the first row, off to my right by only three seats. Our eyes met in recognition and then I squinted to read the name sewn over the breast pocket of his lab coat: "Dr. S. Constant."

I thanked the audience for its applause, indicating I suspected it was led by the hundred-some-odd visitors because my regular students knew me better. Even Sam laughed.

I outlined what would be covered over the following three hours, but before I could proceed, Sam raised his hand. "Dr. Lee," he said, standing, those behind shifting to either side. "I was at your last lecture—the one about Lindbergh and Hauptmann. Well, I just want to comment—I have it on excellent authority that Hauptmann had worked around the Lindbergh estate and must have known which window was the nursery's, that it had a broken latch, and also how high off the ground it was, in order for him to build a proper size ladder. Heck, he might have even broken the latch himself."

I wondered why he was revisiting that case at this point. Showing off? "Yes, I've heard that hypothesis, myself," I said.

"Hypothesis? It's really the opinion of most people."

You should know, I thought, but didn't say. Instead, I bluffed a reading of his coat and offered, "Thank you—ah—Dr. Constant."

For the benefit of the guests, I repeated most of the preliminary comments I'd made in New Haven—generalities about forensic science, its development, its advances, its future. Then came the lists, the first, relative to the Sheppard case, the next, JFK. This time, there was very little in the way of idea exchange, for everyone seemed too busy taking notes to ask questions or make comments. For Sheppard, the items I chose to elaborate on were:

1. The Sheppard house on a lake was in an exclusive neighborhood, as was the case with the Lindbergh mansion. Were they both selected targets?

2. In the 1950 to 1960 era, motive, means and opportunity were the major elements to be considered in solving crimes. What was the motive in this case? In Sacco-Vanzetti, they were anarchists who needed money. In Lindbergh, Hauptmann was said to be

after money, also. But in Marilyn's murder, why?

3. The upstairs bedroom was clearly the primary crime scene. Was this an organized, preplanned murder or a random, unorganized act?

4. The blood spatter pattern was crucial. Does the pattern show a left-handed killer? Or was it equally possible for a right-handed person to inflict the wounds with backhanded swings?

5. Was Marilyn raped? The position of the body and condition of her clothing suggested it, or did they simply represent signs of a struggle or a pattern of staging?

6. The floating cigarette was questionable evidence. Both Sheppards were nonsmokers. Did the police ever determine if their dinner guests on the night of the murder were smokers, and had they used the upstairs bathroom? Did one of the investigators leave it behind?

7. If no one used the upstairs bathroom, then who deposited the cigarette? What brand? Were there any matchsticks around? Any cigarette ashes? The DNA-STR testing of today might have revealed who the smoker was.

8. Were any footprints or fingerprints found in the house? Wouldn't a struggle between Sam and a "bushy-haired man" have produced some evidence?

9. What was the blunt instrument used to hit Dr. Sam? Was there any trace evidence like hair, tissue or blood on it?

10. Fingernail scrappings from Marilyn would have yielded important evidence. Today, biological findings such as DNA, blood and various tissues can either link or exonerate a suspect in a crime.

11. The time of death was never clear. Stomach contents were not saved.

12. Trace evidence is extremely important to today's homicide investigations. In this case, there was no systematic search for trace materials such as hairs, fibers, soil particles and wood fragments.

13. DNA was presumably found in blood removed from the crime scene. It did not match either of the Sheppard's DNA. Does this prove there was someone else's blood there or does it mean the test is so sensitive that it picks up a DNA result through secondary transfer?

I was helped by a few questions from the audience which of course I welcome. But there was so much to cover this time, and I was already well into the third hour, so I immediately turned to the JFK case:

1. The autopsy of the President was flawed. Probably some of the associated records were modified, and certainly some information was not retrievable.

2. Why did Commander Humes burn his autopsy draft notes of November 24, 1963?

3. Why wasn't there any meaningful follow-up to reports of puffs of smoke coming from the grassy knoll?

4. The smell of gunpowder in the vicinity of the same knoll was reported by more than one observer. Explanation?

5. Many pieces of physical evidence were missing including the brain of President Kennedy. What happened to that evidence?

6. A portion of the tip of the "magic bullet" was sliced off for spectrographic comparisons with other bullet fragments. The test results were never released. Why not?

7. Today's DNA testing might have helped remove or validate some doubts about said bullet. If , for example, both President Kennedy's and Governor

Connally's DNA had been found on the same "magic bullet," one could argue such a bullet caused all the wounds in both men. On the other hand, if the DNA on the bullet matched only one of them, then the "magic bullet" theory is wrong.

I had planned to include a discussion of the ballistics findings in the assassination case, stressing the speculation of a planted bullet casing, the presumed trajectories of the bullets and other scenarios. The real possibility of a conspiracy and the strange aftermath of Jack Ruby killing Oswald before a live national TV audience also were to be covered. But, I had run out of time. Thanking them all for coming, I gave a hint of the content of the next and final lecture: nagging questions about the deaths of Vincent Foster and JonBenet Ramsey. The ensuing applause reaffirmed my belief that I was on the correct instructional path.

I paused in the rear corridor outside Center Hall, shaking hands like a politician while biding time for Sam's appearance, but after half the class had filed past me, I knew he had left by a front exit along with the other half. By then, he had no doubt entered an empty room and clicked away. So what else is new?

Chapter 5

Vincent Foster. Suicide or Murder In Washington?

After Lecture Number 1, I had back-pedaled to get from Dr. Sheppard (1966) to President Kennedy (1963). Now having delivered the second lecture in the series, I skipped forward to the Vincent Foster mystery (1993). In addition to their governmental connection, these last two men shared something else: If Foster, whose death had been officially listed as a suicide, was instead murdered, he would have been the highest ranking Washington official to meet such a fate since President Kennedy. And once more, the word "conspiracy" was to rear its ugly head.

Public opinion was mixed in both cases. It's my personal belief that many Americans simply didn't want to taint the JFK assassination by considering more than the Warren Commission conclusions. They felt safer and more comfortable that way. And they had had enough. At worst, they might have secretly thought a conspiracy involving either foreign or underworld elements as only "possible."

In the Foster case, the death was not publicized enough to generate a firestorm, and there was a reason for this: There were more pressing headlines, as we shall see.

Public opinion crossed my mind because I wondered whether Sam Constant would bother to show up in Washington or Boulder, Colorado, or, for that matter, at the Los Angeles trial of a football legend. In fact, did I want to return to those cities to relive each case or merely to see if Sam would appear? Both. For despite my own forensic findings in, say, the Foster episode, I wanted to refresh my memories of all the odd pieces in a most perplexing puzzle and, at the same time, learn what my traveling companion had to offer.

In 1993, Washington and the country were preoccupied with a cannonade of matters political, economic and military. The Clinton administration forged a doomed national health care plan. Its tax increase package passed by a single vote. The North American Free Trade Agreement was ratified. American troops were withdrawn from Somalia after the deadly ambush of 18 marines. There seemed to be no room for other headlines.

On July 20, 1993, White House deputy counsel, Vincent W. Foster, was found dead in Fort Marcy Park in Arlington, Virginia, seven miles from the Capitol. He was a longtime friend and classmate of President Clinton, a confidant of First Lady Hillary Rodham Clinton and an important player in the handling of the Whitewater scandal. Foster had also been a partner with Hillary Clinton in the Rose Law Firm in Arkansas.

The death was summarily pronounced a suicide because some evidence pointed to a man who was depressed, frustrated and unable to continue his pressure packed position. But many researchers who believed it was a murder suggested that Foster's death was part of a larger Whitewater cover-up.

There were conflicting reports of where his body was found in the park, its position on a steep slope and whether or not his right hand clutched a .38 Colt handgun. Evidently, Foster had inserted a gun into his mouth and pulled the trigger. In consideration of powder burns found on both his hands, it was a feat that some believed could only have been performed by a contortionist. And, as in the case of body location and position at the crime scene, the description of blood on the body, on the gun and on the ground varied from observer to observer.

It was alleged that within 24 hours of the crime, Foster's White House office was stripped of documents, and U.S. Park Police (USPP) investigators were prevented from entering the office or conducting routine interviews. Five days later, a torn suicide note was supposedly found in his office briefcase. Accusations were heaped upon accusations: illegalities, improprieties, prosecutorial incompetence, abuse of power, media bias. Over time, the USPP, the FBI, the initial special counsel Robert Fiske, his successor Kenneth Starr and the U.S. Senate Banking Committee, were all unanimous in labeling the death a suicide.

In his book, *A Washington Tragedy*, Dan E. Moldea wrote:

> The Starr Report concludes that, based on the autopsy report and its subsequent analysis by the OIC (Office of Independent Counsel), along with the photographic evidence, Foster had been killed by a mouth-to-head gunshot wound, and that no other wounds were present. The cited evidence that Foster had shot himself includes the following:
>
> 1. Foster was found with the gun in his right hand, with his thumb, which had a visible indentation, trapped in the trigger guard;
> 2. the evidence "tends to show" that the gun was Foster's property;
> 3. "gunshot residue-like material" was discovered on Foster's right hand—in a manner confirmed by comparison testing with the revolver found in Foster's hand;
> 4. similar residue was found on the soft palate of Foster's mouth;
> 5. traces of lead were detected on Foster's clothing;
> 6. an examination yielded evidence of Foster's DNA on the barrel of the gun;
> 7. blood consistent with Foster's was found on the paper in which the gun had been wrapped by USPP criminalist Peter Simonello;
> 8. blood spatters were discovered on the fingerprint lifts from the revolver;
> 9. there were no signs of struggle at the crime scene, nor on Foster's body or clothing;
> 10. a small bone chip, containing Foster's DNA, was discovered in the trace evidence collected from Foster's clothing;
> 11. there was no evidence that Foster had ingested either drugs or alcohol;

12. traces of gunshot residue were discovered "in a sample of the soil from the place where Mr. Foster was found";
13. additional blood spatter was found in photographs on the vegetation around Foster's body at the crime scene;
14. there was no indication that Foster's body had been wrapped or cleaned;
15. no one saw Foster, conscious or unconscious, with anyone else at Fort Marcy Park. (*All numbers added for clarity*.)

To Kenneth Starr and his associates in the Office of Independent Counsel, this case is dead bang. In the final chapter of their report, they state:

In sum, based on all of the available evidence, which is considerable, the OIC agrees with the conclusion reached by every official entity that has examined the issue: Mr. Foster committed suicide by gunshot in Fort Marcy Park on July 20,1993.[10]

Studies by the OIC's chief criminalist, Dr. Henry Lee, were responsible for item numbers 5, 6, 7, 10 and 13 above. Also included in the *Starr Report* was an upbraiding statement issued by Dr. Lee:

… perfect reconstruction of the circumstances of Mr. Foster's death was not possible at the time of the OIC's investigation. The reasons include the lack of complete documentation of the original shooting scene; the lack of subsequent records and photographs of each item of physical evidence prior to examination; the lack of x-rays of Mr. Foster's body, tissue, and bone fragments in the areas at the scene under and around Mr. Foster's head; the lack of close-up photographs of any definite patterns and quantity of bloodstains found on Mr. Foster's clothing and body at the scene; and the unknown location of the fatal bullet which makes complete reconstruction of the bullet trajectory difficult.

I arrived at Fort Marcy Park early one morning, opening my eyes while seated at a picnic table in the general vicinity of where the body had reportedly been found. I knew it was 1997, immediately after the release of the Starr Report. I also knew my stay in the Washington area would be brief and thus no quarters would be needed. The single reason I "willed" my visit to that spot was to capture the ambiance of the tragedy, better to conceptualize the highlights of the case and its aftermath.

I recalled some of our contributions to the investigation in addition to finding the lead traces on Foster's clothing, the DNA on the gun barrel, Foster's blood on the wrapping paper, the bone chip with Foster's DNA and blood-like spatter on photographed vegetation around the body. We had detected traces of lead and a portion of a sunflower seed husk in an oven mitt taken from Foster's car on the park. These materials matched similar material found in Foster's pants pocket and clearly resulted from the transfer by an intermediate object such as the Colt weapon. I also discovered two other vital pieces of evidence: bloodstains on *both* sides of the lenses of Foster's eyeglasses which were picked up 13 feet below the body and grass and particles of sand on the soles of Foster's shoes.

Thus, on balance, I was satisfied there was sufficient evidence for me to agree with the *Starr Report*—that Foster took his own life—even though some of the claims of the "murder conspiracy" theorists were compelling. There were far too many of these to mull over, but I thought of a few as representative samples and filed them away for use later in Lecture Number 3.

I sat there convinced that, in keeping with one of the themes of this book, the resolution of the case might have been arrived at more easily and certainly might have been more universally accepted had the many discrepancies and unanswered questions not existed. It was Sacco-Vanzetti, Lindbergh, Sheppard and JFK all over again.

My wristwatch indicated I'd been at the park less than an hour, and I anticipated the stay in Colorado would be just as brief, if I were to return there at all. It seemed the more recent the crime, the less time required for my retrospections and, in the case of JonBenet Ramsey's slaying, I'd had—and continue to have—such an ongoing involvement with the investigation, there was no need to have time and place manipulated for my attendance. For example, just last week I was in Boulder conferring with District Attorney Alex Hunter. Before heading home to my office and current 2000 time, my last thought—a disturbing one—was that Sam Constant had never showed for the Foster review.

I sat at my desk, trying to organize my mind which was going off in many directions: the pending criminal investigations, the speeches scheduled for the week, teaching responsibilities, committee meetings, Department business, legislative hearings, travel itineraries and why Sam hadn't made contact with me about the Foster case. What was his opinion? Was it the final act of a man overwhelmed by life, or a murder conspiracy and cover-up? And did Sam not bother to appear because, as a symbol of public opinion, that symbol was too ambivalent to make a difference, that there had been too many theories and opinions advanced in the print and electronic media?

I believed my hectic schedule had nothing to do with his failure to communicate, for he could appear—and disappear—at will. At least that had been his pattern. But he had written me before and perhaps he'd write me again. He wouldn't be alone because, ever since I was asked to conduct a review of the Vincent Foster case, I'd received 17,000 letters and postcards from around the world. Maybe, like those correspondents, he would want to express his opinion in writing. I arose to search through a tableful of mail at the north corner of my office, and it was as if fate had separated a postcard from one of the stacks and deposited it at my feet. It read:

Hello Henry—I seem to write only after I attend one of your lectures. Re: Foster's death, there were, and still are, so many facts, rumors and innuendos swirling about, I thought you didn't need me to compound your confusion, if you have any. Besides, you know by now how I operate. I started out thinking suicide, but the more I thought about it, the more a murder makes sense. Surprised? The case is still relatively recent and time will tell what really happened. Sam

Chapter 6

JonBenet Ramsey. What Is Wrong with the Case?

As murder cases go, Sacco-Vanzetti had its years of appeals, JFK had its years of mishandling evidence and Sam Sheppard had its years of wrongful incarceration. What about JonBenet Ramsey? Was it a perfect crime? Or was its solution bogged down by crime scene issues and/or law enforcement infighting?

The latter crime is presented not only because it has spellbound people everywhere but also because it's a prototypical example of how not to handle a criminal investigation, particularly the all-important crime scene. Many say the case was fraught with forensic errors from the outset. George Washington University law professor Jonathan Turley has characterized it as follows: "The JonBenet Ramsey murder is almost a mandarin saga of complexity and conspiracy. An investigation of the investigation may determine whether improper influence or incompetence undermined the outcome."[11]

The bizarre story began with a frantic 911 call which was received by the Boulder Police Department at 5:52, the morning after Christmas 1996. The caller was Patsy Ramsey who shrieked that her daughter had been abducted from their home during the night. An attractive couple, Patsy and John Ramsey were members of Boulder's socially elite. Their home was a sprawling Tudor-style structure.

Police arrived at 6:10 a.m. and from that point forward, the case was to drag on for years as a stormy mixture of tragedy, investigative ineptness, controversy, accusations of payoffs and alleged cover-up. The Ramseys informed the police that Patsy had descended the stairway from their third floor bedroom to make coffee. On the bottom steps, she reportedly found a three-page note. Hand printed on white-lined paper, apparently with a black felt-tip pen, it read:

Mr. Ramsey,

Listen carefully! We are a group of individuals that represent a small foreign faction. We respect your bussiness (sic) but not the country that it serves. At this time we have your daughter in our posession (sic). She is safe and unharmed and if you want her to see 1997, you must follow our instructions to the letter.

You will withdraw $118,000.00 from your account. $100,000 will be in $100 bills and the remaining $18,000 in $20 bills. Make sure you bring an adequate size attache to the bank. When you get home you will put the money in a brown paper bag. I will call you between 8 and 10 a.m. tomorrow to instruct you on delivery. The delivery will be exhausting so I advise you to be rested. If we monitor you getting the money early, we might call you early to arrange an earlier delivery of the money and hence an earlier pick-up of your daughter.

Any deviation of my instructions will result in the immediate execution of your daughter. You will also be denied her remains for proper burial. The two gentlemen watching over your daughter do not particularly like you so I advise you not to provoke them. Speaking to anyone about your situation, such as the police, F.B.I., etc., will result in your daughter being beheaded. If we catch you talking to a stray dog, she dies. If you alert bank authorities, she dies. If the money is in any way tampered with, she dies. You will be scanned for electronic devices and if any are found, she dies. You can try to deceive us but be warned that we are familiar with law enforcement countermeasures and tactics. You stand a 99% chance of killing your daughter if you try to out smart us. Follow our instructions and you stand a 100% chance of getting her back. You and your family are under constant scrutiny as well as the authorities. Don't try to grow a brain John. You are not the only fat cat around so don't think that killing will be difficult. Don't underestimate us John. Use that good southern common sense of yours. Its up to you now John!

Victory!
S.B.T.C.

Patsy Ramsey stated that after reading the note and screaming, she raced to JonBenet's second-floor bedroom and found the child missing. She quickly checked on their nine-year-old son, Burke, down the hall. He slept soundly. Two other children from John's first marriage were away from home at the time: John Andrew Ramsey, 20, a University of Colorado student was visiting in Atlanta; and Melinda Ramsey Long, 25, a nurse, lived in Atlanta with her husband, a medical doctor.

After being summoned to the home, police officers conducted a search of the premises but failed to examine a small room in the basement. Then, instead of securing the entire house—all of it, a crime scene—they allowed Patsy and John to admit four friends and their pastor into the house, people who were free to roam about as they pleased. Detectives arrived two hours later.

In those early morning hours, the behavior of both Ramseys was characterized as strange. Patsy was described as sobbing, but without tears; John, cool and collected. First officers on the scene reportedly stated they were struck by the way Patsy covered her eyes as if in tears, but peered furtively between her fingers and glanced around the room. They added there was no physical contact between the parents who hardly spoke to nor made eye contact with one another.

Police reports indicate that officers photographed areas of melting snow in the yard. Mention was also made that no footprints were discovered in the immediate vicinity of the house, and there was no indication of forced entry. Two notations, however, described a small broken basement window and a blue suitcase in place directly beneath it. John would later claim he had broken the window during the summer when he accidentally locked himself out of the house.

By 10:30 a.m., no ransom call had been received and it was at that point that John Ramsey's behavior was said to have puzzled the investigators the most. According to a September 1997 issue of *Vanity Fair* magazine, writer Ann Louise Bardack quoted from a report filed by Detective Linda Arndt that John Ramsey left the house alone between 10:30 a.m. and noon to pick up the family mail. Many observers wondered why the police allowed this, and how they could justify letting the father of a kidnapped child venture out of the house and away from the telephone when kidnappers had written they would call the house that morning. Furthermore, it was asked, how could an apparently distraught father leave the scene?

An hour after his return, another major problem occurred when John and two of his friends were asked to search the house again. Ramsey took to the basemant and within minutes was heard screaming. He had discovered JonBenet's lifeless body in the small room that was described as a "wine cellar." The body was wrapped in a white blanket which John pulled away. He next ripped off a small piece of duct tape which covered her mouth. Her body was stiff and cool. She was dressed in a long-sleeved, knit shirt with an embroidered, sequined star on the front. She also wore long white pajama pants with an elastic band.

A garrote of white cord lay deeply embedded in her neck, while another loop was wrapped loosely around her right wrist. There was a double knot in the neck cord at its back midpoint and another knot at its connection to a portion of a wooden paint brush. Presumably the stick could have been used as a handle for tightening. Some of the child's blonde hair was entangled in the cord.

John bolted upstairs carrying JonBenet's body like a rag doll, placed her on the living room floor and hovered over her, moaning without tears. Like his wife before, his eyes reportedly darted around the room to see if anyone was watching.

The final diagnoses in the autopsy report are listed as follows:

I. Ligature strangulation

A. Circumferential ligature with associated ligature furrow of neck

B. Abrasions and petechial hemorrhages, neck

C. Petechial hemorrhages, conjunctival surfaces of eyes and skin of face

II. Craniocerebral injuries

A. Scalp contusion

B. Linear, comminuted fracture of right side of skull

C. Linear, pattern of contusions of right hemisphere

D. Subarachnoid and subdural hemorrhage

E. Small contusions, tips of temporal lobe

III. Abrasion of right cheek

IV. Abrasion/contusion, posterior right shoulder

V. Abrasions of left lower back and posterior left lower leg

VI. Abrasion and vascular congestion of vaginal mucosa

VII. Ligature of right wrist

VIII. Dotted pattern injuries on cheek and body

Many questions have been raised concerning specific aspects of the crime, such as:

1. Was JonBenet sexually assaulted?

2. She died of strangulation and head trauma. Which came first?

3. Was it an inside job, or was there an intruder?

4. Was a stun gun used?

5. Why was the exact amount of John Ramsey's yearly bonus—$118,000—used as the ransom demand?

6. Was the ransom note bogus? A common theme among analysts was that since there was a ransom note left at the Ramsey house, there shouldn't have been a murdered child in the basement. And, conversely, since a dead child was in the house, there shouldn't have been a ransom note on the stairs.

What followed was month after month of bickering by officials, media frenzy, leaks and a 13-month grand jury probe culminating in District Attorney Alex Hunter's October 1999 announcement that, "I and my prosecution task force believe we do not have sufficient evidence to (file) charges against anyone."[12] To date, the case remains unsolved.

I had amassed more than enough teaching material from the firsthand study of both the Vincent Foster and JonBenet Ramsey cases. My concluding lecture in the special series would be held in the auditorium of the State Police Headquarters building, and the rest of the winter semester would be confined to small breakout seminars dealing with specific areas of forensic science. Then, at the start of the next semester, I hoped to delve into the Sacco-Vanzetti and O.J. Simpson cases.

An early morning meeting with several police officials from a nearby city had just concluded, and I escorted them to the door beyond the outer vestibule. Upon reentering my office, I froze. Sam Constant sat on one of two settees which faced each other in front of my desk. I walked around and sat on the other, still feeling the effects of my surprise, not so much in seeing Sam the man, as in seeing Sam the cop. He was dressed like a Connecticut State Police officer!

"Henry," he said, "so what's the good word?"

I answered with a laugh as I partially covered my mouth. "Forgive me, but you … it … caught me off guard."

Sam seemed offended. "What do you mean, 'it'?"

"Your clothing. Stand up. Let's take a look at you."

He rose stiffly, looping his hands to the side before resting them on his hips. He beamed a proud smile and said, "When in Rome, you know."

Speechless, I ran my eyes over his full frame—law enforcement on stilts! I knew his uniform had to be custommade and wondered who had made it for him. But, then again, who made Sam?

The pants were charcoal gray with vertical blue and yellow stripes. Twice the length of our average officer's, I thought. His crisp shirt was of a gray wool blend and bore a multicolored patch of the state emblem. There was a gold badge on the left side of his chest and the right was plastered with various medals signifying specialized training and meritorious service. His shoulders sported blue and yellow epaulets. The leatherwear was patent with brass buckles and snaps, and a holstered gun hung from his belt.

When I realized my mouth was gaping, I clamped it shut. "Well, you certainly look sharp," I said, not sure of my sincerity.

"Don't worry, you won't be embarrassed."

I caught on immediately. "So you're ... ?"

"Yes."

"Then why the uniform in the first place?"

"It sets the proper character for me—a symbolic one—to emphasize my feeling about the two cases you'll be discussing in a bit."

"You know what I'll be lecturing on?"

"Henry," he said impatiently, "let's not go into that again. Of course I do."

"Okay, so you do. And your feeling?"

"The same as most cops'. I've watched *Hawaii-Five-O*, *Quincy* and *Kojak*. I use my gut feeling to solve cases and that tells me that Vincent Foster was murdered and the Ramseys are lying through their teeth."

"Sam, you're incredible."

"And invisible. Now, go do your thing out there."

I did not see him in the auditorium but was certain he lurked somewhere near. The lecture was not unlike the others in structure and style, and the following issues were raised, first about the Foster case, then about JonBenet's.

I. Vincent Foster:

A. Supporting a murder conspirary theory:

1. The "blowback" material was minimal even though Foster apparently fired the gun deep in his mouth. No powder burns were found in the mouth and no teeth were broken from gun recoil.
2. Very little blood was found at the scene, either on his body or on the ground.
3. The body was found in a highly unusual position for a self-inflicted gunshot wound into the mouth: too neat, with his extremities at his sides.
4. The spent bullet was never recovered.
5. Three rolls of 35 mm. film were taken to photograph the crime scene but evidently none of them came out. And some autopsy photos and x-rays had technical errors.
6. There were conflicting reports of the color of the gun owned by Foster, of whether or not there was another entry wound on the body, of whether or not suspicious-looking people were seen around Foster's car just before the body was discovered.
7. The crime scenes were never fully secured.
8. Allegedly, Foster's White House office (a secondary crime scene) was immediately cleared of evidence by administration officials.

B. Supporting a suicide theory:
1. There were no signs of a struggle or of damage to his clothing.
2. Grass, sand and soil debris were found on the sole of his shoes, indicating he walked to the park by himself.
3. High-velocity blood spatter was noticed on his shirt, and all bloodstains on the shirt were intact and definitive. There were no smears or smudges.
4. Black-colored soot and gunpowder residue-like material were observed on his hand.
5. Blood spatter-like residues were found on the gun and the evidence package wrapper of the gun.

6. The three rolls of crime scene negatives were underexposed due to a faulty camera setting. But it was possible to enhance some of the images and they corresponded to the images in the original Polaroid photographs.

7. Physical evidence found on his clothing, in his car and at the scene was consistent with a suicide theory.

II. JonBenet Ramsey:
  A. Supporting an intruder theory:
    1. A basement window had been broken and there were black scuff marks on the inside surface of the wall.
    2. Dotted injury patterns on her body resembled patterns made by a stun gun.
    3. A small amount of foreign DNA was found on her fingernails.
    4. A small amount of foreign DNA was found on her underwear.
    5. A ransom note was found in the house.
    6. The Ramseys passed a polygraph (lie detector) test.
    7. A metal baseball bat was found in the yard. It contained fibers similar to the basement carpet fibers.
    8. There were signs of sexual assault.
    9. A shoe print was found on the floor of the wine cellar.
  B. Supporting an insider theory:
    1. The place where the body was found was clearly a secondary location within the primary scene.
    2. The "wine cellar" in the basement is located in a back room. The layout of the house is such that only a person familiar with the house would be able to find that room.
    3. The language used in the ransom note is unlike that found in the typical ransome note of a kidnapper. The entire note contained disguised printing.

4. The ink and paper used for the ransom message originated from the Ramsey house.
5. A partial note containing similar printing was found in a garbage can in the house.
6. The amount of foreign DNA found on her fingernails and underpants was extremely minute and could have been the result of contamination.
7. Fibers found in various areas of the house showed similar origins.
8. The content of the 911 tape recording was inconsistent with the Ramseys' statements.

A lively discussuion of all the listed issues occupied nearly the full three hours, and after indicating I was still actively involved in the JonBenet case and frequently visited with Boulder DA Alex Hunter, I stressed that much can be gleaned about the direction of an investigation by the variety of forensic specialists consulted. I labeled the JonBenet Ramsey story as a case in point, and then enumerated the following:

DNA experts
Sexual abuse and assault experts
Child abuse consultants
Specialists in violent crime
Forensic pathologists
Psychological profilers
Juvenile witness interview specialists
Advocates for incest survivors
Consultant for chemical breakdown of trace evidence
Linguistic experts
Forensic knot specialist
Stun gun expert
Fingerprint experts
Expert in terrorism (ransom note study)
Crime scene reconstruction experts
Handwriting experts (ransom note)
Fiber experts

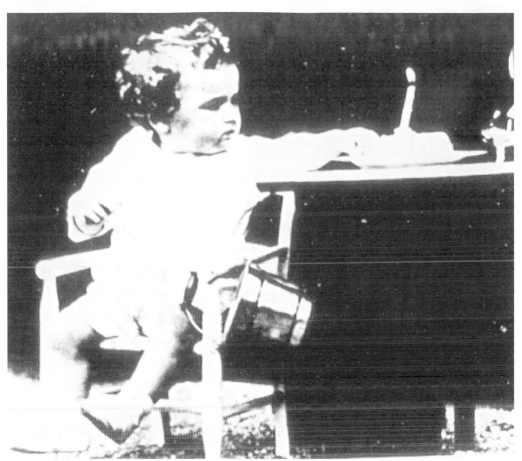

Charles A. Lindbergh, Jr., at age one. (Courtesy of the New Jersey State Police.)

Ladder and second-story window in Lindbergh case. (Courtesy of the New Jersey State Police.)

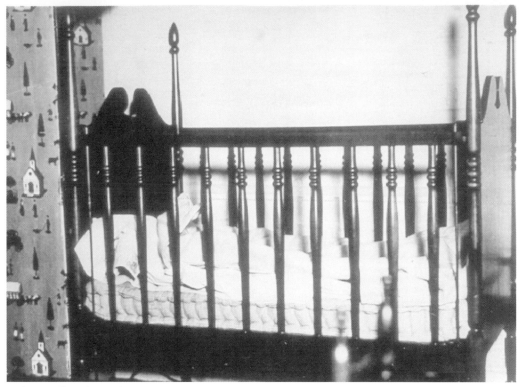

Baby Lindbergh's crib. (Courtesy of the New Jersey State Police.)

Lindbergh ransom note. (Courtesy of the New Jersey State Police.)

Lindbergh wanted poster. (Courtesy of the New Jersey State Police.)

Baby Lindbergh's remains and clothing.

Bruno Richard Hauptmann.

Ten dollar gold ransom bill recovered in Lindbergh case. Note license number written on bill, lower right. Hauptmann's Dodge sedan, upper right.

Hauptmann attic floor showing where wood had allegedly been removed to make the ladder.

(Above 4 photos courtesy of the New Jersey State Police.)

Stamp licked by Dr. Sam Sheppard in 1943. Later used to obtain DNA. (Courtesy of Dr. Mohammed Tahir.)

Attorney F. Lee Bailey (foreground) leaving courthouse in 1966 with Dr. Sam Sheppard (left) and Attorney Russell Sherman. (Photo by Richard T. Conway. Reprinted with permission from The Plain Dealer©. All rights reserved.)

Aerial view of Kennedy assassination site.
Texas School Book Depository (TSBD) is at
top center.

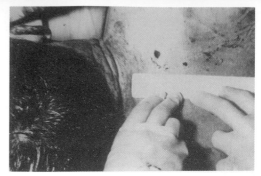

JFK's back wound.

JFK's head wound.

Location of wound and the bullet track
through JFK's head.

(Above 4 photos courtesy of Dr. Cyril Wecht and Dr. Gary Aguilar.)

The Warren Commission.

Entrance to Fort Marcy Park where Vincent Foster's body was found.

Vincent Foster's gun.

Cannon within Foster crime scene.

Foster crime scene reconstruction showing entrance and exit sites and bullet trajectory.

Foster crime scene. Note body, left upper quadrant.

Dr. Lee and FBI agent searching for physical evidence and clues in Foster case.

JonBenet Ramsey Ransom Note

Mr. Ramsey,

Listen carefully! We are a group of individuals that represent a small foreign faction. We ~~do~~ respect your bussiness but not the country that it serves. At this time we have your daughter in our posession. She is safe and unharmed and if you want her to see 1997, you must follow our instructions to the letter.

You will withdraw $118,000.00 from your account. $100,000 will be in $100 bills and the remaining $18,000 in $20 bills. Make sure that you bring an adequate size attache to the bank. When you get home you will put the money in a brown paper bag. I will call you between 8 and 10 am tomorrow to instruct you on delivery. The delivery will be exhausting so I advise you to be rested. If we monitor you getting the money early, we might call you early to arrange an earlier delivery of the money and hence a earlier ~~delivery~~ pick-up of your daughter.

Any deviation of my instructions will result in the immediate execution of your daughter. You will also be denied her remains for proper burial. The two gentlemen watching over your daughter don't particularly like you so I advise you not to provoke them. Speaking to anyone about your situation, such as Police, F.B.I., etc., will result in your daughter being beheaded. If we catch you talking to a stray dog, she dies. If you alert bank authorities, she dies. If the money is in any way marked or tampered with, she dies. You will be scanned for electronic devices and if any are found, she dies. You can try to deceive us but be warned that we are familier with law enforcement countermeasures and tactics. You stand a 99% chance of killing your daughter if you try to outsmart us. Follow our instructions and you stand a 100% chance of getting her back. You and your family are under constant scrutiny as well as the authorities. Don't try to grow a brain John. You are not the only fat cat around so don't think that killing will be difficult. Don't underestimate us John. Use that good southern common sense of yours. It is up to you now John!

Victory!

S.B.T.C

The Ramsey house.

JonBenet Ramsey. (Courtesy of Zuma Press and Dr. Cyril Wecht.)

Dr. Lee and District Attorney Alex Hunter at news conference discussing Ramsey case.

Ink, paper experts
Spider expert
Plant experts
Legal consultants
Medical experts

I ended the session by stating that, despite such a dazzling array of experts, there has been no closure in Boulder. Dismissing the students, I retired to my office and sat facing a stack of written materials about the Ramsey murder. Some of it consisted of my own notes that I'd compiled each time I returned from Colorado. After cramming as much information as I could into a three-hour lecture and responding to astute questions from my students, one would have thought I'd spent enough mental energy on the case for one day. But my mind drifted to its initial stages three years ago when I was called in as chief forensic advisor by District Attorney Alex Hunter.

Since that time, I'd met all the key players, examined evidence, took in most of the media coverage, and heard different theories about the tragedy. Yet, whether or not it was a murder or an accidental death with staging of the scene remains an open question in my mind. Maybe I should ask Sam. What might *his* opinion be, or is he just like the others—still debating the guilt of either the Ramsey parents or an intruder?

But one thing is clear to me: Alex Hunter has carried a heavy cross from the outset, and he had the courage not to push the grand jury for an indictment. And why? Lack of sufficient evidence. He is an honest and fair gentleman—a truth seeker who is known for thoughtful deliberation.

Section 3
O. J. Simpson

Chapter 1:
Historical Summary
Relationships

Chapter 2:
The Crimes

Chapter 3:
The Preliminary Hearing

Chapter 4:
The Trial

Chapter 5:
Evidence
Closing Arguments
Verdict

Bundy crime scene.

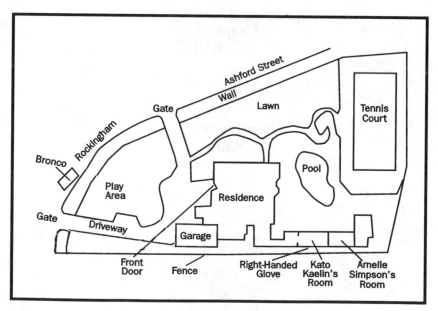

The Rockingham estate.

Chapter 1

Historical Summary

In the last three crimes discussed, the central figure was the victim: John F. Kennedy, Vincent Foster and JonBenet Ramsey. In this one, the second of our pair of bookends, the central figure is the suspected killer: O.J. Simpson. An African-American football hero, he had been a running back at the University of Southern California, and in 1968, he was named the Heisman Trophy winner, emblematic of college football's most outstanding player. Simpson went on to professional stardom with the Buffalo Bills. In 1985, his first year of eligibility, his name was enshrined in the Professional Football Hall of Fame. After retirement as a player in 1979, he maintained celebrity status as a television network sports commentator and a highly successful pitchman. He was also a movie actor, appearing in roles opposite the likes of Paul Newman and Steve McQueen. Over a high-profile career, the "Juice" had established himself as an American idol, respected by an adoring public who had seen him running through defensive lines, leaping through airports in TV commercials or hamming it up in three *Naked Gun* movies.

At age 47, O.J. seemingly had it all: fame, wealth and power. And then came the fall. The time was 1994 when, at home, former President Richard Nixon and former First Lady Jacqueline Kennedy Onassis had just died. And, abroad, Nelson Mandela had been sworn in as South Africa's first black President and the Channel Tunnel linking England and France took its first passengers. The place was Los Angeles, the city where a black motorist, Rodney King, had been beaten by police officers a few years earlier, and where blacks rioted in Watts more than a generation before.

On June 12, 1994, Simpson's former wife, Nicole Brown

Simpson, 35, and her friend, Ronald Goldman, 25, were savagely killed near the front gate of her Bundy Drive condominium in the Brentwood area of Los Angeles. Simpson became an early suspect, but it wasn't until five days later that the possibility of his complicity became evident when a white Ford Bronco led police cars and a fleet of TV news helicopters in a slow, 60-mile chase across the southern California 405 freeway. O.J. was in the car which was driven by his boyhood friend and ex-football teammate, A.C. Cowlings. Simpson rode in the back seat pointing a gun at his head. The improbable drama was viewed by a national TV audience of an estimated 95 million people.

Earlier that day, O.J. had failed to appear for arraignment on charges of double homicide. When the Bronco eventually pulled into his Rockingham Avenue estate, he was taken into custody, and the much-admired face of a confident, smiling O.J. Simpson had been transformed into a somber television image of confusion and darkness. He had been stripped of his superstar mantle and cloaked beneath the weight of a new and unseemly role: murder defendant.

More than a year after jury selection began, and after a sensational trial which covered 133 days of televised courtroom testimony, Simpson was acquitted of all charges. Fifty-thousand pages of transcript, 126 witnesses and 857 pieces of evidence were produced. The verdict rendered by a predominently African-American jury was met by a public reaction clearly split along racial lines, and many observers feel the outcome dealt a serious blow to race relations in America.

For over a year, millions of viewers tuned in to watch a falling star on a collision course with the "mountain of evidence" amassed by a resolute prosecution team. Part melodrama, part soap opera, there was a little for everyone. And the daily spectacle, along with its nightly coverage by news anchors, pundits and spin doctors, all combined to transfix the nation.

I had became part of the Dream Team put together by Attorney Robert Shapiro to represent Simpson. At the trial,

individual events seemed to happen swiftly within a drawn-out time sequence, like widgets being constructed on a barely moving assembly line. Therefore, although the pace of the trial appeared to lag, its component parts moved very quickly. What consumed much of the time were the incessant delays in resolving suppression motions and various questions of law by the presiding judge, the Honorable Lance Ito.

While in Los Angeles, I stayed at a hotel not far from the Criminal Courts Building. I was not in town for large blocks of time because of other responsibilities in Connecticut and those related to my consultations in other criminal cases around the world. But there were frequent cross-country flights to be made, and I was always put up at the same hotel. When not in court or reexamining evidence, I was in day and night planning sessions with other team members.

Since the full court proceedings were available and I had personally participated in the trial, I had given some thought to reconstructing all of it from memory. But that approach would have lacked the immediacy of the cases revisited up to this point. The JonBenet Ramsey story was different. It was still ongoing. But for O.J. Simpson, I required the whisk back in time and, fortunately, it happened.

One other thing: A simple recollection would have precluded any encounter with Sam Constant. I'd only seen him in warped time and had gotten used to the notion that he could be part of the magic, but not of anything more rational. And I did want to get his take on the Simpson case, especially in regard to racism and domestic violence and whether or not these twin issues influenced the outcome of the trial. If Sam had not, by then, won over my abiding trust, he had at least piqued my curiosity about his opinions. Not that I'd ever considered them "the last word." But if my assumption were correct—that somehow his was the voice of public opinion—then it was valuable to hear him out. After all, as a scientist, who says I have to be on his side?

Relationships

Nicole Brown Simpson

Simpson's first marriage to his teenage sweetheart, Marguerite Whitley, ended in 1979, the same year he retired from professional football and the same year their two-year-old daughter, Aaren, accidentally drowned in a swimming pool. The couple's union produced two other children, a son Jason and a daughter Arnelle. She would later become an important witness in defense of her father.

Nicole Brown first entered Simpson's life in 1977 when she was 18-years-old. He was 30 and still married to Marguerite, but the knot was unraveling.

Simpson's new love was born in Frankfort, Germany, to a German mother and military serviceman, but she was raised in California. A stunning blonde, she was elected homecoming princess at Dana Point High School, south of Los Angeles. After the divorce, she moved in with Simpson and they married in 1985. Their daughter, Sydney, was born the next year and a son, Justin, followed two years later. The children were living with Nicole at the Bundy Drive condo at the time of the crimes.

Until their divorce in 1992, the beautiful Caucasian and the handsome African-American occupied a mansion on Rockingham Avenue, in the tony Brentwood section of West Los Angeles, their marriage appearing to transcend interracial considerations. Nicole seemed happy, just as she did in the months before her murder when she could be seen tooling around in her $90,000 white Ferrari with its licence plate L84AD8, "Late for a Date."

But throughout the marriage, there were signs of serious trouble and the veneer of glitz, glamour and marital paradise gave way to public revelation of an abusive relationship. Police had responded a reported nine times to calls alleging domestic violence, an issue which was to become one of the cornerstones of the prosecution's case in the trial. Two 911 calls were made in 1993—after their divorce—and released as a tape by the Los Angeles Police Department two weeks after the double murder. The calls were less than a minute apart and occurred during one of their reconciliation attempts when she lived in a rented home on Gretna Green Way, six blocks from Bundy, the eventual crime scene. O.J. had come upon a photo album of Nicole's former boyfriends and became enraged. In the transcripts, "The guy who lives out back" refers to "Kato" Kaelin who rented guest quarters from Nicole. They had met on a skiing holiday in Aspen, Colorado. The transcripts are herewith presented in their entirety in order to demonstrate the sheer terror and fury of those moments. Later, during the trial, they would frame the picture of O.J. Simpson as a violently jealous stalker.

Nicole: Can you send someone to my house?

911: What's the problem there?

Nicole: My ex-husband, or my husband, just broke into my house, and he's ranting and raving outside in the front yard.

911: Has he been drinking or anything?

Nicole: No, but he's crazy.

911: Did he hit you?

Nicole: No.

911: Do you have a restraining order against him?

Nicole: No.

911: What is your name?

Nicole: Nicole Simpson.

Less than a minute later:

Nicole: Could you get somebody over here now, to … Gretna Green. He's back. Please.

911: What does he look like?

Nicole: He's O.J. Simpson. I think you know his record. Could you just send somebody over here?

911: What is he doing there?

Nicole: He just drove up again. (She begins to cry.) Could you just send somebody over?

911: What is he driving?

Nicole: He's in a white Bronco, but first of all he broke the back door down to get in.

911: Wait a minute, what's your name?

Nicole: Nicole Simpson.

911: OK, is he the sportcaster or whatever?

Nicole: Yeah.

911: Wait a minute, we're sending police. What is
     he doing? Is he threatening you?

Nicole: He's f-----g going nuts. (Sobs.)

911: Has he threatened you or is he just harassing
     you?

Nicole: You're going to hear him in a minute. He's
     about to come in again.

911: OK, just stay on the line.

Nicole: I don't want to stay on the line. He's go-
     ing to beat the s--t out of me.

911: Wait a minute, just stay on the line so we can
     know what's going on until the police get
     there, OK? OK, Nicole?

Nicole: Uh-huh.

911: Just a moment. Does he have any weapons?

Nicole: I don't know. (Sighs.) He went home. Now
     he's back. The kids are up there sleeping
     and I don't want anything to happen.

911: OK, just a minute. Is he on drugs or any-
     thing?

Nicole: No.

911: Just stay on the line in case he comes in. I
     need to hear what's going on.

Nicole: Can you hear him outside?

911: Is he yelling?

Nicole: Yep.

911: OK. Has he been drinking?

Nicole: No.

911: OK. (Can be heard contacting police units.)
     All units: more on the domestic violence
     at … South Gretna Green Way. The sus-
     pect has returned in a white Bronco.

Monitor comments. Incident 48231. OK, Nicole?

Nicole: Uh-huh.

911: Is he outdoors?

Nicole: Uh-huh, he's in the backyard.

911: He's in the backyard?

Nicole: Screaming at my roommate about me and at me.

911: OK. What is he saying?

Nicole: Oh, something about a guy I know and hookers and keys and I started this s--t before and ...

911: Um-hum.

Nicole: And it's all my fault and now what am I going to do, get the police in this? And the whole thing. It's all my fault. I started this before. (Sigh.) Brother ... (inaudible) kids ... (inaudible).

911: OK, has he hit you today or ...

Nicole: No.

911: OK, you don't need any paramedics or anything. OK, you just want him to leave?

Nicole: My door. He broke the whole back door in.

911: And then he left and came back?

Nicole: He came and he practically knocked my upstairs door down but he pounded it and he screamed and hollered and I tried to get him out of the bedroom because the kids are sleeping there.

911: Um-hum. OK.

Nicole: He wanted somebody's phone number and I gave him my phone book or I put my phone book down to write down the phone number that he wanted and he took my phone book with all my stuff in it.

911: OK. So basically you guys have just been
arguing?

(O.J. continues yelling inaudibly.)

911: Is he inside right now?

Nicole: Yeah.

(O.J. continues to yell.)

911: Is he talking to you?

Nicole: Yeah.

911: Are you locked in a room or something?

Nicole: No. He can come right in. I'm not going
where the kids are because the kids ...

911: Do you think he's going to hit you?

Nicole: I don't know.

911: Stay on the line. Don't hang it up, OK?

Nicole: OK.

(Inaudible.)

911: What is he saying?

Nicole: What?

911: What is he saying?

Nicole: What else?

(Sound of police radio in background.)

Nicole: O.J., O.J., the kids are sleeping.

911: He's still yelling at you?

(Sound of yelling. Nicole sobs into telephone.)

911: Is he upset with something you did?

Nicole: (Sobs.) A long time ago. It always comes
back.

911: Is your roommate talking to him?

Nicole: No one can talk to him, listen to him.

911: Does he have any weapons with him right
now?

Nicole: No, uh-uh.

911: OK, where is he standing?

Nicole: In the back doorway, in the house.

911: OK.

O.J.: I don't give a s--t anymore ..."

Nicole: Would you please, O.J., O.J., O.J., could
      you please (inaudible), please leave.

O.J.: I'm not leaving ...

Nicole: Please leave, O.J. Please, the kids, the kids
      are sleeping, please.

911: Is he leaving?

Nicole: No.

911: Docs hc know you're on the phone with
      police?

Nicole: No.

911: Where are the kids at right now?

Nicole: Up in my room.

911: Can they hear him yelling?

Nicole: I don't know. The room's the only onc
      that's quiet ... God.

911: Is there someone up there with the kids?

Nicole: No.

(Yelling continues in the background.)

911: What's he saying now? Nicole, you still on
      the line?

Nicole: Yeah.

911: Do you still think he's going to hit you?

Nicole: I don't know. Hc's going to leave. He just
      said that. He just said he needs to leave.

O.J.: Hey! I can read this bull s--t all week in the
      National Inquirer. Her words exactly.
      What, who got that, who?

911: Are you the only one in there with him?

Nicole: Right now, yeah. And he's also talking to
      my, the guy who lives out back is just stand-
      ing there. He came home.

911: Are you arguing with him, too?

Nicole: No! Absolutely not!

911: Oh, OK. OK.

Nicole: That's not arguing.

911: Yeah. Has this happened before or no?

Nicole: Many times.

911: OK. The police should be on their way. It just seems like a long time because it's kind of busy in that division right now.

(Yelling continues.)

911: to police: Regarding Gretna Green Way, the suspect is still there and yelling very loudly.

911: Is he still arguing?

(Knock on door.)

911: Was someone knocking on your door?

Nicole: It was him.

911: He's knocking on your door?

Nicole: There's a locked bedroom and he's wondering why.

911: Oh, so he's knocking on the locked door?

Nicole: Yeah. You know what, O.J. That window above you is also open. Could you just go, please? Can I get off the phone?

911: You want, you feel safe hanging up?

Nicole: (inaudible.)

911: You want to wait till the police get there?

Nicole: Yeah.

911: Nicole?

Nicole: Yeah.

911: Is he still arguing with you?

Nicole: Um-hum. He's moved a little (inaudible).

911: But the kids are still asleep?

Nicole: Yes. They're like rocks.

911: What part of the house is he in right now?

Nicole: Downstairs.

911: Downstairs?

Nicole: Yes.

911: And you're upstairs?

Nicole: No, I'm downstairs in the kitchen ... in the kitchen.

(Yelling continues in the background.)

911: Can you see the police, Nicole?

Nicole: No, but I will go out right now.
911: OK. You want to go out there?
Nicole: Yeah.
911: OK.
Nicole: I'm going to hang up.
911: OK.

The general opinion was that the district attorney's office had launched a media barrage to turn public opinion against O.J. and used the above tapes as its centerpiece. I suppose they thought it necessary to counter public sympathy for him which was expressed during the Bronco chase.

Apparently the campaign worked because before the 911 tapes were aired, I was informed that 60 percent of Americans believed Simpson was innocent, but after the tapes were released, 60 percent believed he was guilty. Sam should know for sure. I hope I get to ask him about it.

However, the tactic may have backfired because, while it shifted the polling numbers, it thwarted grand jury proceedings and moved the case to a preliminary hearing. (A preliminary hearing is more favorable for the defense than a grand jury.) The defense had filed a motion claiming grand jurors had possibly been exposed to prejudicial information by hearing the tapes along with the rest of the country. Ironically, a tie-in with a case we previously revisited is of interest here not only because the same issue was at stake, but also because a famous defense attorney was common to both cases: F. Lee Bailey.

My good friend, member of the Dream Team and former dean at the Santa Clara University School of Law, Gerald Uelmen, wrote in his book, *Lessons from the Trial: The People v. O.J. Simpson*:

The chief authority I cited for this motion induced a real sense of déjà vu. It was the 1966 decision of Sheppard v. Maxwell, the landmark case which F. Lee Bailey had argued to the U.S. Supreme Court thirty years before. The trial of

**Dr. Samuel Sheppard for the murder of his wife
had been preceded by widespread dissemination
of clearly inadmissible evidence, including his re-
fusal to take a lie detector test, and the claim there
were "bombshell witnesses" who would describe
his "Jekyll-Hyde" personality and fiery temper.
In setting aside the conviction, the Supreme Court
criticized the trial court's failure to "take strong
measures" to protect the defendant's right to receive a fair trial by an impartial jury free from
outside influences. At a retrial, Dr. Sheppard was
acquitted.[1]**

The 911 tapes represented the most dramatic example of
domestic violence since an early morning incident on New Year's
Day in 1989 when Simpson severely beat his wife and was ordered by the court to undergo therapy. He complied. Both pieces
of evidence were introduced by the prosecution at the preliminary hearing and again early in the trial to demonstrate Simpson's
volatility, to document his abusive nature and to establish that he
was capable of stalking and eventually killing his ex-wife.

When not engaged in reconciliation with Nicole, O.J. dated
several women, particularly Paula Barbieri, a 20-year-old Caucasian model. She later denied rumors that they had been roman-
tically involved. In contrast, Nicole did not form a public romantic relationship with anyone else after the end of their final attempt at reconciliation a month before her murder.

Ronald Lyle Goldman

The brutal murder of 25-year-old Ron Goldman was a classic example of a person who was at the wrong place at the wrong
time. He had struck up a friendship with Nicole six months before, but there was no evidence they had been linked romanti-
cally. Tall, handsome and fun loving, he aspired to become a
model.

Ron was a waiter at a nearby fashionable restaurant, the

Mezzaluna, where on the night of the crimes, Nicole had hosted an evening dinner party for her family. Her parents had driven in from Orange County to watch their granddaughter, Sydney, perform in a dance recital at the Paul Revere School in Brentwood earlier that day. At 9:30 p.m., Nicole's mother, Juditha Brown, phoned the restaurant to inquire about her reading glasses which were lost. The glasses were found by an employee and placed in an envelope. A few minutes later, Nicole called Goldman who was preparing to leave work to go on a date with a female co-worker. Goldman agreed to deliver the glasses to her condo after he had changed clothes at his nearby apartment. He canceled the date and arrived at Bundy only to become a victim in the double tragedy.

Brian "Kato" Kaelin

As a tenant at Gretna Green Way, Kaelin was offered a room when Nicole moved to her Bundy condo in 1993. He was considered no more than her baby-sitter, confidant and good friend, but, regardless, O.J. prevailed upon the blond Hollywood bit player to move into guest quarters at his Rockingham estate, rent-free. Simpson had convinced him that it would be inappropriate for a single man to occupy the same condo with a recently divorced woman.

Kaelin later testified at the preliminary hearing and the trial. The shaggy haired, jeans-clad houseguest combined nervousness, humor and a halting delivery to evoke several instances of raucous laughter from those in the courtroom, even at times from Simpson, himself. Prior to Kaelin's testimony, his value as a prosecution witness may have been overestimated.

Robert Kardashian

One of Simpson's oldest friends, Kardashian was and continued to be his closest advisor during the trial; after it was over, the friendship was terminated. The business entrepreneur had selected O.J. to be an usher in his wedding and was with O.J. when he first met Nicole. The one-time practicing attorney was heavily relied upon by the members of the defense team because of his ability to provide valuable inside information. It was at Kardashian's house in Encino that O.J. sought refuge after Nicole's funeral; it was from his house that he left with A.C. Cowlings on the famous slow pursuit just before the police arrived with an arrest warrant; and it was Kardashian who produced the so-called suicide letter just prior to the Bronco escapade. Excerpts from the rambling, handwritten letter are as follows:

> To whom it may concern: First, everyone understand, I have nothing to do with Nicole's murder. I loved her. I always have and always will. If we had a problem, it's because I loved her so much.

> Unlike what has been written in the press, Nicole and I had a great relationship for most of our lives together. Like all long-term relationships, we had a few downs and ups. I took the heat New Years 1989 because that's what I was supposed to do. I did not plead no contest for any other reason but to protect our privacy and was advised it would end the press hype.

> I think of my life and feel I've done most of the right things, so why do I end up like this. I can't go on. No matter what the outcome people will look and point. I can't take that. I can't subject my children to that. This way they can move on and go on with their lives. Please, if I've done anything worthwhile in my life, let my kids live in peace from you, the press.

> Don't feel sorry for me. I've had a great life, great friends. Please think of the real O.J. and not this lost person. Thanks for making my life special. I hope I helped yours.
>
> Peace and love, O.J.

Faye D. Resnick

Labeled the "mystery woman" by the media, Resnick was Nicole's best friend, sometimes roommate and reportedly the last person who spoke to Nicole in a phone conversation shortly before her murder. Resnick was rumored to have had close ties with the Westside L.A. drug culture. For never disclosed reasons she moved into Nicole's condo on June 3 and stayed until the afternoon of June 8 when she suffered a drug overdose and was admitted to a rehabilitation center. She had been unemployed for some time and had no assets, and the ongoing question during the trial period was how could she have afforded to support an expensive cocaine habit over a period of months, if not years.

Resnick became an important character witness in view of her friendship with Nicole (and O.J.), her lengthy phone call with Nicole at 9 p.m. on June 12 and press reports she had flown to Europe or South America after the killings. Some even believed Resnick was somehow in on the crimes.

There were other things related to this woman. Her diaries for the six days she lived with Nicole were stolen. She was to be given a set of keys to the condo, but the spare set kept in the drawer of a living room table was missing. And then there was the phone conversation on that fateful night: was Resnick acting as a go-between, an informant for Nicole's time schedule?

Early on in the saga, some observers believed O.J. had been framed. If so, one hypothesis held that elements of organized crime had arranged Nicole's murder and that Goldman had simply stumbled onto the crime scene. But why would they want Nicole dead? Was Faye Resnick the mob's informant and did it provide her with a steady supply of drugs?

I had settled into my hotel room on June 29, 1994, the evening before the start of the preliminary hearing. It was as if I'd never left. The retrogression felt strange, stranger than my trip back to the Sacco-Vanzetti era, for example. This time, the timespan covered only five years; I had been involved

with the defense from its inception; and I had vivid recollections of the entire experience. I could have opted for a reliance on memory, but for reasons I've already mentioned—immediacy, spontaneity, freshness—I willed it this way. But a question or two bothered me: Will I be watching myself on the witness stand? How could I observe the defense team in action if I had been part of it originally? For such technicalities to be ironed out, I was confident I'd be as phantom-like as was the case at the Warren Commision hearings in the 1960s.

I wasn't sure whether I preferred the modern conveniences of a hotel suite with soft towels and two television sets, or the homey comforts of rooming houses generations ago. But the same supplies were at hand: books, magnifying glass, briefcase, personal papers. It had just crossed my mind that the phone was in my room and not out in the hall when I recoiled from its ring. I fumbled the receiver as Sam Constant's voice took me by surprise.

"Henry, my friend," he shouted, "everything copacetic?"

I was happy, even relieved to hear his booming words. "Hi, Sam, how are you doing?"

"Fine, just fine. Ready for the fireworks? He's guilty, you know."

"No, I don't know. Not yet, anyway." Up to his old tricks, I thought. But that's Sam, and I should have gotten used to it by then. "How do you know he's guilty?"

"Me, personally?"

"Yes."

"Simple. He *looks* guilty."

At the time, that was the prevailing attitude among Caucasians while the reverse applied to African-Americans, so I didn't know what else I'd expected from the likes of Sam. I wanted to change the subject but he continued, "Plus I don't like it when men hit women."

I waited for more before finally asking, "Where are you?"

There was a pause. "Are we going into that again?"

Another pause. "But if you need an answer: here and there and everywhere."

"Pardon me for asking." I gave it my best sarcastic delivery.

Sam sounded unfazed. "You going to the hearing tomorrow?"

"Of course. Are you?"

"Maybe, maybe not. I'm not even sure of the trial. Maybe I'll pop in. Seems like a no-brainer. Whoops! I should have held my tongue. You're part of the defense team."

"Sam, the day you hold your tongue is the day when the whole world goes silent." I felt proud of the way I put it and knew that he wouldn't be offended.

He proved it with a chuckle. "No matter," he said. "So if I don't show up in public or—wait, let's phrase that another way—if you don't see me in public, okay to come over there sometimes?"

"Be my guest." I thought my response was too offhand and added, "Really, Sam, I mean it. Anytime."

"Thanks. Let's leave it at that. Bye."

I waited for his usual personal click but heard only the phone's.

Before turning in for the night, I took out some old notes from my briefcase and referred to them as I recalled the details of the crimes and the events just before and just after them.

Chapter 2

The Crimes

The sequence of important events that occurred on Sunday, June 12, 1994, involved O.J., Nicole, Goldman, Kato Kaelin, limousine driver Allan Park and an Akita dog also named Kato.

Well in advance, O.J. had made arrangements for an 11:45 p.m. flight from L.A. to Chicago. On the next morning, June 13, he planned to attend a convention of the Hertz rental car company whose TV commercials featured him hurtling over airport benches. A limousine was scheduled to pick him up at 10:45 p.m.

Earlier he played a round of morning golf at the Riviera Country Club and, in the afternoon, attended daughter Sydney's dance recital. But he had not been invited to the dinner at the Mezzaluna.

At about 9 p.m., he and Kato Kaelin drove to a Santa Monica McDonald's for hamburgers. O.J. ate his on the way home while Kaelin saved his for later. Kaelin last saw O.J. that night at 9:40.

Meanwhile, Nicole's party of 10 people dined from 7:00 to 8:30 and, after dinner, she walked with her children to a nearby ice-cream parlor before heading for home.

Later at Bundy, several neighbors heard the persistent barking and wailing of a dog around 10:15 or 10:20. One neighbor reportedly saw Nicole's brown and white Akita on the loose at 10:45, its paws covered with blood.

At 12:10 a.m., two passersby looked down the moonlit walkway of Nicole's condo and, through the open front gate, saw a woman crumpled in the alcove at the foot of several steps leading to a landing. Later, police would discover a male body sprawled against a wrought-iron fence to the right of the walkway.

Nicole Brown and Ron Goldman had been stabbed and sliced to death, their bodies lying in pools of blood. Blood had also trickled onto the grout between the bricks of the long exterior walkway. Later, a medical examiner detailed their fatal wounds. Among Nicole's was a slashed neck associated with severed carotid arteries. The knife wound had penetrated one of her vertebrae. Goldman had been stabbed 28 times, no doubt an indication of the fierce struggle he put up. Several wounds had pierced his lung but the most damaging was a deep flank injury with laceration of his abdominal aorta.

Throughout the slaughter, the two Simpson children—seven-year-old Sydney and five-year-old Justin—remained asleep in an upstairs bedroom.

At approximately the same time that the Akita was spotted roaming the streets near Bundy Drive—10:45—Town and Country limousine driver Allan Park rang the intercom buzzer at the gate surrounding O.J.'s Rockingham estate. There was no answer. He had arrived at 10:25, 20 minutes early. And over the next 10 to 15 minutes, he did not see the Bronco parked on North Rockingham. Park stated that at 10:54 he saw a large black man running across the front of the mansion. The lights went on and then O.J. answered the intercom. Six minutes later O.J. appeared at the doorstep, immaculately dressed and carrying four bags of luggage. The two left for the airport between 11:10 and 11:15 p.m.

Several key points must be added to the time line: One, phone records showed that at 10:03, Simpson called his girlfriend, Paula Barbieri, from the cellular phone in his Bronco. Two, Kato Kaelin would later testify that at 10:52, he heard three thumps on the outer wall of the Rockingham guesthouse. And three, several neighbors corroborated each other's statements regarding the time of the dog's protracted barking. Two of them linked the timing to reruns of the "The Mary Tyler Moore Show" and "The Dick Van Dyke Show."

Obviously, the barking dog and Park's statements would

become important to the prosecutors in their attempt to set the time of the murders. They would allege that Simpson killed two people at Bundy Drive at 10:15 and disposed of the weapon and bloody clothes. Then he had sufficient time to drive to Rockingham Avenue to meet Allan Park, the limousine driver. Some disputed such a window of opportunity in a traffic-congested city like L.A., while others pointed out that traffic would have been less sluggish at night. Yet, defenders of Simpson countered with the question of how, after his arrival at home, he could have tidied up and presented himself at the front door in just six minutes? And these same supporters asked why Park didn't see or hear the Bronco pull up to Rockingham?

After police arrived at the blood-splattered scene and cordoned off the area, they used white towels to soak up the blood in order to allow forensic experts easier approach to the bodies.

From a forensic point of view, a *big* mistake.

By 1:30 a.m., authorities were anxious to locate O.J., not only to inform him of the deaths, but also to interrogate him but, at that point, he was on the red-eye special to Chicago aboard American Airlines flight number 668. Contacted by phone at 7:30 a.m. Central daylight saving time, Simpson hurriedly checked out of Chicago's O'Hare Plaza Hotel and flew back to L.A. on American Airlines flight number 1691. He landed at Los Angeles International Airport at 11:08 a.m. and pulled into Rockingham at 11:30 where he was briefly handcuffed and then taken to police headquarters for questioning.

On the flight to Chicago we learned that Simpson had encountered an old friend, Howard Bingham. They engaged in general small talk both during the boarding procedure and at the luggage carousel. Bingham would later state that Simpson appeared calm and normal.

At the crime scene, bloody paw prints lined Bundy Drive in front of Nicole's condo. A restaurant menu lay beside her. Near Goldman's body were a bloody leather glove (left-handed), a dark-blue knit cap, a white envelope, a torn piece of paper and a pager.

Bloody shoe prints led from Nicole's body through the walkway to the back alley. A trail of five blood spots lined the shoe prints to the side. Weeks later, blood spots were noted at the bottom of the back gate which also contained a possible blood smudge near its top. At its deadbolt lock area was a second smudge.

A white Ferrari was parked inside the garage and a black Jeep Cherokee was parked in the driveway. Both hoods were cold.

Had Nicole been expecting another guest or just Goldman? The residence had not been ransacked, the stereo was playing, the lights were dim and candles were lit in the living room and around the tub in the upstairs bathroom. One of the first police officers to arrive on the scene noted a dish of unmelted ice cream inside the condo unit. These points were never explained during the investigation.

One of the passersby who spotted Nicole's lifeless body notified neighbors who in turn called the police. Within minutes several West L.A. police officers arrived at Bundy, and around 2 a.m., detectives arrived. Among them was Detective Mark Fuhrman who along with Detectives Philip Vannatter and Tom Lange would prove to be pivotal witnesses during the trial. The latter two arrived about 4 a.m. Fuhrman and his boss at West L.A. Homicide, Ron Phillips, briefed the others, shared their notes and led them on a walk-through of the crime scene.

After it had been determined that the female victim was O.J. Simpson's former wife, Keith Bushey, the West Bureau commander telephoned that O.J. should be informed "in person." Accordingly, Fuhrman, Phillips, Vannatter and Lange drove to Rockingham in two cars, arriving at 5:05 a.m. Three hours before that, the L.A. Bureau Chief had phoned to relieve Fuhrman and Phillips of the case; he reassigned it to Vannatter's and Lange's

Robbery/Homicide Unit. And, strangely, Fuhrman's name never appeared in the report of the night's activities as submitted by the latter two detectives.

At least two versions of what transpired that morning at Rockingham would be introduced at the trial, particularly as they related to the actions of Detective Fuhrman. But a generic account would include the following. Upstairs and downstairs lights were on in the house. All four men approached the estate's iron gate and rang the doorbell repeatedly. There was no answer. A white Bronco was parked at an odd angle on the street. Fuhrman stated he walked alone to the vehicle and in the course of his inspection, found a one-foot-long piece of picket fence near one of its wheels, an apparent bloodstain on the door at the driver's side and several dark stains on the doorsill. Also, in the car's cargo area were a package addressed to Simpson, an old shovel and a folded piece of heavy gauge plastic.

Without a search warrant, it was decided that Fuhrman would scale the five-foot high wall. He did and then let the others in through the main gate. They rang the bell at the front door and received no answer. The four detectives next walked to the rear of the house toward three bungalows rimming the property just inside a Cyclone fence. They knocked at the doors of houseguest Kaelin and Simpson's 25-year old daughter, Arnelle. Kaelin informed them that during the night at approximately 10:45, he heard three thumping noises on the wall above his bed. Arnelle, who lived next-door, admitted three of the detectives to the house while Fuhrman remained behind to question Kaelin further. Fuhrman and Kaelin then entered the house together and Kaelin was asked to wait at the bar for more questioning by Vannatter.

Around 6 a.m., Fuhrman decided to investigate a dark, narrow walkway between the bungalows and chain-link fence. On leaf-covered ground, he saw a right-handed leather glove with dark, wet material on it. Fuhrman believed that the material was blood and that the glove matched the one at the Bundy crime scene. He noticed nothing unusual about the leaves or ground in the immediate vicinity. Continuing some distance beyond the glove, he brushed against some cobwebs. Over the next few minutes, he summoned the other detectives back individually to examine the glove.

Vannatter instructed Fuhrman to drive to Bundy to check on whether the glove there matched the one at Rockingham. Fuhrman complied and discovered it to be a perfect match. He stated that while at Bundy, an LAPD photographer took a picture of him as he knelt and pointed to the bloody glove. (This conflicted with subsequent testimony that the photo was snapped *prior* to Fuhrman's discovery of the glove at Simpson's estate.)

Upon the detective's return to Rockingham at approximately 7:15 a.m., he and others located several drops of blood on the street near the Bronco, on the driveway, on the cement walkway outside the front door and on the light-stained floor inside the house. Fuhrman and one of the other detectives checked the rest of the house and found nothing amiss except a pair of black socks on the floor of the master bedroom.

Detective Vannatter officially declared Simpson's estate a secondary crime scene.

Even before certain cogent points will be brought up either at the preliminary hearing or at the trial itself, I must begin asking some burning questions. There are so many, but a few will do for now, and I share in the importance of many that were put to Johnnie Cochran when he requested them from members of his defense team. Cochran, as gifted and famous an attorney as they come, would later assume the role of lead defense counsel. In his excellent book, *Journey To Justice*, he lists some of the questions submitted and which would possibly be used during the trial. One set, faxed to him by the well-known and distinguished appellate lawyer, Alan Dershowitz, is worthy of mention. I leafed through the book which had been included among those sent along on my trip, found the questions and skimmed over a few:

> **1. How do you explain the Rockingham glove still being damp with blood at 6:00 [the next morning]**

if it had been dropped there at 10:45 P.M. on a dry
night?
2. What exactly is the state's theory as to how the glove
got there? Why was there no blood near it?
3. Why did Fuhrman not tell the truth about time of
photo showing him pointing at glove?
4. Why was Fuhrman alone outside crime scene for
18 minutes? Isn't it equally reasonable that the real
killer dropped second glove outside of crime scene
[rather] than behind O.J.'s house?
5. In light of knife wounds, shoe prints, etc., isn't it at
least equally reasonable that more than one killer
was involved? If state is wrong about its one-killer
theory, isn't it at least equally reasonable that it is
also wrong about *who* did it?
6. If the killer was covered with blood—as he had to
be—how do you explain absence of large amount
of blood either on way to car (if killer changed before getting into car) or in Bronco (if it were O.J.
and he got into Bronco before changing)?[2]

But on the other side of the ledger were some allegations
I was sure the prosecution would make, so I listed them, too:
1. Simpson cut his finger during the killings and
dripped blood at the Bundy crime scene. DNA results pointed to a "match" with Simpson's DNA.
Prosecution scientists claimed that the chances of
a match with a person other than Simpson would
be less than one in 170 million.
2. Simpson lost his left glove at Bundy during the
struggle, then deposited his right glove along the
walkway near the guest cottages. He was hurriedly
trying to hide it in the dark.
3. Blood found in the Bronco established that Simpson
drove the vehicle from the crime scene.
4. The barking dog fixed the time of deaths after which

Simpson had adequate time to return to Rockingham, dispose of the weapon and his bloody clothes, drop the glove and meet his limo driver.
5. **The limo driver stated he saw a tall black person emerge from the area near the side of the house. Simpson had just "hidden" the glove.**
6. **Simpson's whereabouts were unaccounted for between 9:40 p.m. and 10:56 p.m. on the night of the murders.**

Early that Monday afternoon, June 13, Detectives Vannatter and Lange tape-recorded an interview with Simpson in the interrogation room at police headquarters. Most of it dealt with routine questions and vague answers about the relationship between O.J. and Nicole, O.J.'s whereabouts on the day of the killings, his Chicago trip and—of most importance—how he had sustained a cut on the middle finger of his left hand. Simpson gave varying versions including injuring it when he broke a glass in his Chicago hotel room. The interview concluded, Simpson agreed to be fingerprinted, to have his injured finger photographed and to allow the LAPD to draw a blood sample.

If Simpson had something to hide, why did he agree to an interview by the police without a lawyer present? And why would he give a voluntary blood sample and allow his finger to be photographed? Because he wasn't smart?

From that point to the celebrated Bronco chase four days later, the principal events in the drama were the appointment of defense attorney, Robert Shapiro, as lead defense counsel, and the funerals of the victims. O.J. attended Nicole's with his children, Sydney and Justin. Shapiro immediately set about to assemble Simpson's Dream Team, a process to be addressed later.

Chapter 3

The Preliminary Hearing

After the grand jury was dismissed for reasons discussed earlier, a six-day preliminary hearing was held. Such a hearing is intended to determine whether there is sufficient evidence to prosecute a defendant for a crime. In a grand jury courtroom, there is no judge present and no defense attorneys are allowed. There is no cross-examination of witnesses nor evidence presented on behalf of the defendant. It is a prosecutor's paradise. In contrast, preliminary hearings level the playing field and better enable the defense to size up the prosecution's case.

The hearing began on Thursday, June 30, and was presided over by Los Angeles Municipal Judge Kathleen Kennedy-Powell. The prosecution was led by Marcia Clark and her boss in the D.A.'s office, Bill Hodgman, an excellent trial attorney and the head of L.A.'s Special Trials Unit. Clark, who ultimately would gain worldwide fame as lead prosecutor in the trial, had been appointed by Gil Garcetti, the Los Angeles district attorney. Clark possessed a splendid reputation; she had never lost a case in over 10 years. Robert Shapiro, known for his interpersonal and negotiating skills, headed the defense team and was joined by legal scholar Dean Uelmen, Bob Kardashian, Skip Taft (Simpson's personal attorney) and two of Shapiro's associates, Sara Kaplan and Karen Filipi.

Of course, I knew the outcome of the preliminary hearing in advance—as well as the later trial. But, as usual, I tried to keep an open mind, for it imparted a vibrant quality to my attendance, as vibrant as my being there the first time, bearing witness to history as it repeated itself. I had never seriously questioned how, why and in what form I'd turn up at

these events—crime scenes, hearings, trials—because I feared somehow that might break the spell. But now, near the conclusion of our collection of seven famous cases, I demanded more of myself. At least I should plan to give it more thought, sometime near the end of the O.J. Simpson story. There was only one problem, though: I could think about it until doomsday, but where do I actually go for answers? Who's the logical one to hold the key to what's going on? Sam Constant! Eventually, I'll dig it out of him.

Meanwhile, I sat not too far from the defense table and tried to look inconspicuous, even while realizing no one could see me.

The Exclusionary Rule

It has never been the intention of this book to argue for or against a legal procedure in the investigation or adjudication of the crimes we have selected. But an exception arises when such an issue illuminates other aspects we *do* wish to stress. In the case of O.J. Simpson, these include blatant contradictions in testimony, falsification of a legal document by some of the investigators and mishandling and/or fabrication of evidence.

A good deal of the preliminary hearing dealt with the Fourth Amendment "exclusionary rule," a constitutional provision which holds that illegally obtained evidence cannot be used in a trial against a defendant. It was Professor Uelmen who spearheaded the defense's claim that all evidence collected at Rockingham should have been excluded because no search warrant had been obtained before Detective Fuhrman went "over the wall." Uelmen has written:

> The requirements of the Fourth Amendment are really quite simple. Police and some politicians frequently refer to them as "technicalities," but I think they are more appropriately called "simplicities." All a police officer needs to remember are three rules:
> 1. Write out the facts that show why you believe evidence of a crime is in the place to be searched in an

"affidavit," under oath.

2. Take the affidavit to a judge, who will then issue a search warrant if your facts are sufficient. If you don't have time, you can just call the judge on the telephone. She will swear you in by telephone, tape record your recitation of the facts, and give you oral authorization to search.

3. Execute the search warrant by going to the exact place it describes, then searching for and seizing the exact things it describes, and then report back to the court what you seized.[3]

These guidelines were not followed by some of the detectives. They maintained that the purpose of the trip to Rockingham was to notify Simpson of his ex-wife's death and to arrange for the care of his children who, by that time, were safeguarded at police headquarters. Upon discovery of what they believed to be blood—less, in size, than the edge of a penny—on the "haphazardly" parked Bronco, they stated they feared other victims might be in the mansion, possibly injured and bleeding to death, unconscious or kidnapped. They then labeled the situation an emergency and therefore did not require a search warrant.

After the detectives gained access to the property, they soon awakened Kato Kaelin in order to ask where Simpson was but, "None of the four officers were even interested in his answer. They expressed no concern about any injured persons on the premises. ... They did not look for injured persons anywhere in the house." [4]

Furthermore, Professor Uelmen obtained the following sworn testimony from Arnelle Simpson at the hearing:

Uelmen: "Did you tell the officers they had your permission to search the premises or to seize any property on the premises?"

Simpson: "No, I did not."

Uelmen: "Did any officer ask you if he could take any item from the premises?"

Simpson: "No."

Uelmen also made the point that the search warrant affidavit, which Detective Vannatter wrote out *after* the search was conducted, contained a misleading description of what was found. Vannatter stated that a blood spot observed on the Bronco door was "later confirmed by scientific investigation personnel to be human blood." But no such testing had been performed.[5] He also wrote that drops leading to the mansion's entrance and the material found on the glove which Fuhrman "discovered," were of human origin. Again, no specific tests for human blood were done until weeks later. But the most erroneous claim was that O.J. had fled the state in order to avoid prosecution shortly after the homicides. Although both Kaelin and Arnelle had informed the detectives that the flight to Chicago was a prearranged business trip, Vannatter said, "It was determined, by interviews of Simpson's daughter and a friend Brian Kaelin, Simpson had left on an unexpected flight to Chicago during the early morning hours of June 13, 1994, and was last seen at the residence at approximately 2300 hours of June 12, 1994." According to Uelmen, the officers were willing to misrepresent the circumstances to avoid having evidence suppressed in court. However, he reasoned, false statements in the affidavit would prejudice the jury against the detectives' testimony later at the trial.[6] The defense felt that Fuhrman may have planted the glove, but Uelmen believed the intention was to supply probable cause for a search warrant rather than to frame Simpson. Or was the rationale, as F. Lee Bailey suggested, to plant evidence "which he (Fuhrman) alone could testify to, thus insuring he would remain on the case?" [7]

In this connection, the prosecution ridiculed the planting of the glove entirely, because, it said, the detective had no motive to frame O.J. with a murder charge. Yet, Fuhrman's past racist comments would be revealed during the trial, and many observers to this day insist such views were sufficiently virulent to motivate a frame-up. In trial testimony, Kathleen Bell would recall Fuhrman's remark at a Marine Corps recruiting station— that he would stop any interracial couple and "make up" a reason to do so. And, after he described the arrest of an African-American motorist who he thought appeared out of place in Westwood,

Fuhrman was asked by Laura Hart McKinny, possessor of the so-called Fuhrman tapes (which is more fully explored later), "So you're allowed to just pick somebody up that you think doesn't belong in an area and arrest him?"

Fuhrman answered, "I don't know. I don't know what the Supreme Court or the superior court says, and I don't really give a shit. If I was pushed into saying why I did it, I'd say suspicion of burglary. I'd be able to correlate exactly what I said into a reasonable cause for arrest."[8] These admissions were bland, however, compared to his more racist vitriol that will be revealed later (See The Trial).

Dean Uelmen seemed to summarize the defense's push for evidence exclusion when he stated: "If we were to carve out an exception to the Fourth Amendment for detectives who don't know what they have, in effect we would turn the Fourth Amendment on its head and say, 'The less you know, the more you can search.'" He then cited California's Supreme Court in *People v. Smith*: "The belief upon which an officer acts must be the product of facts known to or observed by him, and not a fanciful attempt to rationalize silence into a justification for a warrantless entry."

The Mystery Envelope

The owner of a Los Angeles cutlery store had contacted the police to inform them that six weeks before, O.J. had entered the store to purchase a folding stiletto knife from one of its salespersons, Jose Camacho. Police then bought a similar knife at the store and consulted with Dr. Irwin Golden, the coroner who had performed the autopsies on Nicole and Goldman. The conclusion drawn was that the knife O.J. had purchased was, indeed, the murder weapon because it "fit" with the size of the wounds.

During Camacho's testimony at the preliminary hearing, he disclosed that he had been paid $12,000 by the *National Enquirer* for his story. This impeached his credibility as a witness, and he would not be the last of potential witnesses jumping on a "quick cash" bandwagon. Jill Shively was another person who fell into this category. At the hearing, she declared she had observed O.J.'s Bronco leaving the Bundy scene, but on the same day of her testimony, she sold her story to both TV's *Hard Copy* for $5,000 and to the *Star* for $2,600. She never testified at the trial.

The knife O.J. had purchased was, in fact, stored in a hidden compartment of a cabinet in his bedroom, and, as was later documented, had never been used. The defense was not required to notify either the court or the prosecution of any exculpatory evidence (i.e., favorable to the defense) it had uncovered, but arrangements were made to have a legal official seize the knife, put it in a Manila envelope under seal and deliver it to the court. For the longest time, members of the media and a national TV audience speculated on the contents of the envelope. Was it the real murder weapon? But after the prosecution learned of forensic testing that proved the knife was "pristine," the envelope and its contents were not considered during the trial.

The testing results were probably the only evidence that wasn't leaked to the news media during the whole preliminary hearing and trial.

The "mystery envelope" episode arose on the first day of the hearing, and it set the stage for obvious animosity between Robert Shapiro and lead prosecutor, Marcia Clark. When she requested permission from the court to open the envelope in full view of a national television audience, Shapiro said, "It seems like a bit of grandstanding."

An indignant Clark snapped back, "Excuse me, I can't believe I heard Mr. Shapiro say that." The prosecutor had demonstrated she would not and could not be intimidated, and her performance through the hearing and into the trial bore that out consistently.

Upon court order, one forensic scientist was asked to conduct a detailed examination of the knife and it was I who undertook the task. My conclusion was that it had never been used for any purpose whatsoever. No blood, tissue or hair

fragments were found on it and the original price sticker was in place on the blade without any change of shape or form. In short, I found the knife to be in the same condition as it had been at the time of purchase.

Another thing worth mentioning is that when I processed the knife utilizing the cyanoacrylate fuming method, 14 latent fingerprints appeared. Whose were they? Neither the defense nor the prosecution pursued this finding.

Selected Witnesses

The hearing produced several instances of contradictory testimony by Detectives Vannatter and Fuhrman. Furthermore, many court observers believe that there may have been indications of fabrication and tampering with evidence, as revealed in statements given by witnesses under oath. When Vannatter was asked why he brought Fuhrman and Detective Phillips with him from Bundy to Rockingham, after Fuhrman had been relieved of responsibility in the case, Vannatter testified, "they were assisting us." Fuhrman, on the other hand, stated that Vannatter and Detective Lange, "didn't know the area" and that they had asked him "to lead us up there."

Furhman explained his actions regarding his initial inspection of the white Bronco. He walked over to the vehicle *alone* and noticed it was parked "in a very haphazard manner," with its rear jutting out into the street a foot or so compared to the front wheels. But Professor Uelmen maintained the detective's testimony all but proved that the car might have been entered or moved because photographs taken more than two hours later showed the Bronco was parked perfectly parallel to the curb.

Fuhrman said he inspected the Bronco with a flashlight, noticing a stain above the handle on the driver's side. Another stain consisted of "three or four little lines, red-stained lines" at the doorsill below. He told no one of the lower stains. It was later demonstrated that the "lines" were visible only with the door open. *After* observing the stains, he said, he looked through the window and saw the package, shovel and plastic.

Vannatter's description was at marked variance with Fuhrman's. The lead detective testified that *both* he and Fuhrman went to the Bronco and looked through the windows. Vannatter then left to join the other detectives at the gate, but was called back to the car by Fuhrman who pointed out the stain above the door handle. Vannatter stated he never saw the stains that Fuhrman had seen near the bottom of the driver's door.

The two key investigators in the case gave conflicting statements. This fact alone raised the issues of possible perjury and possible tampering with or planting of evidence. And their very different versions of what happened at Rockingham that morning raised the important question of credibility. Who was telling the truth? Was either one? Could either one be believed during trial testimony? If they had simply told the truth and indicated their real reason for checking the Rockingham estate, the trial might have had a different outcome.

The defense wanted to establish the fact that the detectives' trip to Rockingham was made not only for the purpose of informing Simpson of his former wife's murder, but also because he was a suspect all along. In Robert Shapiro's cross examination of Vannatter, he brought this to light. The detective agreed with the defense attorney that the police did not personally inform the Goldmans of their son's killing, and they did not take photographs of Kato Kaelin's car or Kaelin, himself, as they did the white Bronco and O.J. Simpson.

Shapiro asked, "If Mr. Goldman had been the sole victim of this case under the same circumstances, would the same investigation be taking place?"

Detective Tom Lange also testified at the hearing. The LAPD had not called the coroner until 10 hours after the murders, and he substantiated such a delay. Lange also admitted to inadequate securing of the Bundy crime scene and the discovery of five spots of blood which were neither Nicole's nor Goldman's. He added there was no way to tell when they had been left there.

In terms of honesty and integrity, the testimony of Detective Lange was in complete contrast to that of Vannatter and Fuhrman.

Two LAPD criminalists were questioned by Dean Uelmen. Dennis Fung stated he received a call to go to Rockingham, not to the Bundy crime scene. The call was made at 5:30 a.m., and he arrived at 7:10. He tested the Bronco for only one blood spot. The other criminalist, Gregory Matheson, bolstered the defense's contention that there may have been contamination of blood samples and that the LAPD was careless in its collection and storage techniques. Matheson said his blood typing and serology testing of a blood droplet at the Bundy location showed that it could have come from one out of every 200 people, and that O.J. belonged in that group. Professor Uelmen, however, teased from the criminalist the fact that the police lab's database is heavily skewed toward criminals and is not representative of the general population.

"The tests … are exclusionary tests, is that correct?" Uelmen asked.

"That's correct," Matheson replied. "There's nothing here that would individualize a stain to one specific person."

"So any attempt to analogize this to fingerprints or precise identification of a person would be inaccurate?"

"That's correct," the criminalist answered.

Other information gleaned from Matheson was that, statistically, the stains at Bundy could have been produced by blood from any of 40,000 to 80,000 individuals in the Los Angeles area; the blood of 0.48 percent of the general population had the same characteristics as O.J.'s blood and that found at Bundy; there was a possibility the drops were a mixture of more than one person's blood; and the time when the blood drops were deposited could not be determined.

One of the more dramatic and, some say, pitiful sequences in the preliminary hearing occured when L.A.'s deputy coroner, Dr. Irwin Golden, testified. He had performed both autopsies. It had been estimated by the defense that the coroner's office had made 16 mistakes in the handling of the case, including Dr. Golden's stating the knife purchased by O.J. could have been the murder weapon; mislabeling forensic evidence (fluid from Nicole's body); discarding Nicole's stomach contents; and changing his opinion about the time of the deaths. Eventually, he opined that 75 percent of the forensic criteria would set the time at *after* 11:00 p.m.

The coroner also suggested that based on his findings of "two … different types of stab wounds on the victims," two different weapons may have been used. Thus, the possibility of two perpetrators existed.

In all, 21 witnesses testified at the six-day preliminary hearing. On the last day, July 8, Shapiro delivered his closing argument which included:

> If in fact the killer lived at the Simpson residence (Rockingham), the court would have to believe the following: that in a window period of less than an hour, the killer was able to leave the crime scene that has been described with a victim with two arteries in the neck cut, two jugular veins cut, and massive blood from both victims. A clear inference would be that the murderer was indeed covered with blood. The murderer would then have to do the following: abandon the bloody clothing, because they have not been found or presented; abandon the murder weapon, because that has not been found or discovered; abandon bloody shoes, because they have not been found or discovered, and then go back to his house and leave a bloody glove in his backyard. That just doesn't stand up to logic. . . . This is a case that the police admit is still under investigation, where other suspects are being sought, where the medical examiner admits that two weapons could have been used—a clear inference that there could have been more than one killer.

I don't want to go through each and every area of impeachment with the witnesses, but I think it is very, very clear that everybody who has participated in this investigation has not done so in a professional manner. From the time the Los Angeles Police Department arrived on the crime scene, it was nearly 10 hours later until they started the scientific investigation and even took the temperature of the body.

… This is a case that is not ready yet to come to court.

But at the conclusion of that day's proceedings, and after Marcia Clark had presented the State's case, Judge Kennedy-Powell ruled that O.J. Simpson would be bound over for trial on two counts of first-degree murder. She stated, "The people have more than established their burden. The defendant should be held to account."

I remember thinking when I was there six years before, that both the prosecution and the defense were engaged in a sort of chess game, and that if the preliminary hearing had been supplanted by a grand jury, the prosecution would have had a field day. This is not to disparage the performance of Marcia Clark and her associates. On the contrary, they were outstanding, and they gave convincing notice that they would be a formidable team during the trial. But a grand jury's only lawyers are the prosecutors and no defense evidence is presented.

I thought the same things the second time around. And because, in contrast to 1994, I was in attendance on each of the six days, I had gained additional insights. The prosecution had played it "close to the vest," presenting just enough evidence to warrant a full trial. Furthermore, it had scuttled the defense's attempt to invoke the Fourth Amendment exclusionary rule. But the defense, in turn, gained something

that might prove to be crucial later on: It raised the issue of veracity as it related to some members of the LAPD.

The hearing over, I went directly to my hotel just as I had done on all the other nights. But this time was different. As I rounded the corner of the twelfth floor corridor, Sam Constant straightened from his leaning position near the door to my room. He wore the same Yankee Doodle outfit he had on at the Dedham, Massachusetts, trial: white shirt, red vest, blue pants and golden leggings. He seemed animated in body and voice.

"Well, are you convinced?" he asked.

I was tired but didn't feel as annoyed as I might have sounded. "First—hello, Sam. Second—to answer your question—no. And I'm assuming you're talking about guilt."

"You got it, old buddy. But not 'talking about.' Certain about."

Once again, I wondered why he didn't know the outcome of things, just as I did. And, once again, I reminded myself that if mercurial Sam knew outcomes for sure, he wouldn't fit as the poster boy for public opinion.

"Sam, there's nothing proven yet. That's the beauty of our system. No matter how poor the odds might seem, everyone is entitled to his day in court. Then it's up to the prosecution to prove guilt. It's not up to the defense to prove innocence. So a defendant is innocent until proven guilty; you've got it the other way around."

He looked as though he'd been shot. Tensing, he brushed aside an imaginary object in the air. "For crying out loud," he exclaimed, "you're for the defense! What else would you say?"

"But it's made clear to everyone who asks me to help out: I call it as I see it. As a forensic scientist, it's the only way—the correct way—I can work."

"Yeah, right. Well, everyone's entitled to his opinion." Then, as an apparent afterthought, he continued, "Guess I should know—I go around collecting them till I'm blue in the face."

I felt adventurous. "You don't help *make* them, too?"

"Never. Like I said, 'Everyone to his own opinion.' I got mine."

I felt reckless. "Yeah, right."

Sam seemed to ignore the sarcasm and said, "By the way, Henry, I might write a book about this case."

Before I could respond, the click came and he had vanished.

Chapter 4

The Trial

There have been numerous selections for the "Trial of the Century," but "People v. O.J. Simpson" wins the title of "Media Trial of the Century," hands down. It also stands alone as champion among trials pressured by an undercurrent of major social issues—in this case, racism and domestic violence. An African-American football hero stood accused of killing two Caucasians. He had a veritiable history of spousal abuse. Around the world, the verdict was met by reactions split along racial lines and, to a lesser extent, along gender lines. But, the more relevant and perhaps enduring questions are: Was the predominently African-American jury swayed by these considerations? Despite societal influences, was there reasonable doubt that Simpson committed the crimes? It is more than a coincidence that the prosecution began its case with evidence of domestic violence, and the defense, with testimony of family members who spun stories of unity, love and warm memories.

From the formal arraignment on July 22, 1994, during which O.J. pleaded "absolutely 100 percent not guilty," to the start of the trial in January 1995, a plethora of motions, hearings and rulings led to the following developments:

1. Mark Fuhrman's personnel and military records would not be made available.
2. The prosecution would seek a sentence of life without parole rather than the death penalty.
3. The jury would be sequestered beginning January 11, 1995.
4. Superior Court Judge Lance A. Ito, who had been assigned to hear the case, upheld the legality of the search of Simpson's Rockingham estate.

5. Judge Ito ruled the defense was entitled to its own DNA testing of the blood sample evidence. Thus, the sample was split: 90 percent for the prosecution and 10 percent for the defense.

In August 1994, court papers revealed DNA test results which showed that O.J.'s blood had the same genetic markers as samples from the drops leading away from the Bundy crime scene.

In September, jury selection began.

In November, a jury of eight women and four men was chosen. It contained eight African-Americans, one Caucasian, one Hispanic and two persons of mixed race.

In December, an alternate jury of seven African-Americans, four Caucasians and one Hispanic was picked. As the trial progressed, there were many juror dismissals, but the composition of the jury that began deliberations 10 months later was still decidedly African-American.

In January 1995, Judge Ito ruled against the defense which had attempted to bar evidence of domestic violence, not only during the relationship of Nicole and O.J., but also during the marriage to his first wife, Marguerite. The defense retaliated by accusing the prosecution of character assassination. A week earlier, a hearing had been held to determine whether or not Fuhrman could be questioned about alleged racial slurs he had made. At one point, Deputy District Attorney Christopher Darden and defense lawyer Johnnie Cochran, both African-Americans, had an acrimonious exchange about the use of "the n-word." Ito's decision allowed the introduction of Fuhrman's possible racism if the defense could prove its relevance.

The trial began in earnest on January 24, 1995, with Judge Lance Ito presiding. A Japanese-American with a reputation for legal acumen and compassion, he would—during the long, televised, often heated debates—become transformed from a cheerful, jocular man to a grumpy judge prone to outbursts of anger and indignation. Bearded and bespectacled, he became an easy target for media and commercial parody.

Other players, on both sides, changed during the course of

the ordeal, either in appearance, disposition or outlook—in some cases, all three. The lead prosecutor was 41-year-old Marcia Clark, twice-divorced, and the experienced, no-nonsense attorney from the preliminary hearing. At the start of the trial, her television image was that of a tough, confident leader, a rising star who even submitted to a hair, makeup and wardrobe overhaul for the cameras. But the courtroom battles and her own contemporaneous child custody fight took their toll and, by the end, she had lost weight and appeared exhausted and bedraggled.

One of the original members of the prosecution team, Bill Hodgman, a skillful, high-ranking district attorney, had already withdrawn as an active participant in the case. The seasoned veteran was rushed to the hospital after collapsing from the stress of an especially caustic courtroom session, even before official proceedings began.

Some legal scholars feel that if that honest and highly regarded D.A. had remained as the lead prosecutor, the trial would not have turned into a media circus.

Thrust into Hodgman's position, Christopher Darden, 38, was a talented lawyer who, some said, allowed his Afro-Americanism to interfere with his legal performances. Soft-spoken and introspective, he would become the butt of frequent attacks over race by Johnnie Cochran, the hard-hitting defense attorney. Darden had been in charge of the A.C. Cowlings grand jury investigation to determine if the close friend of O.J. had committed any crimes when he drove the white Bronco in the slow-speed chase. (The grand jury decided he had not.) Halfway through the trial, the prosecutor, who had become increasingly sullen, stated he regretted having accepted a role in the trial and never wanted to practice law again. And his once warm relationship with Cochran had soured.

It was Attorney Robert Shapiro who, within a few days of the murders, assembled the defense's Dream Team. An experienced strategist, he had defended the son of Marlon Brando in a highly publicized murder trial. Shapiro's goal was to utilize a team approach with some of the country's brightest and most experienced individuals, a cast drawn from law, medicine, science and academia. There were private investigators, computer experts, forensic experts and special litigators, but within the core of the team, there was Johnnie Cochran, Jr., the esteemed criminal defense lawyer from Los Angeles. A former assistant to the district attorney in the mid 1970s, he had established a solid reputation among judges, prosecutors, defense attorneys and L.A. community leaders. There was old warrior F. Lee Bailey, the mastermind of Dr. Sam Sheppard's acquittal in his second trial, and defense counsel for many high-profile defendants such as the Boston Strangler in the 1960s. Shapiro and Bailey had had a close friendship culminating in Bailey's serving as godfather to Shapiro's eldest son. Gerald Uelmen, a learned professor and law school dean, was added to provide academic credentials to the team. A former prosecutor, Uelmen had, in 1972, defended Daniel Ellsberg in the Pentagon Papers case.

Then there was the highly gifted Barry Scheck and his associate, Peter Neufeld. Their energy and enthusiasm were well-known within the legal and forensic communities. As attorneys, they had worked together on many cases, particularly as experts in the forensic application of DNA technology to legal issues. Others were Harvard Law professor, Alan Dershowitz, an authority on appellate and constitutional law and defender of high profile clients such as Claus von Bulow and boxing champion Mike Tyson; and, Bob Blasier, a Harvard graduate, former assistant D.A. in California and superb organizational technician.

Rounding out the principals were Dr. Michael Baden, the brilliant pathologist and former chief medical examiner of New York; Dr. Barbara Wolf, the Director of Anatomic Pathology at Albany Medical Center; Dr. Edward Blake, a DNA expert and forensic consultant; and, finally, the unnamed (at the time) top forensic scientist in the country.

But the Dream Team was not immune to the strain of the trial. For reasons not relevant to the purposes of this book, there was a "changing of the guard" at its top level: Cochran assumed control for the defense. But soon his marital woes were dragged into daily newspaper headlines; his playing of "the race card" was roundly censured, some blaming him for accelerating racial disharmony; and by the trial's end, he was surrounded by bodyguards after receiving death threats. Old friends Shapiro and Bailey feuded publicly and, for most of the trial, hardly spoke to one other. And there were other instances of nasty accusations and counter accusations within the fractious defense camp.

Proclaiming that jealousy was Simpson's motive for killing his wife, Marcia Clark and Chris Darden delivered their opening statements in a courtroom that was much smaller than it appeared on television. It was jammed with reporters and spectators along with friends and relatives of the Brown, Goldman and Simpson families. The prosecutors stressed O.J.'s physical abuse and stalking of Nicole that were at the heart of her opposition to his attempts at reconciliation. They asserted that the "last straw" was Nicole's and her family's rejection of him at his daughter's dance recital the afternoon of the killings. It was then, they said, that a bitter O.J. Simpson decided to take Nicole's life. They believed that Ron Goldman happened upon the scene at the wrong time and he was killed as well. Clark fixed the time of the deaths at 10:15 p.m., June 12, 1994.

She called attention to cuts on O.J.'s left middle finger and graphically depicted a trail of blood drops which, she said, extended from the Bundy crime scene to his bedroom at Rockingham. Clark claimed the blood contained DNA which "matched" the defendant's. Later, defense lawyer, Barry Scheck, would insist the "match" was scientifically invalid because of the faulty way the samples had been collected, and because they had been processed at the LAPD crime lab. He called the lab a "cesspool of contamination," and suggested that the entire "mountain of evidence" professed by the prosecution was a molehill that was "contaminated, compromised and corrupted."

The following day, Johnnie Cochran presented his opening

statement, challenging Clark's description of O.J.'s feeling about Nicole and his demeanor at the recital. The defense attorney held that the defendant had been upbeat and showed a videotape of a friendly, smiling father at the school's festivities. Cochran said that Simpson's positive mood persisted, and on his plane flight to Chicago, he bantered with passengers and signed autographs.

As for the cuts on the finger, Cochran explained that Simpson had shattered a drinking glass in his Chicago hotel room upon hearing of Nicole's murder.

The defense then took exception to the time line postulated by Clark on the previous day. Cochran stated emphatically that the murders took place *after* 10:15 p.m., allowing Simpson insufficient time to commit the crimes, drive to his home, dispose of the weapon and bloody clothes, clean up and meet limousine driver Allan Park.

Thus, battle lines had been drawn. The prosecution declared evidence would show overwhelmingly that an intensely jealous O.J. Simpson was indeed the killer. Meanwhile, the defense contended that at the time of the murders, Paula Barbieri was O.J.'s main romantic interest, not his ex-wife; and that the State was so anxious to corral a celebrity, it overlooked evidence that would completely exonerate him.

As has been previously stated, the overarching purpose of this book is to demonstrate, through reviews of classic crime cases spread over the twentieth century, that the same human and forensic errors have recurred and that they may have shaded the outcome. Our intent has been to revisit each crime, each investigation and, when applicable, each adjudication, in order to achieve our purpose and, yet, to avoid exhaustive reportage. The Simpson case is no exception, and in this vein, what follows is the testimony of important witnesses and suggestions about the roles they may have played in dealing with key pieces of evidence.

During the opening statements on the first two days, I was impressed with the confidence of each camp and the composure of the defendant. But those observations aside, the

initial discussion about DNA stirred my interest in more ways than one, and I was sorry Sam wasn't there to hear me out. Many of the DNA results had come back "inconclusive" because of an insufficient quantity of DNA in the samples or because of deterioration. And this came about because of mishandling after collection. The way to collect a valid sample is first to moisten the bloodstain with a wet fabric swatch, thus absorbing the blood. Then, an absolute necessity for preserving DNA is to dry the swatch as soon as possible in order to prevent bacteria and fungi from consuming the human DNA. This had not been carried out at that time by the LAPD. Testimony would later show that the crime scene security and evidence gathering had not been in accord with established protocol. Instead, samples had been collected first at Rockingham, then at Bundy. The collectors then returned to Rockingham and stored their samples in plastic bags kept in their unrefrigerated van. It was not until 12 hours later that they arrived at the lab to begin drying out the samples.

While we're on the subject, it was later revealed that blood was discovered on the back gate of Nicole's condo and on the sock found in O.J.'s bedroom—but not until weeks after the crimes. Furthermore, analysis of the stains would show three things that were among several throughout the trial that together would prompt my later comment on the witness stand: "Something is wrong here." One concerned the five drops of blood found on the walkway at the Bundy crime scene. Testing showed that the DNA in these drops matched that of O.J. Simpson. The blood drops had been transferred to cotton swatches and, in theory and practice, should have dried overnight. However, during the reexamination of evidence, reddish blood transfer imprints were found on some of the paper packages. (During the trial, the paper packages were referred to as "bundles.") This fact clearly indicates that some of the blood swatches collected from the crime scene were not dried when placed in the paper packages.

Another was that the stains on several items, including the back gate and sock, contained EDTA, a preservative added to collection vials and test tubes to prevent coagulation of blood. And the third was that the blood from the back gate and sock had much higher concentrations of DNA than that in the blood samples collected on June 13, the morning after the crime. Why the presence of EDTA and the higher concentrations of DNA?

By the way, that comment I made was one that would receive mixed reactions depending on which side of the fence people stood. Those who thought Simpson got away with murder would criticize it. Those who believed either that he was not guilty or that there was reasonable doubt in the case would embrace it as a kind of mantra. In any event, it was my considered opinion at the time. I could not certify that evidence had been planted but, on the other hand, there were too many circumstances without scientific explanation. And I had no doubt Sam would eventually disagree with me.

But, lest it be thought I found fault only with the prosecution's case, quite the opposite was true. After Cochran's opening statement, Carl Douglas, one of Simpson's lawyers, admitted to the court and before a national TV audience that the defense had withheld the names of numerous witnesses from the prosecution. This was in violation of California's reciprocal discovery laws. And, as if that weren't enough, prosecutors identified many of the potential defense witnesses as heroin addicts, felons, thieves plus a court-certified pathological liar.

A word must be said about criminalist Dennis Fung. He was roundly criticized over his performance at the crime scene. But I must point out that detectives are in charge of a crime scene, not the criminalists. Furthermore, many supervisors were at the scene. But it was Fung who took the heat.

Detectives Fuhrman and Vannatter were the best examples of those possibly guilty of human and forensic errors. With respect to Fuhrman, others would add racism; with respect to both detectives, others would add the compulsion to indict, prosecute and sentence at any cost.

Barry Scheck's cross-examination of Fung was unrelenting. In essence, he impeached the criminalist on a number of issues relating to his department's procedure manual and his less than professional collection and preservation of vital evidence. Fung honestly admitted he erred at the preliminary hearing when he claimed to have performed many of the procedures. In fact, they had been done by Andrea Mazzola, an inexperienced trainee. It had been only her second assignment for evidence gathering, but apparently Fung wanted that kept under wraps.

The criminalist conceded he had covered Nicole's body with a white cotton blanket he obtained from inside her condo unit, thus introducing the possibility of cross-contamination. He stated he handled all evidence with gloves but Scheck promptly ran a vidiotape obviously depicting Fung handling evidence with his bare hands.

Chain of custody issues were also brought into question. He had previously testified that Vannatter had brought the vial of O.J.'s blood to the Bundy crime scene in a gray envelope and he, Fung, took custody of it. Later, he recanted, saying he was not certain—that perhaps the vial was in a paper bag, or in no container at all. Again, Scheck went to the videotape, and again something different appeared: The vial had been put in a garbage bag and carried to the van by Mazzola.

In addition to the above irregularities, there were others attributed to crime scene evidence collection issues.

1. The collection procedure followed by Mazzola was considered problematic.
2. A number of samples collected from each site was not inventoried.
3. There might have been degeneration of the blood samples left in the unrefrigerated van.
4. Blood and other evidence were left unlocked in a storage cabinet.

5. The blood spots in the Bronco were not recorded and were discovered later.
6. The bloodstains on the sock were not discovered until two months later.
7. Blood spots were not observed on the back gate on June 13 but were seen in a photograph taken on July 3.

It is generally acknowledged that of all those who testified, *prosecution* witness Mark Fuhrman turned out to be the most valuable witness for the *defense*.

Simpson's lawyers pounded away at the detective's documented history of using racial slurs and his proclivity to "bag" suspects in virtually any way possible. Some believed the bloody glove on the walkway of Simpson's estate, the blood smears on the Bronco, the blood drops near the front of Simpson's residence and the blood smears on the back gate at Bundy might have been planted.

That Fuhrman was a perjurer and racist were brought out in no uncertain terms. Two approaches for proof will suffice: F. Lee Bailey's cross-examination of the detective and the so-called Fuhrman Tapes. Bailey's performance was a classic:

Q: Do you use the word "nigger" in describing people?
   A: No, sir.
Q: Have you ever used that word in the past ten years?
   A: Not that I can recall, no.
Q: You mean if you called someone a nigger you have forgotten it?
   A: I'm not sure I can answer the question the way you phrased it, sir.
Q: You have difficulty understanding the question?
   A: Yes.
Q: I will rephrase it. I want you to assume that perhaps at some time since 1985 or 1986, you addressed a member of the African-American race as a nigger. It is possible that you have forgotten that act on your part?

A: No, it is not possible.

Q: Are you therefore saying that you have not used that word in the past ten years, Detective Fuhrman?

A: Yes, that is what I'm saying, sir.

Q: And you say under oath that you have not addressed any black person as a nigger or spoken about black people as niggers in the past ten years, Detective Fuhrman?

A: That's what I'm saying, sir.

Q: So that anyone who comes to this court and quotes you as using that word in dealing with African-Americans would be a liar, would they not, Detective Fuhrman?

A: Yes, they would.

Q: All of them, correct?

A: All of them.

This exchange had set the stage for what was to follow: a series of audiotapes admitted as evidence that would prove to be devastating to the State, judicially, and to Fuhrman, personally. The irony, however, was that the cross-examination took place on March 15, 1995, while the audiotapes did not surface until July 7, 1995.

After a series of complicated legal maneuvers, the tapes and their transcripts were obtained by the defense from Laura Hart McKinny who, at the time of their recording, had been piecing together material for a screenplay about the experiences of female police officers. She had met Fuhrman in a restaurant in early 1995 and enlisted him to assist in the development of background material for her project. He subsequently met with McKinny over a 10-year period—up to 1994—for a 13-hour series of taped interviews.

The transcripts contained 42 instances of Fuhrman using the word "nigger," and 18 instances in which he admitted his participation in police misconduct in order to incarcerate "criminals." Among them were the use of deadly force, beating confessions out of suspects, covering up the misconduct of other police officers, and of particular relevence: *the planting of evidence and the framing of innocent people.*

Excerpts of Fuhrman's utterances—heard by the court but not the jury—were as follows:

> We got all this money going to Ethiopia for what? To feed a bunch of dumb niggers that their own government won't even feed. ... Let 'em die. Use 'em for fertilizer. I mean, who cares.

> Well, I really love being a policeman when I can be a policeman. It's like my partner now. He's so hung up with the rules and stuff. I get pissed sometimes and go, 'you just don't fucking even understand. This job is not rules. This is a feeling. Fuck the rules, we'll make them up later.' He's a college graduate, a Catholic college. He was going to be a fucking priest. He's got more morals than he's got hair on his head. He doesn't know what to do about it ... he doesn't know how to be a policeman. 'I can't lie.' Oh, you make me fucking sick to my guts. You know, you do what you have to do to put these fucking assholes in jail. If you don't, you fucking get out of the fucking game.

Speaking about the same partner:

> He goes, 'I got a wife and kid to think about.' I says, 'Fuck you. Don't tell me because you've got a wife and kid ... you're either my partner all the way or get the fuck out of this car. We die for each other. We live for each other, that's how it is in the car. You lie for me, up to six months suspension. Don't ever get fired for me. Don't get indicted for me. But you'll take six months for me, 'cause I'll take it for you. If you don't, get the fuck out of here. It shouldn't have to be said.'

In one of the last interviews, on July 28, 1994, Fuhrman

blurted, "I am the key witness in the biggest case of the century. And if I go down, they lose the case. The glove is everything, Without the glove—bye-bye."

Judge Ito ruled, however, that from the 61 excerpts available, the only words he would allow the jury to hear were a sentence extracted from a statement Fuhrman made, and a question and answer taken from an exchange about where Black Muslims live.

Ito permitted the last sentence in the following excerpt:

People there don't want niggers in their town. People there don't want Mexicans in their town. They don't want anybody but good people in their town, and anyway you can do to get them out of there that's fine with them. We have no niggers where I grew up.

The single allowable question and answer about Black Muslims was:

Q: Why do they live in that area?
A: That's where niggers live.

These two portions of the tapes were played in court with the jury present on September 5, 1995. On September 6, Fuhrman appeared on the stand and invoked his Fifth Amendment priviledge against self-incrimination. The following day, the defense announced that O.J. would not testify on his own behalf. And on September 22, in making a formal statement to Judge Ito that he waived his right to testify, Simpson said, "I did not, could not and would not have committed this crime."

A few days after F. Lee Bailey's cross-examination of Fuhrman, Robert Shapiro cross-examined the burly detective, Phil Vannatter, and brought out two significant points favorable for the defense. First, on the morning of June 13, 1994, Vannatter had spent considerably more time at Rockingham than he had at Bundy, a fact supporting the defense hypothesis—denied by Vannatter—that O.J. was an early suspect. His hurried trip to

Rockingham, said the defense, was not made exclusively to inform O.J. of his former wife's murder. It was, they alleged, a "rush to judgment" by him and other investigators. And, second, when Vannatter obtained O.J.'s blood sample at the downtown Parker Center later that day, he did not follow procedure and book it into evidence. Instead, he carried the vial in his pocket for three hours before relinquishing it to criminalist Fung at Rockingham.

As I left the courthouse late that day, I fretted over several questions—the same ones I had in "real" time, five years before. What happened to the blood during that three-hour interval? Did it remain innocently in his pocket? Is he the only one in the world who would put a defendant's blood sample in his pocket and bring it back to the crime scene— and get away with it? Was that time interval related in any way to the 1.5 ml of blood which couldn't be later accounted for?

Back at the hotel, I entered the questions in my laptop computer as the start of a long list I'd been thinking about. Although the content of my teaching classes in Connecticut had already been formulated for the current semester, I would find the list invaluable during the following one, when I expected to cover both the Simpson and the Sacco-Vanzetti cases.

It was time for dinner and I was about to begin my usual routine of shower, eating out and returning for note transcription, when I heard three loud knocks on the door. I didn't know why, but what flashed through my mind was the "thump, thump, thump" which Kato Kaelin had described during the trial. But the face of the world's most famous houseguest was not there when I peeked through the peep sight. Instead, I saw the lower half of a red, white and blue necktie. Sam!

I threw the door open. "Well, I'll be darned," I said. "I thought you had disappeared for good. It's been over a year, you know. Since, let's see ... the preliminary hearing. Why haven't you come to the trial?"

I'd long ago come to the conclusion that Sam was a

master at not missing a beat. "Preliminary hearing—main event—who cares? It's all a waste of time. Why not just lock up the slasher and be done with it?" He started to pant, but I didn't think it was anything physical.

"Come on in," I said. "Have a seat." I thought the break in the direction of the conversation would calm him down. I was wrong.

Sam sat on a chair which he had yanked from the desk, and when he crossed his legs, it seemed to stretch out his upper body. I'd been sitting all day and, still standing, I noticed that our eyes were on the same level.

"I suppose you think otherwise?" he continued.

I'd almost forgotten the original question. "Not if he's found guilty," I said.

"Henry, c'mon. I understand you said there was 'something wrong' there, but it's so obvious when you think about it. The murder of that blonde woman was 17 years in the making. I wonder how many times he *really* punched her out." He grew somber and shook his head once. "Not that I feel sorry for her—carrying on and marrying a black man. I feel sorry for the Goldman family though—their boy got in the way."

"I agree with you," I replied. "I always feel the pain when victims and their families suffer. That's part of the reason why I chose forensic science as my career—to help these people. But at the same time, we have to adhere to the principles of science and call the facts as we see them."

I wasn't sure my statement registered with Sam, but I wasn't about to tangle with him about the wheels of justice once again so I quickly changed the subject. "You'll be around when it's over?"

"You bet. Mainly to bid you adieu. And don't forget, I'm writing a book." He rose and walked to the door.

Why walk to a door, I thought, when he can leave from anywhere. "I look forward to seeing you soon," I said, straining to pat him on his shoulder but never quite reaching it.

Feeling embarrassed, I added, "Care to join me for dinner or will you be clicking away?"

"The latter," he said, before disappearing.

I felt as though a cyclone had just roared past me—or, not a cyclone, but a humanoid who was late in catching his plane flight and had to spew out his convictions before he left. I recalled not having an opportunity, during our previous encounter, to inquire about how exactly my visits came about, and why I was invisible during some of them—questions I'd promised myself to ask some day. But, once again, Sam had not given me the opportunity. It would have been nice to ask him, also, how he was going to write a credible book about the case when he hadn't been present at any of the courtroom sessions. But did he have to be? Again, the whole question of physical presence and invisibility—as it applied to both of us.

After dining at one of the half-dozen restaurants I'd frequented in the Los Angeles area, I returned to the hotel and, working from notes I'd jotted down during the trial, uploaded additional questions into the computer. There were many more than I'd expected and it was getting late, so I decided to save some for another time and to input only the following:

1. Regarding the 1.5 ml of missing blood, could it have been spread around as droplets on the Bronco and at Rockingham, and then later added to the sock and back gate?

2. Marcia Clark said O.J. drove the Bronco home wearing the murder clothes and shoes. Why was only a small amount of blood found in the Bronco, especially on the steering wheel?

3. Then O.J. walked upstairs. Why wasn't there any of the victims' blood on the carpeting, light switches or doorknobs? The Rockingham house had wall-to-wall beige-white carpeting.

4. If the glove was as described and O.J.'s sock had wet blood on it, why wasn't there a blood trail from the fence to the glove at Rockingham?

5. What happened to the weapon and bloody clothes?

6. Mark Fuhrman had been dismissed from the case, yet insisted on going to Simpson's estate. Why, considering the others knew how to get there?

6. If O.J. was the killer and didn't want to be detected, why didn't he enter his house from the back?

8. Again—Fuhrman had been taken off the case. Why, then, was it he who investigated the Bronco, leaped the fence, questioned Kaelin and allegedly found the glove?

9. Why were there only five drops of O.J.'s blood evenly deposited on the Bundy walkway? If he cut himself, there should have been more drops initially and less as time passed. And there certainly should not have been an even distribution.

10. Why did it take 10 hours to notify the coroner?

11. Why, following a probably fierce struggle with an athletic Ron Goldman, didn't Simpson have more signs of injury on his body, such as scratches and bruises?

12. How could anyone who had just viciously killed the mother of his children act so calm for so long after the incident?

13. Simpson allegedly jumped the fence near the guest house in his haste to return home and, at the same time, avoid being detected by limousine driver Allan Park, who was out front. The fence is very high and is covered by a large number of vines and other vegetation. Why was there no damage to such vegetation? And besides, who other than Bruce Lee can jump that high?

14. Since O.J. had cuts on his finger, why were there no cuts on the glove itself?

15. A second type of bloody shoe prints was found in the blood at Bundy. Whose was it?

16. How could Allan Park not have noticed the Bronco parked near the front gate at Rockingham?

Chapter 5

Evidence

Many authorities believe that physical evidence does not lie unless it has been contaminated, carelessly collected, mishandled, tampered with or planted. All these may apply to the Simpson case. The State's case had been built on circumstantial, rather than direct, eyewitness evidence, and the jury heard it all expressed as the much-heralded "mountain of evidence."

But against that, the defense raised its own "mountain" of reasonable doubt in the faulty handling of physical evidence and other mistakes made by some of the investigators as they rushed to erroneous conclusions.

Opposing interpretations of major evidence were as follows:

1. Violent past:

Prosecution—O.J. repeatedly beat Nicole during jealous rages. Her sister Denise wept during her testimony about the couple's stormy relationship. Photographs were introduced of Nicole's swollen face as a result of the alleged beatings.

Defense—The conviction for spousal abuse occurred five years earlier and O.J. had paid his debt. No other claims of marital discord and physical abuse were reported or documented.

2. Time line:

Prosecution—The wailing dog indicated Simpson committed the murders at 10:15 p.m.; and he had sufficient time to drive the 25 miles to Rockingham, dispose of the weapon and bloody clothes, clean up and meet the limo driver.

Defense—It was physically impossible to accomplish all those things in that time interval. Furthermore, it was ludicrous to assume that a dog's barking could establish, beyond a reasonable doubt, the time of the deaths. The real time of the murders was more likely

10:30 p.m. Or to assume that Simpson could have showered and appeared neatly dressed and composed in just six minutes, that is, from the time the driver spotted the black person entering the home to the time Simpson emerged from the front door.

In addition, the scene at Bundy was consistent with an active and disorganized crime scene where fighting and struggling took place. It had to have taken longer to kill two people there than the prosecution claimed.

3. Trail of blood:

Prosecution—Simpson's blood was found at the Bundy crime scene, on and in the Bronco and scattered about his estate. These facts linked him to the murder scene, to the getaway car and back to his house.

Defense—At worst, the blood droplets were planted; at best, the samples were improperly collected and handled. There were no traces of blood on doorknobs, on light switches or on the light-colored carpeting in the house. If Simpson had been the killer, he would have been drenched in blood. The tiny smear in the Bronco and those elsewhere were not logically compatible with a brutal double homicide.

4. DNA:

Prosecution—The odds of matching the characteristics of the blood found at Bundy with the blood from anyone other than Simpson was set at less than one in 170 million.

Defense—That was irrelevant since the blood may have been compromised. In any event, it was improperly collected and handled. Also, the prosecution expert erred in the statistical calculation.

5. The vial of Simpson's blood:

Prosecution—Detective Vannatter put the vial in his pocket because he wanted to present it directly to criminalist Fung who was at Rockingham.

Defense—Vannatter carried the vial in his pocket for

three hours instead of following protocol and booking it up the stairs from where it had been drawn. And why was Fung asked to go to Rockingham before going to the primary crime scene, in the first place? Also, there were 1.5 ml of the blood unaccounted for.

6. The bloody glove:

Prosecution—Simpson lost one of his gloves at the crime scene and then tried to hide the other one behind the guesthouse at Rockingham.

Defense—There was no unequivocal proof that the gloves belonged to Simpson; in fact, they did not fit. (In a dramatic sequence, Simpson struggled in trying on the gloves in open court and exclaimed, "They're too small.") There was no blood on the ground leading to or around the glove at Rockingham. The blood on that glove was still wet, seven hours after it was allegedly used during the crimes. This violates scientific fact because the blood should have been dry by then. The glove may have been planted at Rockingham.

7. The sock:

Prosecution—Blood was detected on one of Simpson's socks which had been thrown on the floor in his bedroom on the evening of the murders.

Defense—A video supposedly taken within 24 hours of the crimes revealed there were no socks on the floor. However, crime scene still photos showed the socks. Then, nearly two months later, bloodstain evidence was found on reexamination of one of the socks. But expert forensic testimony demonstrated that the sock had the typical pattern of "compression transfer," indicating there had not been a foot in it when it was stained; and the blood contained the preservative, EDTA. The delayed detection of a bloodstained sock, the pattern of the blood, its EDTA component and the absence of blood on the carpet where the sock was "found"—all pointed to a questionable source for the blood on the sock.

Front gate at Bundy crime scene.

The bloody glove between guesthouse and fence at Rockingham.

Front gate at Rockingham estate. Note blood markers.

Dr. Lee and Attorney Scheck arriving at courtroom.

Some members of the Dream Team.

Robert Shapiro, Michael Baden and Johnnie Cochran in conference.

Dr Lee explaining evidence to members of Dream Team.

Knife contained in the mystery envelope.

White Bronco parked at Rockingham.

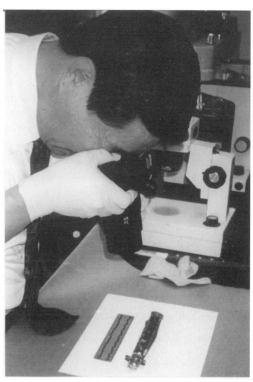

Dr. Lee photographing knife taken from mystery envelope.

Dr. Lee examining evidence while Peter Neufeld observes. Note Ron Goldman's boot in foreground.

Bloodstained envelope containing Juditha Brown's eyeglasses. Note pattern evidence.

Showing transfer of blood from wet swatches.

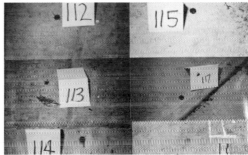

Composite of blood drops on Bundy walkway.

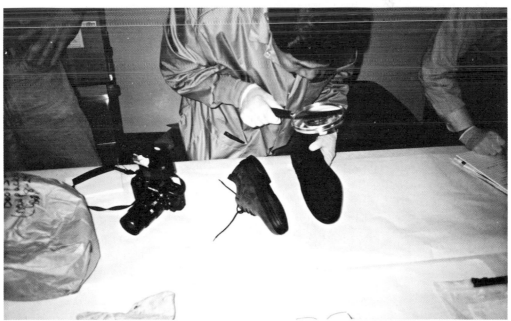

Dr. Lee examining Bruno Magli shoes.

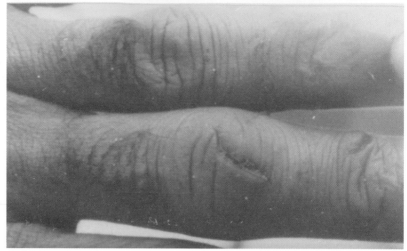

O.J.'s cut finger.

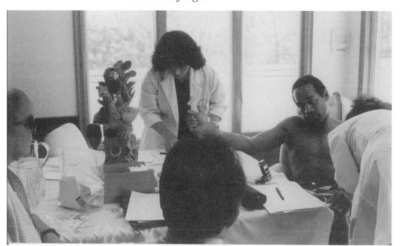

O.J. being examined.

Dr. Micheal Baden examining O.J.'s hand.

Dr. Lee examining evidence while Robert Blasier, Barry Scheck and Peter Neufeld look on.

From left to right: Barry Scheck, Henry Lee, Peter Neufeld, Robert Blasier and Michael Baden.

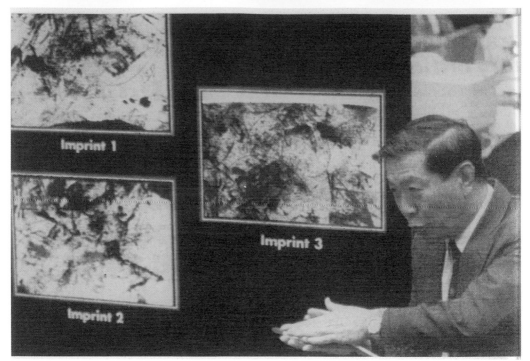

Dr. Lee testifying on imprint evidence.

Dr. Lee testifying while Johnnie Cochran looks on.

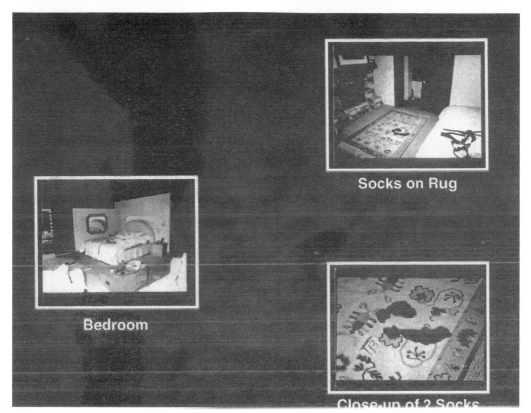

Socks on Rug

Bedroom

Close-up of 2 Socks

Socks and suspenders at Rockingham. Note change in position of suspenders on bed.

Envelope found at Bundy crime scene. Note change in its position.

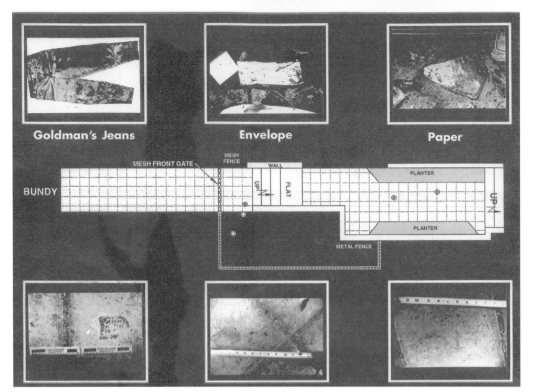

Bundy crime scene evidence: Goldman's jeans, the envelope and two types of shoe prints found on walkway.

The verdict. Barry Scheck, O.J., Johnnie Cochran and Robert Shapiro.

At one point in the trial, Judge Ito ruled that defense forensic experts could inspect and conduct nondistortive testing of all the physical evidence related to the case. However, he allowed only three days to complete these tasks. Thus, boxes of evidence were flown from L.A. to the Albany Medical Center in New York where Dr. Michael Baden, Margaret Lee, Dr. Barbara Wolf and Dr. Effie Chang assisted me in the examination of their contents. We began the macroscopic and microscopic examinations on a Friday afternoon and worked until midnight. We then continued all day Saturday until the early hours of Sunday. During that engrossing period, we uncovered many instances of incompatibility between prosecution claims and what we had all observed.

When I was on the witness stand, Barry Scheck led me through an analysis of the forensic evidence. I utilized a red ink dropper to demonstrate various aspects of blood spatter patterns, and I also challenged the integrity of some of the evidence including the swatches of blood I had been allowed to examine at the LAPD crime lab. I found blood imprints which had been transferred from one of the swatches to the inside of a paper package. Therefore, the blood on the swatch had been wet when it should have been dry. I believed there were gaps in the case and so informed the court. However, I did not agree with the defense theory that such a wet transfer constituted positive proof that DNA evidence had been planted. It was at this point that I uttered the oft-repeated statement, *"Only opinion I can give under these circumstances—something wrong."*

Closing Arguments

Most authorities feel that Johnnie Cochran's and Barry Scheck's closing arguments were, by far, more persuasive than Marcia Clark's and Chris Darden's.

Speaking for the prosecution, Clark was initially obligated to distance herself from Mark Fuhrman, and she attempted to dismiss the impact of his testimony. First she resorted to rhetorical questions and answers:

Q: Did he lie about the n-word?

A: Yes.

Q: Do we wish no such person belonged to the LAPD ?

A: Yes.

Q: Do we wish no such person were on the planet?

A: Yes.

Clark then tried to pick apart the planted glove theory and devoted considerable time on motive, referring to the crimes as "not efficient murders" but as "slaughters." She implored, "Open up the windows. Let the cool wind of reason come in."

But as eloquent as Clark was at times, she failed to tear apart the defense's direct assertions and many inferences that the LAPD conspired to frame Simpson.

For his part, Darden's final argument was perhaps his finest hour of the trial, describing himself as "the messenger for Nicole," and O.J. Simpson as "a time bomb ticking away."

But in Cochran's close, he took exception to Darden's metaphors by saying, "The message can't be trusted." And he lambasted the LAPD with the words, "an infected investigation by a corrupt detective and a bumbling cesspool of a lab." In the style of a revivalist preacher, he moved deftly from Biblical quotations to the utterances of Abraham Lincoln and Cicero and, in the process, challenged the prosecution's "mountain of evidence." "If he had bloody clothes, bloody gloves, bloody shoes," Cochran asked, "then where's the blood on the doorknob? On the carpet?"

The lead defense attorney ridiculed the prosecution's claim that Simpson wanted to disguise himself by donning a knit hat.

Let me show you something. This is a knit cap. Let me put this knit cap on. You have seen me for a year. (He put on the hat.) If I put this knit cap on, who am I? I'm still Johnnie Cochran with a knit cap. And, if you looked at O.J. Simpson over there—and he has a rather large head—O.J. Simpson from two blocks away is still O.J. Simpson. It's no disguise. It makes no sense. It doesn't fit. *If it doesn't fit, you must acquit.*

It was one of several times when Cochran used that phrase and, along with Dr. Henry Lee's "something wrong," was to become the most memorable of the trial.

Barry Scheck used some of his time in expounding on Dr. Lee's earlier reference to cockroaches in a bowl of spaghetti. Scheck contended that blood showed up on the rear gate and the sock *after* the murders, and asked, "How many cockroaches do you need?" He continued:

> Every explanation that they're desperately trying to come up with is a highly improbable influence. The most likely and probable explanation is not for the timid or the faint of heart: Somebody played with this evidence! There's a reasonable doubt for this case. Period. End of sentence. End of this case.

Verdict

Sixteen months had passed from the commission of the crimes to final arguments. Two-hundred-sixty-six days had passed since the jury members had been sequestered. Judge Ito finally released them for their deliberations, exhorting, "You are not partisans or advocates, but impartial judges of fact." And in a mere three minutes of their leaving the courtroom, they had elected a foreperson.

Ito recessed the trial until 10 a.m. on the following Monday and four hours into their deliberations, the jury had reached a decision. The judge's clerk announced, "We, the jury, find the defendant, Orenthal James Simpson, not guilty."

The last thing I remembered before leaving the courtroom was the strangely similar images of crying spectators on both sides of the room. But for the Brown and Goldman families, the tears were for anguish and rage; for the Simpsons, relief and jubilation.

Personally, I commiserated with the victims' families but, equally, I shared the sense of relief and believed the prosecution had not proven O.J. guilty beyond a reasonable doubt.

Aside from that, I felt numb as I entered my hotel room, my mind having abruptly cooled down after months of ready alert. It was a feeling hard to decipher because I was well aware of the verdict heard once before. But if my revisit brought an immediacy not achieved through simple recollections of the proceedings, then the same immediacy must be expected to rub off on any reactions to those past events, including the verdict.

I loosened my tie and kicked off my shoes, mulling over whether to shower first or have a cup of tea. After aimlessly removing all my clothes, I had the answer.

The shower over, I sat at the desk and added a few more questions to the list of 16 I'd started.

17. Should any jury convict if it believes evidence may have been tampered with?

18. The prosecution insisted that footprints in blood at the Bundy crime scene were produced by Bruno Magli shoes. But did they belong to O.J.? The prosecution spent months trying to prove he owned that brand of shoe, and they couldn't.

19. Why hadn't anyone secured the Bronco early on the morning of June 13? And why weren't photographs taken of the vehicle's interior?

20. Speaking of the Bronco, if there had been a bloody scuffle between Simpson and Goldman, why was there less than a drop of Goldman's blood "found" in the vehicle?

21. Expert testimony was given that the gloves would not have shrunk despite being covered with blood. Then how come they didn't fit Simpson's hands?

I wasn't particularly surprised at the knock on the door but *definitely* surprised at Sam's expressionless face.

"Welcome," I said, "I thought you'd be apoplectic by now."

Sam rushed in and, twisting the chair at the desk, sat down facing me as I bent into the edge of the bed. He tapped his fingers on his knee.

"You know, Henry, this case was different from the start. Ordinarily, I'd be seething for days, maybe weeks, but that won't happen this time. If it were just a matter of a battered wife, that's one thing, and I'd be hard to contain. But I don't react to motive alone. Plus the abuse occurred years ago. No, this was a murder trial and there were elements to it that made me fighting mad. And embarrassed."

He stopped the tapping and cocked his head. "Can you imagine me embarrassed?"

His pause told me he expected an answer, so I gave one. "No," I said, then followed with my own studious question: "Embarrassed about what?"

"About Fuhrman's intense bigotry."

"And mad?"

"Cochran played the race card, and a wife beater got off the hook."

I wasn't looking for an argument but had to say, "Now, wait a minute. I believe you just said that wife beating was irrelevant to the case."

"Yes, I did. It should not have influenced the verdict—and it didn't—but it certainly defined Simpson."

It wasn't the first time I thought public opinion was irrational at times. And it wasn't the first time I thought Sam would evaporate without warning, so I quickly switched to my pent-up questions.

"I see," I said, "but let me ask you—we've been buddies for some time now, right?"

Sam's features came alive and that pleased me. "Eighty years by my calculation."

"Then please answer me a question or two. One, are you responsible for pulling me back in time?"

"That's easy. You might say so—but then, again, you might not."

Hmm, vintage Sam, again. "Okay, next question. You said you're going to write a book about this case. I didn't see you once in court. How can you do it?"

He smiled and said, "Everybody else can do it that way, so why not me?"

I couldn't help but feel he was merely editorializing on the rash of O.J. Simpson books written from a secondhand perspective because, of course, he might have been in the courthouse in spirit—literally.

"Last question, then. Where do you get the power to do it?"

"Do what, write a book?"

"No. Pull me back in time."

"That's easy, too. From here, there and everywhere." The smile which had never left his face, broadened.

Oh, brother. There was no way I could be guaranteed of anything definitive from the mouth of Sam Constant, so why waste my time? But, maybe a straight answer to something less deep. "Will I see you again?"

"Why not? Pick out more cases and I'll be there. Only make sure I care about them, like the William Kennedy Smith alleged rape case down there in Florida, or the woodchipper murder over in your neck of the woods, if you'll pardon the pun. You investigated them, right?"

"Right."

"Did you do the Lizzie Borden ax killings?"

"In the 1890s?" I asked, taking the bait.

Sam chuckled and, lifting himself, gave my shoulder a gentle poke with his elbow as he headed toward the door.

"Very funny," I said, realizing he was trying to be humorous. Plus human.

He turned and put a finger to his lips. "By the way, Henry, do you think we learned anything from these cases?"

I didn't hesitate. "You bet your life we did: We should do a better job in conducting crime scene and forensic investigations."

And when my eyes opened on a Monday afternoon in my Connecticut office, I also realized it was the first time I had disappeared before hearing Sam's click.

Epilogue

Now that you have shared in the journeys to seven of the most famous crime venues, we hope they have been worth your while. Every attempt has been made to portray the stories accurately and to offer my comments from the perspective of an impartial forensic scientist and not from that of a social historian.

Each crime was committed on American soil, each was controversial and each generated worldwide attention. And, whether the episode took place 80 years ago or within the last decade, its final verdict is still debated among scholars and students alike. But do some or all of them manifest other similarities and consistencies?

On the matter of public opinion, you have all met the fictional Sam Constant. Some may have found him pessimistic and rigid. Some, fickle, even capricious. A few, understanding and forgiving. Others, carefree and humorous. Yet, while any combination of these characterizations may apply, the one constancy he exhibits is inconstancy. And that is as it should be because the public may be rigid one week, and forgiving the next. As an aside, I must admit that, even though I participated in Sam's creation, I grew fond of him as the book took shape—fonder than I am at times of public opinion in the real world.

But the more pertinent feature was the probable effect of public sentiment on the outcome of the cases. Sacco-Vanzetti and the Lindbergh kidnapping are the best examples. Sacco and Vanzetti embraced anarchism, a political activity which may have cost them their lives. Many still hold that they were executed not because of murder, but because they were unpatriotic. The dynamic in the Lindbergh case was different. The aviation hero was adored at the same time a vilified Bruno Hauptmann was executed. But within a year or two—after Lindbergh moved abroad and befriended certain Nazi leaders—his popularity plummeted while Hauptmann's guilt began to be questioned.

In the investigatory phase of all the crimes, there may have been instances of unsound and/or unethical practices such as not securing the crime scene; faulty identification, collection and mishandling of evidence; staging of the crime scene; and planting of evidence.

Of those four cases that went to trial, there was and continues to be the suspicion that several irregularities occurred: suppression of evidence, tampering with evidence, perjury, falsification of and/or destruction of records, breach of autopsy protocol. In short, many allege a miscarriage of justice in all four instances.

And then there is what I call, "The Phenomena of Two." In two cases, a verdict of not guilty was returned in the criminal trial but guilty in the civil trial (Sheppard, Simpson). Twice, ill-fitting apparel figured prominantly in the trial (a cap in the Sacco-Vanzetti case and a pair of gloves in the Simpson case). In two, the same executioner, Robert G. Elliott, was called upon (Sacco-Vanzetti, Hauptmann). Finally, the following applied to two cases each: ransom notes, suicide notes, barking dogs, children as victims, killer or killers still at large, the same defense attorney (F. Lee Bailey).

What of the future? Throughout this book, beginning with the Prologue, we have stressed the issues of science and human behavior, two spheres that are not always compatible. Yet, in the march of forensic history that matches the cases we have reviewed, these spheres have come closer together. For example, during the first half of the twentieth century, suspects were interrogated until they confessed. In the 1960s and 1970s, motive, means and opportunity were utilized to pinpoint possible suspects. Psychological profiling and informants were major resources in the 1980s. Then in the 1990s and into the twenty-first century, the thrust has been in crime scene reconstruction, physical evidence, data bases, image enhancement, new latent print technology and artificial intelligence. Yet, although more recent cases are informed by science (e.g., DNA), they are still determined by fallible human beings who interpret and define and have the potential to manipulate the data. Given these shortcomings, therefore—past and present—was justice served in the seven classic cases we have revisited, and can it be reasonably served in the years ahead? Perhaps, but legitimate debates will persist.

Dr. Henry Lee

APPENDIX

Forensic Science: Past, Present and Future

Chapter 1

Introduction and Definitions

As will soon become apparent, this appendix is not intended to replace comprehensive forensic science texts and manuals in circulation. Its purpose, rather, is first to convey the essence of the discipline as a whole and, second, to allow the reader to hold up for review the cases in this book, like silhouettes against the ever brightening light of modern technology.

Will a pattern of similarities emerge? Would contemporary invesigative techniques have made a difference in the outcome of the Sacco-Vanzetti case? Would the authorities have *held* to the tenets of forensics to begin with? Were they applied in the cases of O.J. Simpson and Dr. Sam Sheppard or in the kidnapping of the Lindbergh baby?

Although the first book of forensic medicine was published in 1400 in China, the scientific investigation of crimes has become more sophisticated only in the past 100 years. One can hardly label some of the primitive investigative practices of the nineteenth century and before as activities of an ancient school of forensics per se, or even as rudiments of the science as we know it today. In those days, for example, the law arrested a suspected murderer and tortured him/her until a confession was obtained. Or the suspect was tossed into a pond and if he floated, he was deemed to be innocent of the crime. Still again, he might have been dragged to the side of the victim: if the corpse's wounds bled, he was proclaimed guilty.

The decade of the 1990s witnessed enormous advances in the field of forensic science and, like medical care, has moved away from generalization toward specialization. The term "criminalistics" is often used interchangeably with "forensic science" but technically is only a part of the overall field. Thus, the broad definition of forensic science encompasses, in addition to criminalistics, many other specialties as discussed below. Highlights of each specialty contain certain terminologies which will be addressed later under "General Concepts."

1. Criminalistics

   Criminalistics involves the recognition, collection, identification, individualization and evaluation of physical evidence using the techniques of natural science in matters of legal significance. It includes the reconstruction of events based on the analysis of physical evidence and the interpretation of crime scene patterns. Some of its subspecialties are:

   (a) Drug Analysis

      Standard methods of analytical chemistry are called upon to identify the presence of controlled substances and to quantify these materials. In addition to the analysis of unknown powders, liquids and vegetative materials, the drug chemist may also identify controlled substances in the form of tablets and capsules. Clandestine laboratories use chemicals to produce illegal substances: the quality and quantity of these reagents may be determined by the drug analyst.

   (b) Forensic Chemistry

      This subspecialty deals with the identification and analysis of toxic substances, accelerants, gun powder residue, explosives and other chemical substances. Comparisons are made among known and unknown materials and, often, attempts are made to trace unknown substances to a specific origin.

   (c) Trace Analysis

      The trace analyst combines the methodologies of microscopical, instrumental and chemical techniques in the examination of hair, fibers, glass, soil, plant material, minerals and other substances present in small quantities or size. While it is difficult to make absolute individualizations in these areas (see "Individualization" below), the trace analyst can make identifications with a high degree of certainty and can often establish with confidence partial individuality of a specimen.

(d) Firearms Examination

The examination of firearms, discharged bullets, cartridge cases, shotgun shells and other ammunition and various weapons are all conducted by the firearms examiner. Generally, the examiner tries to answer three questions: (1) What kind of ammunition was used? (2) What kind of weapon fired the bullet? (3) Did this gun fire this bullet or cartridge case? Garments and other objects are also examined to detect firearm discharge residue and to determine the distance between the target and the weapon when it was fired. Many firearms examiners also perform tool mark comparisons. With increasing frequency, tools of many kinds are used as weapons or in the perpetration of crimes. Whenever a tool has been used to move an object, to scratch or injure a surface or to make an impression on an object, it may be possible to identify the tool.

(e) Latent Fingerprints

Latent fingerprint examiners are responsible for processing fingerprints at the crime scene or on the evidence submitted to the forensic science laboratory. There are many chemical and physical methods available to detect and visualize such prints, and upon completion of these steps, the examiner compares the results with known fingerprints submitted from the suspect, victim or other individuals involved in the case. An absolute identification can be made based on these comparisons.

(f) Voice Analysis

In cases involving tape-recorded messages

containing personal threats, false alarms, bomb threats or other criminal violations, it may be necessary to employ the skills of a voiceprint examiner to tie the unknown voice to a particular suspect. Patterns produced in speech are unique to the individual and can be displayed in a spectrogram or voiceprint and then compared.

(g) Forensic Serology

Forensic serologists apply the principles and techniques of biochemistry, serology, immunology, hematology and molecular biology to the identification and individualization of blood and other body fluids. The questions which are generally answered by the examination are: (1) What type of stain is it? (2) What species does the stain belong to? (3) Does the questioned stain have the same blood groups and isoenzymes or DNA patterns as a certain known sample? (4) Can serological reconstruction be used to help individualize the sample in terms of origin?

(h) DNA Analysis

This relatively recent technique has been a boon to forensic inquiry and can be utilized to extend the reach of justice even beyond the grave (e.g., Marilyn Sheppard's exhumed body, to be discussed later). Blood, semen, bones and soft tissues, hair roots, and any material which contains nucleated cells may be analyzed for their DNA content (See "DNA Typing" below). This procedure allows for a high degree of individualization and can be applied to a wide variety of samples of various sizes and conditions. Such techniques can also often separate genetic material of spermatozoa from other cells in sexual assault evidence.

(i) Imprint/Impression Evidence

Criminalists who specialize in impression evidence are concerned with various types of two-or-three dimensional markings such as footwear impressions, tire impressions and footprints. Evidence impression marks are compared with known markings made by the object suspected of causing the imprint or impression. Some types of impression evidence such as fingerprints and tool marks fall within the province of other subspecialties discussed above.

(j) Questioned Document Examination

Such an examination played a major role in our consideration of the two cases involving children: the Lindbergh baby and JonBenet Ramsey. The questioned document examiner is involved in the scientific examination of handwriting, typewriting, printing, photocopying or other mechanical production of written material. This specialist may also analyze the ink, paper and other components of documents such as wills, letters and ransom notes. Other examinations include identifying the source or writer of the document, determining if a signature is authentic or forged, fixing the age of the document, deciphering obliterated or erased writing, detecting alterations and examining indented writing and burned or charred documents.

(k) Crime Scene Investigation

This is detailed in Chapter 3, below.

2. Forensic Medicine

This specialty concerns itself with the application of pathology, a branch of medicine, to the investigation of deaths. Laws require the investigation of unexpected and/or unattended deaths to be overseen by either a coroner or a medical examiner. Coroners are usually elected officials and are not typically required to have any medical training; as such, they ordinarily direct the investigation and rely on trained pathologists for medical opinions. Medical examiners, on the other hand, are forensic pathologists who, through autopsy, toxicological analysis and other kinds of investigation determine the cause and manner of a death.

In some countries, forensic medicine also includes examinations to establish the manner and cause of injuries received as the result of accidents or violent crime.

3. Forensic Anthropology

Physical anthropology is the science pertaining to the human skeleton and how it has developed and evolved throughout the history of the human race. Forensic anthropologists are physical anthropologists who specialize in recovering and examining human skeletal remains where legal questions are involved. The examination of recovered bones can reveal whether they are human; the type of injury, if any, to the bones; the approximate age, height and stature of the person; his/her sex; and information about medical conditions and any childbearing history. These experts can also ascertain whether the skeletal remains were deposited recently or whether they belong to people who died many decades or even centuries ago.

Facial reconstruction is often included within this specialty. Based on traditional databases of human bone features, clay has been used to reconstruct skulls for identification purposes. But recent advances in computerized databases and imaging technology have provided new approaches to reconstruction, including the study of age progression.

4. Forensic Odontology

Forensic odontology is the application of dentistry to the problem of human identification. Two types of examination are commonly performed: (a) Comparison of the dental x-rays of an unidentified human body with the antemortem dental records of known persons in order to identify remains that are difficult or impossible to identify by more conventional means. These cases generally result from the finding of skeletal remains or from remains recovered from events such as fires, explosions, accidents and mass disasters. (b) Analysis and comparison of bite marks. Criminals will often inflict bites on the skin surfaces of their victims during violent crimes such as rape, sex-related homicide or child abuse, or they may leave bite mark evidence at a crime scene in food remains.

5. Forensic Toxicology

The forensic toxicologist identifies, analyzes and studies the effects of drugs, chemicals and poisons on the human body. He/she is often required to identify and quantify a drug in a criminal or civil substance abuse context. Toxicological analyses of postmortem tissue and fluid samples are important in assisting the medical examiner in questions of drug, chemical or poison involvement in a particular death. In addition, food poisons, environmental contaminants and industrial chemicals are within the forensic toxicologist's field of study.

6. Forensic Entomology

Entomology is the study of the life cycles of insects. After an organism dies, various insects lay their eggs on the exposed surfaces of the body. The behavior of these insects is predictable, and the waves of insect infestation of a human body follow certain known patterns and time intervals. Forensic entomologists use this information to estimate the time since death in human remains that have not been discovered or protected for some days after the death. New developments in DNA typing of maggots and insects help in this regard.

7. Forensic Photography

Those who are trained specialists in photographic documentation of crime scenes, accident scenes and physical evidence are forensic photographers. Often associated with crime scene investigation teams or with full-service forensic science laboratories, these photographers are involved in photograph enhancement, specialized photography utilizing alternate light sources, photographic and video conversion or enhancement and image processing and enhancement.

8. Others

Today, forensic science encompasses a variety of other specialties, including: Forensic Biology, Forensic Engineering, Forensic Psychology, Forensic Nursing, Forensic Accounting, Forensic Computing and Forensic Genealogy.

Chapter 2

General Concepts

The dimensions of a forensic scientific investigation may include any or all of seven major activities: (1) recognition, (2) preservation, (3) identification, (4) comparison, (5) individualization, (6) reconstruction and (7) interpretation.

1. Recognition

This is the ability to separate important and potentially informative facts from all background and other unrelated materials. Evidence is selected on the basis of what is likely to help in distinguishing among various investigative leads and possible theories of a case. The recognition process involves the basic principles of forensic examination: pattern recognition, physical property observation, information analysis and, sometimes, field-testing. Recognition is perhaps the most important step in the analysis of forensic evidence; no amount of further laboratory examination is likely to shed much light on the case without recognition.

2. Preservation

If crucial evidence is not recognized and properly collected and preserved, it will be lost, and any important links between a suspect and the crime will never be known or established.

3. Identification

Identification is a process common to all the sciences. It may be regarded as a classification scheme in which items are assigned categories containing like items and then given names. Different items within a given category all have the same generic name. In this way, botanists can identify plants by categorizing them and naming them. Likewise, chemists identify chemical compounds. Some types of physical evidence require that scientific tests be conducted to identify them. Examples of such evidence include drugs, arson accelerants, bloodstains and seminal stains. Other types of physical evidence are identified by comparing their physical and morphological characteristics with those of known standards or previously established criteria such as fingerprints, footprints, projectiles, weapons, wounds or bite marks.

The techniques used for identification include one or more of the following: (a) physical measurements, (b) physical properties, (c) chemical properties, (d) morphological (structural) properties, (e) biological properties, and (f) immunological properties. In many cases, identification simply initiates the forensic process. In others, identification may be definitive as in the case of narcotic or drug identification, injury determination or identification of a biological sample.

4. Comparison

Comparison is employed when the class characteristics of questioned evidence are measured against those of known standards or control materials. Some methods used to compare physical evidence may be listed as follows. Our intention here is not to overwhelm but to indicate the level of sophistication today compared to the time of, say, Sacco-Vanzetti or Lindbergh.

(a) Chromatographic methods: paper, thin layer, GC, HPLC, electrophoresis.
(b) Spectroscopic methods: emission spectography, plasma emission, UV-VIS, IR, FTIR.
(c) Composition analysis: AA, Plasma emission, NAA, Mass spectometry, SEM- EDAX, x-ray diffraction.
(d) Microscopical examination: stereoscope, compound microscope, phase contrast microscope, comparison microscope, SEM, IR and UV microscopes.
(e) Biological methods: enzyme assay, electrophoresis, serological typing, DNA analysis.

If all the measurable class characteristics are the same, as between the questioned sample and the known control, then the two samples are considered to have potentially come from the same source or origin. If there are significant differences in some of the class characteristics, however, then the questioned samples can absolutely be excluded as deriving from the same source. In other words, the exclusionary value of comparison in the forensic field is considered absolute. Depending on the nature and type of physical evidence, in some cases no further analysis can be made beyond the comparison step because of inherent limitations. Classification of drugs, single fiber analysis and determination of insect type are examples of this kind of forensic examination.

5. Individualization

Individualization refers to the demonstration that a particular sample is unique, even among members of the same class. It may also refer to the demonstration that a questioned piece of physical evidence and a similar known sample have a common origin. Thus, in addition to class characteristics, objects and materials possess individual characteristics that can be used to distinguish members of the same class. The nature of these characteristics varies from one type of evidence to another, but forensic scientists try to take advantage of them in efforts aimed at true individualization. With some types of evidence, partial individualization is possible. Sometimes this approach may be nothing more than a refined identification or classification such as a genetic marker determination of a bloodstain, DNA typing of semen evidence or trace elemental analysis of paint chips. The term "identification" is occasionally used to mean personal identification (the individualization of persons). Fingerprints, for example, are used to identify an individual. Such terminology is unfortunate, however, since this process is really an individualization. Likewise, dental evidence and dental records may be used by a forensic odontologist to make a personal individualization in situations where dead bodies otherwise cannot be readily identified, such as in mass disasters, fires or explosions.

6. Interpretation

This self-explanatory activity seeks to assimilate and give meaning to all the information accumulated up to this point in the investigation.

7. Reconstruction

Reconstruction utilizes the results of crime scene examination, laboratory analysis and other independent sources of information in order to reconstruct case events. Reconstruction often involves the use of inductive and deductive logic, statistical data, pattern analysis, results of laboratory analysis on a host of evidence materials and information from the crime scene itself.

The developing fields of artificial intelligence and expert systems have created a new dimension in reconstruction. These systems provide forensic modeling and representation of laboratory analysis results, reasoning and enacting of crime scenes, comparing and profiling of suspects and other decision making activities. Advances in computer hardware and software have added systematic problem solving to the forensic scientist's repertoire. Computer technology allows communication between the user and the expert system—in a sense, each helps the other solve a specific forensic problem.

Reconstructions are desirable in criminal cases in which eyewitness evidence is absent or unreliable. They are important in many other types of cases also, such as automobile and airplane accidents, fire and arson investigations and major disasters.

Chapter 3

Crime Scenes
 1. Definitions
        Historically, it has been customary to designate the
crime scene as the area where a criminal act has taken place.
Actually, the crime scene may comprise more than one site;
such was the occasion in a recent abduction-rape-homicide
case. A teenage girl was abducted by a classmate as she left
school for home. Subsequently she was raped and murdered
by the boy in his car. The victim's body was then transported to a wooded area 20 miles from her home and set
afire to destroy the evidence. Each of those locations—the
abduction site, the perpetrator's vehicle and the site where
the body was found—should be considered crime scenes.
In general, the location of the original crime is considered a
primary scene and any subsequent location is considered a
secondary scene.
        In the macroscopic sense, crime scenes could also re-
fer to areas other than physical locations. For example, the
victim's body, the suspect's body or any part of a vehicle
used in connection with the crime are considered crime
scenes. In addition, other locations or persons involved in
the crime are regarded as continuations of the crime scene(s).
        In the microscopic sense, any piece of physical mate-
rial related to the crime is also deemed a crime scene, such
as a cigarette butt or the scrapings of a victim's fingernails.
Each case, therefore, may contain many of these microscopic and macroscopic crime scenes and each could yield
information useful to the solution of the crime.
        After the boundary of a crime scene is defined, the crime
scene(s) should be secured and processed. Any action taken
should meet all legal and scientific standards and requirements. While sometimes the precise boundaries of a crime
scene are not well-defined, it is very important for the investigator to conceptualize both primary and secondary

scenes. In many well known cases—including most in this book—important evidence was never recognized because the investigator(s) lacked the proper skills to determine the boundaries of the crime.

Once the locations and boundaries are determined, the sequence of events can be established, physical evidence can be recognized and collected and, lastly, the crime can be reconstructed.

2. Classification

A macroscopic crime scene may be classified according to the type of offense (e.g., homicide, rape, burglary); physical location (e.g., indoor, outdoor, underwater, buried); nature of the scene (e.g., body, house, train, bank, car); or condition found (e.g., organized or disorganized, active or passive, normal or staged). Each classification is helpful but none provides an all-inclusive listing of the elements comprising a crime scene. Of more importance, it is essential that an investigator develop the skills necessary to profile the scene and to determine the number of scenes in a particular case along with the nature, boundary and condition of each scene.

A microscopic crime scene amounts to nothing more or less than physical evidence, and there are many ways to classify it, such as by its physical state, by the type of crime and by the types of questions to be resolved. It is imperative for a crime scene investigator to appreciate both the value and the limitations of physical evidence, to understand the interaction between macroscopic and microscopic scenes, to comprehend all the facets of evidence transfer and to possess the ability to locate microscopic scenes within the macroscopic scene in a facile manner.

Why is crime scene classification important? The answer lies in its assistance to investigators who must define a crime scene accurately and must understand the principles of physical evidence transfer. This broad statement is best appreciated when coupled with the axiom that most clues leading to the solution of a crime are contained in the macroscopic scene and the physical evidence. In addition, the investigation of a crime, particularly a homicide, is most effectively performed when all members of the investigating team understand crime scene classification and can therefore work in unison. Through experience and familiarity with various crime scenes plus a systematic analysis of a scene at hand, one can determine what kind of physical evidence exists there; where to detect evidence at a particular type of crime scene within the classification; how to recognize, collect, preserve and process that evidence; and finally, how to reconstruct the scene.

Physical Evidence

In recent years, police agencies around the world have become increasingly dependent on forensic laboratory results for evidence not obtainable from other sources. In the crime scene search and initial investigative stages, police officers, detectives or crime scene technicians are usually the ones who decide what types of evidence will be collected and how much of it will be submitted to the forensic laboratory for analysis. In the adjudicative phases of a case, the types of physical evidence introduced in court and the scope of forensic analysis presented through expert testimony are usually determined by prosecutors and/or defense attorneys. With advances in technology, the role of forensic science in criminal investigation has likewise advanced, shifting from a passive to an active one. The forensic science profession has thus become an integral part of the criminal justice system (See Figure 1).

A. Types of Physical Evidence at Crime Scenes

Virtually any type of material can become physical evidence. It may be as small as a pollen particle or as large as a train; in the physical state of a gas, a solid or a liquid; or in the form of a pattern or a distinct object. Because of its diversity, physical

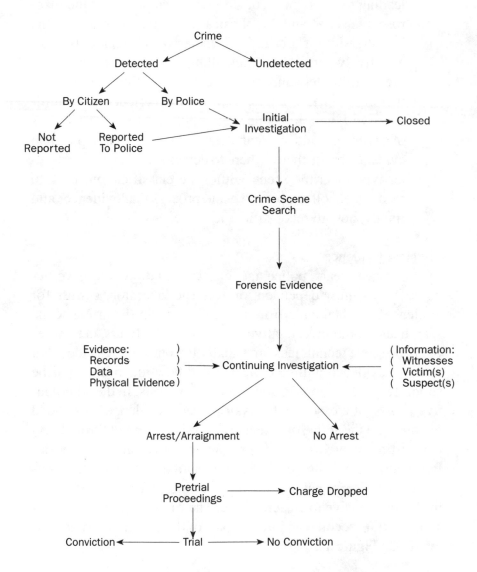

FIGURE 1. Steps in the investigation, identification & adjudication of a crime. Forensic science expertise may be involved in every step of this process.

evidence does not lend itself to easy classification but, in general, the following four forms may be found at a crime scene: transient, pattern, conditional and transfer.

1. Transient Evidence

Transient evidence, usually present in every crime scene, is temporary in nature and can be easily changed or lost in time. Therefore, the sooner police arrive at the scene, the greater will become their chances of discovering this type of evidence. Examples are:

(a) Odor: Putrefaction, perfume, gasoline, cyanide, body, urine, burning, explosives, cigarette or cigar smoke.

(b) Temperature: The temperature in a room; of a car hood or engine; of coffee, tea or water in a cup; of water in a bathtub; of a cadaver; of fire debris.

(c) Imprints and Indentations: Moist footprints on hot or dry road surfaces, fingerprints on meltable material, teeth marks in perishable foods, tire marks on a beach at low tide or footprints in snow.

(d) Markings: Postmortem lividity marks or rigor mortis before they become fixed, blood splatters on moveable objects, a lip print on a smoldering cigarette butt or bloodstains on clothing immersed in water.

Transient evidence is usually detected by the first responding police officer or the first witness at a crime scene and must be recorded and documented as soon as possible. Most transient evidence can be recorded by notes and verified by other officers at the scene. Certain transient evidence can be recorded by photography or videotaping; other types should be collected and preserved with special care to prevent further change or loss.

2. Pattern Evidence

Pattern evidence is produced by direct contact between a person and an object or between an object and another object. Most physical patterns are in the form(s) of imprints, indentations, striations, markings, fractures or deposits. This kind of evidence is especially valuable in the reconstruction of crime scene events. Often, it may be used to disprove a suspect's alibi or a witness's version of what transpired, to associate or dissociate the involvement of persons or objects in particular events or to provide investigators with new leads. Pattern evidence can be further subdivided into two major groups: dynamic transfer patterns and static contact patterns. The following patterns may be found at crime scenes:

(a) Blood spatter
(b) Glass fracture
(c) Fire burn
(d) Furniture position
(e) Projectile trajectory
(f) Track—trail
(g) Tire marks or skid marks
(h) Clothing or article distribution
(i) Modus operandi (see below)
(j) Gun powder residue
(k) Material damage
(l) Body position
(m) Tool marks
(n) Cut, tear and ripping

3. Conditional Evidence

This third type of physical evidence is produced by a specific event or action and, if not documented carefully, may be changed or lost. It is extremely important in crime scene reconstruction and in determining the set of circumstances within a particular event. Some examples follow.

(a) Light: Vehicular headlights on or off prior to an accident, lighting conditions at an indoor crime scene.
(b) Smoke: Color, direction of travel, density, odor.
(c) Fire: Color of the flames, direction of the flames, speed of the flame spread, temperature and condition of the fire.

(d) Location: Location of a weapon or cartridge case in relation to a victim's body, sequence and location of bloodstains on several objects, location of a victim's vehicle, distribution of broken glass or location of injuries or wounds.

(e) Vehicle: Doors locked or unlocked, windows opened or closed; radio on or off—if on, station to which tuned; ignition key in or out; odometer mileage.

(f) Body: Degree of rigor mortis, distribution of lividity, degree of decomposition, body temperature, body position and types of wounds.

(g) Scene: Condition of furniture, doors and windows; any disturbance or signs of a struggle.

4. Transfer Evidence

This type of physical evidence is produced by physical contact between person(s) *or* object(s) or between person(s) *and* object(s). As we have seen under previous headings, a classification system, although imperfect, is essential in order to systematize information and to impart a mutuality of understanding among all tiers of the criminal justice system. Seven commonly used classification schemes for transfer evidence are described below. Each is useful in offering a different conceptual perspective for transfer evidence, although some are more useful than others.

(a) By Type of Crime: An obvious way to classify physical evidence is by the type of crime from which it originates. Thus, there is homicide evidence, burglary evidence, assault evidence and rape evidence, to name a few. Although this scheme has value in certain situations, it should be remembered that any type of physical evidence may occur in connection with nearly every variety of crime. But different evidence types are not restricted to defined crime classifications. Bloodstains, for example, frequently occur in assault and homicide cases, but they may be just as important as evidence at a burglary scene. Similarly, semen stains are frequently considered the primary type of evidence in rape and other sex crimes but in some cases a different type of physical evidence may be even more important. There is some correlation between the type of crime and the type of evidence, and this connection should be appreciated by investigators when searching for transfer evidence.

(b) By Type of Material: Here, there are categories such as metallic evidence, glass evidence or plastic evidence. This scheme, however, has limitations. A fingerprint found on glass, for example, is handled and examined in essentially the same manner as one found on plastic or other nonporous surfaces. Or, a tool mark on a metal surface would be handled and compared in the same way as one found on some other material, such as wood. In both of these cases, the nature of the material is less significant than the evidence produced by the way something interacted with that material.

(c) By General Nature of the Evidence: Evidence may be classified as physical (e.g., a firearm, tool, tool mark, cartridge case); as chemical (e.g., a drug sample); or as biological (e.g., hair, marijuana, bloodstains). Such schemes are of greatest value to an investigator when they serve as reminders for the best method of collection and preservation of the evidence (See Table 1).

(d) By Physical State of the Evidence: Like all other matter, physical evidence may be classified as solid, liquid or gas. Most evidence encountered at a crime scene would be labeled "solid" (e.g., clothing, tools, firearms, glass, paper). Significant liquid evidence would include liquid blood samples or liquid accelerants. Gas samples are rarely collected even though gaseous evidence does frequently appear. Several types of devices are available to sample gases at crime and fire scenes.

Biological
Blood
Semen
Saliva
Sweat/Tears
Hair
Bone
Tissues
Urine
Feces
Animal Material
Insects
Bacterial/Fungal
Botanical

Chemical
Fibers
Glass
Soil
Gunpowder
Metal
Mineral
Narcotics
Drugs
Paper
Ink
Cosmetics
Paint
Plastic
Lubricants
Fertilizer

Physical (Impression)
Fingerprints
Footprints
Shoe Prints
Handwriting
Firearms
Printing
Number Restoration
Tire Marks
Tool Marks
Typewriting

Miscellaneous
Laundry Marks
Voice Analysis
Polygraph
Photography
Stress Evaluation
Psycholinguistic Analysis
Vehical Identification

TABLE 1: Classification of Evidence by Its General Nature

(e) By Type of Question to be Resolved: Examples include those instances when evidence will be used to reconstruct an event, to provide a specific element in the perpetration of a crime, to link a suspect to a victim or crime scene, to exclude or exonerate a suspect, to provide investigative leads, or to supply proof in a court of law.

(f) By the Way Evidence Was Produced: An important consideration when classifying evidence in this manner is the way individuals involved have interacted with their environment, with each other and with the type of evidence created by these interactions. Scrutiny of such behavior allows for an interpretation of the events which have occurred, and this becomes useful in crime reconstruction.

(g) By Specific Type of Evidence: This scheme includes, among others, the following:

1. Tool Marks
2. Fingerprints
3. Organic compounds
4. Glass
5. Tire Tracks
6. Paint
7. Plastics
8. Wood
9. Dust
10. Semen
11. Paper
12. Soil
13. Fibers
14. Weapons
15. Construction materials
16. Documents
17. Metal
18. Hairs
19. Blood

20. Minerals
21. Inorganic compounds
22. Voiceprints
23. Videotapes

5. Associative Evidence

Specific items located at a crime scene or during an investigation may be used as evidence to associate a victim or suspect with a particular scene or with each other. Examples of associative evidence include a suspect's wallet found at the crime scene or one of the victim's personal belongings found in the suspect's possession.

B. The Role of Physical Evidence in Case Investigations

The following represent some of the major types of intelligence which physical evidence may provide.

1. Information on the Corpus Delecti:

The corpus delecti, which means the "body of the crime", refers to those essential facts which show that a crime has taken place. Crime scene patterns and physical evidence often may be used to establish the essential facts of a case. For example, tool-marks, broken doors and windows, ransacked rooms and missing valuables are examples of physical evidence that would be important in establishing a burglary. Similarly, in an assault case, the victim's blood on a weapon and torn clothing could be important pieces of evidence to prove that an assault had taken place. The presence of semen on a vaginal swab and physical injury patterns on the victim's body could be used to establish the crime of rape.

In Connecticut's famous Woodchipper Murder in 1986, 56 bone fragments, 2,660 hair strands and a tooth linked Richard Crafts to the slaying of his wife, Helle.

2. Information on the Modus Operandi:

Many criminals have a particular modus operandi (method of operation or MO) which consists of their own characteristic way of committing a crime. Physical evidence can help in establishing an MO. In burglary cases, for instance, the means used to gain entry, tools that were used, types of items taken and other telltale signs such as leaving a cryptic message or marking, are important case features in postulating an individual criminal's modus operandi. In arson cases, the type of accelerant used and the way in which fires are set constitute physical evidence that helps to establish the patterns or signature of an arsonist. Cases that have been treated separately can sometimes be connected by careful documentation of similar MOs especially in serial killer or serial rapist investigations. A case in point is that of Ted Bundy, the Florida serial killer who had an individualized way of picking his victims, committing the murder and disposing of the bodies.

3. Linking a Suspect with a Victim:

This is one of the most common and important types of linkage that physical evidence may help to establish, particularly in the investigation of violent crimes. For example, the finding of a suspect's semen on a victim's body through the matching of DNA profiles and the identification of the victim's blood, hairs, clothing fibers or cosmetics on a perpetrator's clothing will provide links between the victim and suspect. Sometimes, trace evidence such as blood, saliva or hair, may be transferred from the perpetrator to the victim. An example of this occurred in the 1981 Wayne Williams case in Atlanta, Georgia, when the same type fibers were used to link 20 murders. It is important, therefore, that all physical evidence be treated separately and carefully to avoid secondary cross contaminations.

4. Linking a Person to a Crime Scene:

Numerous types of evidence may be deposited by the person committing a crime including fingerprints, blood, hair, fibers and soil particles. In a 1989 triple homicide in

Derby, Connecticut, for example, the size 8-1/2 hand print and bloody shoe print of the murderer, Derek Roseboro, helped solve the case.

In addition, weapons or other items may leave evidence behind, such as cartridge casings or tool marks. Depending on the crime, various kinds of evidence may be carried away intentionally (e.g., stolen property) or unintentionally (e.g., transfers such as carpet fibers on the criminal's shoes.)

5. Disproving or Supporting a Witness's Testimony:

Physical evidence examination can often indicate conclusively whether a person's version of a set of events is credible. For instance, the examination of a car which fits the description of a hit-and-run vehicle might reveal blood on the underside of the bumper. If the owner of the vehicle claims he hit a dog, laboratory tests on the blood will reveal whether the blood came from a canine or a human.

In Hawaii, a police sergeant murdered his wife but claimed she had jumped from a moving van. Examination of the van's ceiling and sun visor revealed over 500 blood spatters, however, and the husband's story was disproven.

6. Identification of a Suspect:

The best evidence for identifying a suspect is fingerprints. A fingerprint found at a scene and later identified as belonging to a particular person results in an unequivocal identification of that person. The term "identification" as used here really means "individualization" or identifying a single source of the evidence. In one particular bank robbery, a latent fingerprint was recovered from the tellers' counter. Although the perpetrator had not been identified initially, a search of AFIS (Automated Fingerprint Identification System) was made and a suspect was arrested within 17 minutes.

Other examples of evidence used for identification purposes include bite marks on a victim's or suspect's body, or the DNA profile pattern match of a semen sample with a suspect's known blood sample.

7. Providing Investigative Leads:

Physical evidence analysis may be helpful in directing an investigation along a productive path. Not all the scientific evidence found at a scene may necessarily be linked to a suspect but some of it could provide direct and indirect leads to the solution of the crime. For example, in a hit-and-run case, a five-layer paint chip found in the victim's clothing can be used to provide information about the color and possibly the model and year of the automobile involved.

More specifically, in the World Trade Center bombing in New York City in 1993, yellow paint chips were discovered at the scene. The FBI Laboratory identified them as coming from a rental truck company. When the suspects arrived to claim their deposit, they were apprehended.

8. Identification of a Substance:

The results of examining a piece of physical evidence may provide information that contributes to the identity of a specific substance such as cocaine, heroin, LSD, morphine or any other drug or poison. Laboratory analysis of fibers can sometimes yield information about the manufacturer of the fabric or garment.

Chapter 4

New Technologies in Criminal Investigation

As of 1999, nearly 40 percent of all households in the United States had been touched by crime. Each of these households was violated by at least one burglary, larceny or motor vehicle theft; or one of its family members was a victim of rape, robbery, assault or murder. In order to achieve the most accurate interpretation of crime statistics, trends should be examined over the longest time period possible, and population growth should be taken into account by using crime rate as a basis for comparison.

Over the last century, the crime rate has increased 200 percent while, over the same period, the clearance rate for crime has remained relatively low. The Uniform Crime Report (UCR) indicates that the rate of clearance for all UCR indexed crime in the United States is only 19 percent. In other words, for over 80 percent of crimes, the criminal is never apprehended. Why? One reason is that technological developments in crime solution have lagged significantly behind developments in other broad areas such as business and industry or government. But since the 1970s, a systematic national effort to apply new technologies to criminal justice has been forged through burgeoning research and development initiatives. Hundreds of new technologies continue to emerge, thus redefining the means and methods by which police departments conduct their criminal investigations.

Contemporary progress in chemistry, molecular biology, instrumentation, microcircuitry, computer technology and electronics has virtually revolutionized the capability of the forensic science laboratory. The following represents a mere sample of the most notable advances.

1. DNA Typing and Databases:
DNA (deoxyribonucleic acid) typing for forensic purposes was first introduced for casework in 1985. This new technique enabled forensic laboratories to identify an individual at the molecular level. DNA fingerprinting and

the blueprint of life were born. Aside from that found in sets of identical twins, the DNA of a person is absolutely unique, encoding all the information that gives each of us our physical characteristics and allows us to function and be recognized as human. The different combinations of chromosomes that a child inherits from his parents are on the order of two to the twenty-third power. DNA typing results have provided crucial information in many homicide and rape trials.

Because history has shown that many rapists and other felons are repeat offenders, some state and federal jurisdictions have passed legislation enabling the collection of DNA samples from these criminals prior to their release. A DNA profile data bank provides a new investigative tool for law enforcement, because by comparing the DNA pattern from semen samples collected from a rape victim or from bloodstains left at a crime scene to DNA records on file, a suspect may be identified in much the same manner as when fingerprints are compared.

In a majority of jurisdictions, the law restricts the offender DNA database to felony level sexual assault related convictions. However, several states have expanded the scope of their sex offender databases to include DNA profiles from a wide range of convicted felons.

In an effort to balance the privacy interests and concerns associated with an individual's DNA profile, many states have implemented stringent regulations concerning the accessibility to and use of the database profiles. As technologies continue to expand and become increasingly more common and accepted, the use of individualizing records, such as DNA databases, will likely expand.

2. Casing and Bullet Databases:

Violent crime involving the use of weapons, particularly drug related offenses, prompted the introduction of database systems that can store individual characteristics associated with firearms evidence and help solve many of these violent crimes.

In many of the all too common drive-by shootings or street crimes associated with the illegal drugs trade, the only available evidence has been a few cartridge cases recovered from the shooting scene. Until the advent of these databases, such evidence was of little value unless the police were able to recover the weapon used in the shooting. Currently, these databases can be used to associate cartridge cases from one crime scene to another, or to associate those cases to a particular gun from which a known cartridge case sample has been obtained. Known databases consist of test shots obtained from any weapon submitted to the firearms unit of the laboratory as well as from guns seized by police and ordered to be destroyed.

Following the success of databases that stored individualizing information on casings, new databases are being developed to store and search individualizing characteristics identified on the bullets themselves. This technology is helpful in those instances where the casings were not recovered but a bullet was recovered and determined to be identifiable.

3. New Latent Print Technology:

Fingerprinting is an area in which many new and exciting developments have occurred in the past several years. Individualization by fingerprints has been widely accepted by both scientists and courtrooms. Innovative applications of physical and organic chemistry have led to new methods for developing and enhancing fingerprints. More than 200 new chemicals have been applied to prints for better visualization. Lasers, alternative light sources, cyanoacrylate fuming, ninhydrin analogs and other modalities used for the visualization of fingerprints at crime scenes have helped in discovering and retrieving this type of valuable physical evidence.

The AFIS reduces the time required for ten-print filing

and searching as well as for the search for a single latent print match. Match rates are thereby dramatically increased. A further advance is the Live-scan System. Live-scan allows police officers to compare a suspect's fingerprints, taken at the point of arrest, with millions of fingerprints in the AFIS files within minutes.

4. New Instrumentation:

With each leap in instrument technology, forensic investigation is becoming an increasingly exact science. Forensic laboratories now work on an identification and confirmation system. Unknown substances are no longer identified by a process of elimination; as analysis by one method is confirmed by another, it reduces the probability of error beyond reasonable doubt.

An arsenal of sophisticated technologies with menacing acronyms, such as GC-MS, FTIR and SEM/EDX, has permitted scientists to label previously unknown substances with greater ease and sensitivity.

5. Image Enhancement / Artificial Intelligence:

The computer-assisted Image Enhancement System enables the scientist to store, enhance and compare various images such as handwriting, fingerprints, photographs, tool marks, video images and other pattern evidence. The blossoming field of artificial intelligence and expert systems gives investigators the opportunity to move more thoroughly into areas such as crime scene reasoning/logic, profiling, decision making, systematic problem solving and crime mapping.

Postscript

Despite an avalanche of technological discoveries and improvements, high quality and reliable forensics remains in the hands and minds of skilled criminal investigators. The new technology is useless without competent police officers who recognize and collect crucial evidence, without well-trained forensic scientists who decide which analytical methodologies to use and without seasoned investigators to interpret results.

No matter how advanced the forensic frontier, it cannot supercede the human intellect. Innovations and refinements serve, rather, as supportive tools in the quest for justice.

Chapter Notes for Section One

Sacco-Vanzetti
Chapter 1: Historical Summary, Background and Bombings

1.   Bowen, Ezra, Series Editor. *This Fabulous Century*, Volume III, 1920-1930 (NewYork: Time Life Books, 1969), p. 19.

2.   Samuel Eliot Morrison. *The Oxford History of the American People* (New York: Oxford University Press, 1965), p. 859.

3.   Bartolomeo Vanzetti. *The Story of a Proletarian Life*, tr. Eugene Lyons (Boston: Sacco-Vanzetti Defense Committee, 1923), p. 5.

4.   Nicola Sacco and Bartolomeo Vanzetti. *The Letters of Sacco and Vanzetti*, ed. Marion Denman Frankfurter and Gardner Jackson (New York: Viking, 1928), p. 33

Chapter 3: The Plymouth Trial. Dress Rehearsal?

5.   *Boston Globe*, April 24, 1920, morning edition. *Boston Herald*, April 24, 1920.

6.   William Young and David E. Kaiser. *Postmortem*. (Amherst: The University of Massachusetts Press, 1985), p. 33

Chapter 4: The Dedham Trial

7.   Barry C. Reed. *American Bar Association Journal*, August, 1960, 46: 869.

8.   Dr. Frank M. D'Alessandro. *The Verdict of History on Sacco and Vanzetti* (New York: Jay Street Publishers, 1997), p. 127.

Chapter 5: Witnesses and Evidence

9.   *Boston Herald*, April 17, 1920.

Chapter 6: Ballistics Magnified

10. Young and Kaiser. *Postmortem*, pps. 107-108.

Chapter 7: Verdict. Whose Victory?

11. Stewart memorandum, February 18, 1921, Massachusetts State Police files.

12. Ibid.

13. Ibid.

Chapter Notes for Section Two

Chapter 2: Lindbergh. The Murder of an American Hero's Baby

1. *Hartford Courant*, February 6, 2000. p. G12.

2. Ibid

Chapter 3: Sam Sheppard. The Case That Spawned *The Fugitive*

3. *Knight Ridder Newspapers*, April 13, 2000.

Chapter 4: John F. Kennedy. Who Killed Our President?

4. The Saturday Evening Post, December 2, 1967.

5. Burl Osborne. *The Day JFK Died—Thirty Years Later* (Kansas City: Andrews and McMeel, 1993), p. 104.

6. Ibid.

7. The Saturday Evening Post, December 2, 1967.

8. Ibid.

9. Ibid.

Chapter 5: Vincent Foster. Suicide or Murder in Washington?

10. From the book *A Washington Tragedy: How the Death of Vincent Foster Ignited a Political Firestorm* by Dan E. Moldea. Copyright 1998 by Dan E. Moldea. All rights reserved. Reprinted by special permission of Regnery Publishing, Inc. Washington, D.C. pps. 375, 376.

Chapter 6: JonBenet Ramsey. What Is Wrong with the Case?

11. *USA Today*, October 15, 1999.

12. Ann Louise Bardack. *Vanity Fair*, September 1997.

13. *USA Today*, October 15, 1999.

Chapter Notes for Section Three

O. J. Simpson
Chapter 1: Historical Summary and Relationships

1. Gerald F. Uelmen. *Lessons from the Trial: The People v. O.J. Simpson* (Kansas City: Andrews and McMeel, 1996), pps. 22, 23.

Chapter 2: The Crimes

2. Johnnie L. Cochran, with Tim Rutten. *Journey to Justice* (New York: Ballantine Books, 1996), pps. 329, 330.

Chapter 3: The Preliminary Hearing

3. Uelmen. *Lessons from the Trial: The People v. O.J. Simpson*, pps. 29, 30.

4. Ibid., pps. 37, 38.

5. Ibid., p. 35.

6. Ibid.

7. Cochran. *Journey to Justice*, p. 334.

8. Uelmen. *Lessons from the Trial: The People v. O.J. Simpson*, p. 45.

Bibliography
Books & Articles

Sacco-Vanzetti

Avrich, Paul. *Anarchist Portraits*. Princeton: Princeton University Press, 1988.

———. *Sacco and Vanzetti: The Anarchist Background*. Princeton: Princeton University Press, 1991.

Bagdikian, Ben H. "New Light on Sacco and Vanzetti." *The New Republic,* July 13, 1963.

Beffel, John Nicholas. "Eels and the Electric Chair." *The New Republic,* December 29, 1920.

Bowen, Ezra, series ed. *This Fabulous Century.* Volume III, 1920-1930. New York: Time-Life Books, 1969.

Braverman, Shelley. "Forensic Ballistic Errors." *Gun Digest*, 1966.

Broun, H. *Collected Edition of Heywood Braun*. New York: Harcourt, 1941.

Coben, Stanley. *A. Mitchell Palmer: Politician*. New York: Columbia University Press, 1963.

Colp, Ralph, Jr. "Bitter Christmas: A Biological Inquiry into the Life of Bartolomeo Vanzetti." *The Nation*, December 27, 1958.

———. "Sacco's Struggle for Sanity." *The Nation*, August 16, 1958.

Cook, Fred J. "The Missing Fingerprints." *The Nation,* December 22, 1962.

D'Alessandro, Frank M. *The Verdict of History on Sacco and Vanzetti*. New York: Jay Street Publishers, 1997.

Dickenson, Alice. *The Sacco-Vanzetti Case*. New York: Franklin Watts, 1972.

Eastman, Max. "Is This the Truth About Sacco and Vanzetti?" *National Review*, October 21, 1961.

Ehrmann, Herbert. *The Case That Will Not Die*. Boston: Little, Brown, 1969.

———. "The Magnetic Point and the Morelli Evidence." *Harvard Law Review*, January 1966.

———. *The Untried Case: The Sacco-Vanzetti Case and the Morelli Gang*. New York: Vanguard, 1960.

Fast, Howard. *The Passion of Sacco and Vanzetti: A New England Legend*. New York: The Blue Heron Press, 1953.

Felicani, Aldino. "Sacco-Vanzetti: A Memoir." *The Nation*, August 14, 1967.

Felix, David. *Apotheosis in Boston: Sacco and Vanzetti From Case To Legend*. Columbia University Forum VI, Fall 1963.

Fenton, Edwin. *Immigrants and Unions, A Case Study: Italians and American Labor, 1870-1920*. New York: Arno, 1975.

Foner, Eric. "The Men and the Symbols." *The Nation*, August 20, 1977.

Fraenkel, Osmond K. *The Sacco-Vanzetti Case*. New York: Knopf, 1933.

Frankfurter, Felix. *The Case of Sacco and Vanzetti*. New York: Grosset & Dunlap, 1962.

———. *The Case of Sacco and Vanzetti: A Critical Analysis for Lawyers and Laymen*. Boston: Little Brown, 1927.

Frankfurter, Marion, and Gardner Jackson, eds. *The Letters of Sacco and Vanzetti*. New York: Dutton, 1960.

Grant, Robert. *Fourscore: An Autobiography*. Boston: Houghton Mifflin, 1934.

Handlin, Oscar. *Boston's Immigrants*. London: Oxford University Press, 1959.

Harris, Leon. *Uptain Sinclair: An American Rebel*. New York: Crowell, 1975.

Jackson, Brian. *The Black Flag*. London: Routledge & Kegan Paul, 1973.

Jaffe, Julian F. *Crusade Against Radicalism: New York During the Red Scare, 1914-1924*. Port Washington, N.Y.: Kennekat Press, 1972.

Joll, James. *The Anarchists*. London: Eyre & Spottiswoode, 1964.

Joughin, Louis, and Edmund Morgan. *The Legacy of Sacco and Vanzetti*. Chicago: Quadrangle, 1964.

Lowenthal, Max. *The Federal Bureau of Investigation*. New York: William Sloane Associates, 1950.

Montgomery, Robert. *Sacco-Vanzetti: The Murder and the Myth*. New York: Devin-Adair, 1960.

Morison, Samuel Eliot. *The Oxford History of the American People*. New York: Oxford University Press, 1965.

Murray, Robert K. *Red Scare: A Study in National Hysteria, 1919-1920*. Minneapolis: University of Minnisota Press, 1955.

Musmanno, Michael A. *After Twelve Years*. New York: Knopf, 1939.

———. "The Sacco-Vanzetti Case: With Critical Analysis of the Book Tragedy in Dedham by Francis Russell." *Kansas Law Review*, May 1963.

———. "Was Sacco Guilty?" *The New Republic*, March 2, 1963.

O'Connor, Tom. "The Origin of the Sacco-Vanzetti Case." *Vanderbilt Law Review*, June 1961.

Porter, Katherine Anne. *The Never-Ending Wrong*. Boston: Atlantic-Little, Brown, 1977.

Post, Louis F. *The Deportations Delirium of Nineteen-Twenty*. Chicago: Charles H. Kerr, 1923.

Preston, William, Jr. *Aliens and Dissenters: Federal Suppression of Radicals, 1903-1933*. Cambridge: Harvard University Press, 1963.

Reed, Barry C. *American Bar Association Journal*, August 1960, Volume 46.

Russell, Francis. "America's Dreyfus Case." *New York Review of Books*, November 5, 1981.

————. *Sacco and Vanzetti: The Case Resolved*. New York: Harper & Row, 1986.

————. "Sacco Guilty, Vanzetti, Innocent?" *American Heritage*, June 1962.

————. "The American Case of the Century." *New England Quarterly*, Winter 1985.

————. "The Case of the Century: Fifty Years Later." *Harvard Magazine*, July-August 1997.

————. *Tragedy in Dedham*. New York: McGraw-Hill, 1971.

Sacco, Nicola, and Bartolomeo Vanzetti. *The Letters of Sacco and Vanzetti*. Marion Denman Frankfurter and Gardner Jackson, eds. New York: Viking, 1928.

Schlesinger, Arthur M. *The Age of Roosevelt: The Crisis of the Old Order, 1919-1933*. London: Heinemann, 1957.

Sinclair, Upton. *Boston: A Documentary Novel of the Sacco-Vanzetti Case*. Cambridge, MA: Robert Bentley, 1978.

————. "The Fish Pedlar and the Shoemaker." *New York: Institute of Social Studies Bulletin*, Summer 1953.

"Stewart Memorandum." Massachusetts State Police Files, February 18, 1921.

Theoharis, Athan G., and John Stewart Cox. *The Boss: J. Edgar Hoover and the Great American Inquisition*. Philadelphia: Temple University Press, 1988.

Thompson, William G. "Vanzetti's Last Statement." *Atlantic Monthly*, February 1928.

The Sacco-Vanzetti Case: Transcript of the Record of the Trial of Nicola Sacco and Bartolomeo Vanzetti in the Courts of Massachusetts and Subsequent Proceedings, 1920-1927 (5 vols). Trial Transcript. New York: Henry Holt, 1928. Supplemental Volume on the Bridgewater Case. All six volumes were reprinted by Paul P. Appel, Mamaroneck, NY, 1969.

Yeomans, Henry Aaron. *Abbott Lawrence Lowell*. Cambridge: Harvard University Press, 1948.

Young, William, and David E. Kaiser. *Postmortem: New Evidence in the Case of Sacco and Vanzetti*. Amherst: University of Massachusetts Press, 1985.

Lindbergh Kidnapping

Ahlgren, Gregory, and Stephen Monier. *Crime of the Century: The Lindbergh Kidnapping Hoax*. Boston: Branden books, 1993.

Alix, Ernest Kahlar. *Ransom Kidnapping in America, 1874-1974: The Creation of a Capital Crime*. Carbondale: Southern Illinois University Press, 1978.

Allen, Neal. "They Called It the Crime of the Century." *Woman's World*, March 6, 1990.

Badin, Michael M. "The Lindbergh Kidnapping: Review of the Autopsy Evidence." *Journal of Forensic Science*, October 1983.

Battan, David. *Handwriting Analysis.* San Luis Obispo, California: Padre Productions, 1984.

Bedau, Hugo A., and Michael L. Radelet. "Miscarriages of Justice in Potentially Capital Cases." *Stanford Law Review*, November 1987.

Behn, Noel. *Lindbergh, the Crime.* New York: Atlantic Monthly Press, 1994.

Berg, A. Scott. *Lindbergh.* New York: G.P. Putnam's Sons, 1998.

Blackman, Samuel G. "The Case That Shook the World." *Milwaukee Journal,* February 3, 1992.

Boorstin, Daniel J. *Hidden Histories.* New York: Harper and Row, 1987.

Brant, John, and Edith Renauld. *True Story of the Lindbergh Kidnapping.* New York: Kroy Wen, 1932.

Coakley, Leo J. *Jersey Troopers.* New Brunswick, NJ: Rutgers University Press, 1971.

Condon, John F. *Jafsie Tells All.* New York: Jonathan Lee Publishing Corporation, 1936.

Davidson, David D. "The Story of the Century." *American Heritage,* February 1976.

Davis, Kenneth. *The Hero: Charles A. Lindbergh and the American Dream.* Garden City, NY: Doubleday and Co., 1954.

Dewan, George. "The Lindbergh Case Just Won't Go Away." *Newsday,* December 15, 1987.

Doud, Donald F. "A Review of the Lindbergh Case." *Journal of Forensic Sciences 34*, 1989.

Dutch, Andrew K. *Hysteria: Lindbergh Kidnap Case.* Philadelphia: Dorrance, 1975.

Elliott, Robert G., with Albert R. Beatty. *Agent of Death: The Memoirs of an Executioner.* New York: E.P. Dutton & Co., 1940.

Fisher, Jim. *The Lindbergh Case.* New Brunswick, NJ: Rutgers University Press, 1998.

Goldfarb, Ronald. "He Had To Be Guilty." *New York Times Book Review,* June 17, 1985.

Haag, Lucien C. "The Lindbergh Case Revisited: A Review of the Criminalistic Evidence." *Journal of Forensic Sciences.* 28, 1983.

Haring, J. Vreeland. *The Hand of Hauptmann.* Plainfield, NJ: Hamer Publishing Co., 1937.

Hauptmann, Anna. *Story of Anna Hauptmann.* 1935 Lindbergh Collection, New Jersey State Police Museum and Learning Center, West Trenton, New Jersey.

Hermann, Dorothy. *Anne Morrow Lindbergh: A Gift for Life.* New York: Ticknor & Fields, 1992.

Horan, James J. "The Investigation of the Lindbergh Kidnapping Case." *Journal of Forensic Sciences.* 28, 1983.

Hughes, Helen MacGill. "The Lindbergh Case: A Study of Human Interest and Politics." *American Journal of Sociology,* July 1936.

Jones, Wayne. *Murder of Justice—New Jersey's Greatest Shame.* New York: Vantage Press, 1997.

Keenan, John F. "The Lindbergh Kidnapping Revisited." *Michigan Law Review 108,* 1986.

Kennedy, Ludovic. *The Airman and the Carpenter.* New York: Viking Penguin, 1985.

Leighton, Isabel, ed. *The Aspirin Age: 1919-1941.* New York: Simon and Schuster, 1949.

Lewis, Jerry D. *Crusade Against Crime.* New York: Bernard Geis Associates, 1962.

Lindbergh, Anne Morrow. *Hour of Gold, Hour of Lead: Diaries and Letters of Anne Morrow Lindbergh, 1929-1935.* New York: Harcourt Brace Javanovich, 1974.

Lindbergh, Charles A. *Autobiography of Values.* New York and London: Harcourt Brace Javanovich, 1977.

———. *Of Flight and Life.* New York: Charles Scribner's Sons, 1948.

———. *The Spirit of St. Louis.* New York: Charles Scribner's Sons, 1953.

——— *The Wartime Journals of Charles A. Lindbergh.* New York: Harcourt Brace Javanovich, 1970.

Maeder, Jay. "The Resurrection of Richard Hauptmann: Continuing the Arguments in the Case That Won't Go Away." *New York Daily News Magazine,* April 3, 1988.

Manchester, William. *The Glory and the Dream.* Boston: Little, Brown, 1973.

McArdle, Phil, and Karen McArdle. *Fatal Fascinations: Where Fact Meets Fiction in Police Work.* Boston: Houghton Mifflin, 1988.

McElvaine, Robert S. *The Great Depression.* New York: Times Books, 1984.

Milton, Joyce. *Loss of Eden.* New York: HarperCollins, 1993.

Mosley, Leonard. *Lindbergh: A Biography.* New York: Doubleday & Company, 1976.

Moseley, Seth H. "The Night the Lindbergh Baby Disappeared." *Yankee Magazine,* March 1982.

Nicolson, Nigel, ed. *Harold Nicolson: Diaries and Letters 1930-1939.* New York: Atheneum, 1966.

O'Brien, P.J. *The Lindberghs: The Story of a Distinguished Family.* New York: International Press, 1935.

Osborn, Albert D. *Questioned Document Problems.* Albany, NY: Boyd Printing Company, 1944.

Palenick, Skip. "Microscope Trace Evidence—The Overlooked Clue." *The Microscope, First Quarter,* 1983.

Pearson, Edmund. *Studies in Murder.* New York: Random House, 1938.

Prescott, Peter S. "Cobbling Up a Conviction." *Newsweek,* June 24, 1985.

Prosser, William. "The Lindbergh Case Revisited: George Waller's 'Kidnap.'" *Minnesota Law Review*, Volume 46, 1962.

Radelet, Michael L., et al. *In Spite of Innocence: Erroneous Convictions in Capital Cases.* Boston: Northeastern University Press, 1992.

Resinger, D. Michael, et al. "Exorcism of Ignorance as a Proxy for Rational Knowledge: The Lessons of Handwriting Identification 'Expertise.'" *University of Pennsylvania Law Review 137,* 1989.

Ross, Walter S. *The Last Hero.* New York: Harper and Row, 1964.

Sanders, Paul H. "Scientific and Procedural Aspects of the Hauptmann Trial." *American Bar Association Journal*, May 1935.

Scaduto, Anthony. *Scapegoat: The Lonesome Death of Bruno Richard Hauptmann.* New York: G. P. Putnam's Sons, 1976.

Snyder, LeMoyne. *Homicide Investigation.* Springfield, IL: Charles C. Thomas, 1944.

Starrs, James E. "The Prosecution of Bruno Richard Hauptmann: An Imitation of Falconry." *Journal of Forensic Sciences 28,* 1983.

Thomas, Gordon, and Max Morgan. *The Day The Bubble Burst.* New York: Doubleday and Company, 1979.

Treblicock, Bob. "Who Killed The Lindbergh Baby?" *Yankee Magazine,* February, 1994.

Tully, Andrew. *Treasury Agent: The Inside Story.* New York: Simon and Schuster, 1958.

Veron, John. *Lindbergh's Son.* New York: Viking Press, 1987.

Waller, George. *Kidnap: The Story of the Lindbergh Case.* New York: Dial Press, 1961.

Wendel, Paul H. *The Lindburgh-Hauptmann Aftermath.* New York: Loft, 1940.

Whipple, Sidney B. *The Trial of Bruno Richard Hauptmann.* New York: Doubleday, Doran, 1937.

Wright, Theon. *In Search of the Lindbergh Baby.* New York: Tower Publications, 1981.

Zito, Tom. "Did the Evidence Fit the Crime?" *Life Magazine,* March 1982.

Sam Sheppard

Bailey, F. Lee, with Harvey Aronson. *The Defense Never Rests.* New York: Stein & Day, 1971.

Campbell, Anne. *Men, Women, and Aggression.* New York: Basic Books, 1993.

Cooper, Cynthia L. "The Test Culture: Medical Experimentation on Prisoners." *New England Journal on Prison Law 2,* 1976.

Cooper, Cynthia L., and Sam Reese Sheppard. *Mockery of Justice*. Boston: Northeastern University Press, 1995.

Gardner, Erle Stanley. "Are the Sheppards Telling the Truth?" *Argosy Magazine,* August 1957.

———. "The Human Side of the Sheppard Case." *Argosy Magazine,* September 1957.

———. "The Sheppard Case Breaks Wide Open." *Argosy Magazine,* October 1957.

Halberstam, David. *The Fifties*. New York: Villard Books, 1993.

Hare, Robert. *Without Conscience: The Disturbing World of the Psychopaths Among Us*. New York: Simon and Schuster, 1993.

Holmes, Paul. *Retrial: Murder and Dr. Sam Sheppard.* New York: Bantam Books, Inc., 1966.

Israel, Lee. *Kilgallen*. New York: Delacorte Press, 1979.

Kerr, David. *Criminal Investigation and Interrogation*. Cincinnati, OH: Anderson, 1962.

Kilgallen, Dorothy. *Murder One*. New York: Random House, 1967.

Kirk, Paul L. *Crime Investigation: Physical Evidence and the Police Laboratory*. New York: Interscience, 1953.

Kurland, Philip B., and Gerhard Casper, eds. *Constitutional Law, Vol. 63, Landmark Briefs and Arguments of the Supreme Court of the United States* Arlington, VA: University Publications of America, 1975.

Lo Pucki, Lynn M., ed. *Profiles of Ohio Lawyers, Vol. 1, Cleveland and Vicinity.* Cincinnati, OH: Anderson, 1989.

Mihaly, Mary. "The Fugitive Redux". *Ohio Magazine*, February 1995.

Norris, Joel. *Serial Killers*. London: Arrow books, 1990.

Pollack, Jack Harrison. *Croiset the Clairvoyant*. New York: Doubleday, 1964.

———. *Dr. Sam: An American Tragedy*. Chicago: Regnery, 1972.

Radin, Edward. *The Innocents*. New York: Morrow, 1964.

Scranton, Phil, and Kathryn Chadwick. *In the Arms of the Law: Coroners' Inquests and Deaths in Custody*. London: Pluto Press, 1987.

Sheppard, Sam. *Endure and Conquer*. Cleveland, Ohio: World, 1966.

Sheppard, Stephen, with Paul Holmes. *My Brother's Keeper.* New York: McKay, 1964.

Thurston, Gavin. *Coronership*. Great Britain: Rose, 1980.

Transcript, *State v. Sheppard, No. 64571*, Court of Common Pleas, County of Cuyahoga, State of Ohio, 1954.

Turkel, Henry W. "Merits of the Present Coroner System." *Journal of the American Medical Association 153*, November 21, 1953.

Winter, Howard. "Not Guilty As Charged." *Man's Magazine*. October 1955.

John F. Kennedy

Blakey, G. Robert, and Richard Billings. *Fatal Hour: The Assassination of President Kennedy By Organized Crime*. New York: Berkley Books, 1992.

Brown, Walt. *The People v. Lee Harvey Oswald*. New York: Carroll & Graf Publishers Inc., 1992.

Cockburn, Leslie. *Out of Control*. London: Bloomsbury Publishing Ltd., 1987

Davis, John. *Mafia Kingfish: Carlos Marcello and the Assassination of John F. Kennedy*. New York: Signet, 1989.

DiEugenio, James. *Destiny Betrayed: JFK, Cuba, and the Garrison Case*. New York: Sheridan Square Press, Inc., 1992.

Fonzi, Gaeton. *The Last Investigation*. New York: Thunder's Mouth Press, 1993.

Freemantle, Brian. *CIA*. New York: Stein and Day, 1983.

Garrison, Jim. *On the Trail of the Assassins*. New York: Warner Books, Inc., 1988.

Griffith, Michael T. *Compelling Evidence: A New Look at the Assassination of President Kennedy*. Grand Prairie, TX: JFK-Lancer Productions and Publications, 1996.

Groden, Robert J. *The Killing of a President: The Complete Photographic Record of the JFK Assassination, the Conspiracy, and the Cover-Up*. New York: Viking Studio Books, 1993.

Haldeman, H.R. *The Ends of Power*. New York: Times Books, 1978.

Hunt, Linda. *Secret Agenda: The United States Government, Nazi Scientists, and Project Paperclip, 1945-1990*. New York: St. Martin's Press, 1991.

Hurt, Henry. *Reasonable Doubt: An Investigation into the Assassination of John F. Kennedy*. New York: Holt, Rinehart and Winston, 1985.

Lane, Mark. *Plausible Denial: Was the CIA Involved in the Assassination of JFK?* New York: Thunder's Mouth Press, 1991.

————. *Rush to Judgment*. New York: Thunder's Mouth Press, 1992.

Lifton, David. *Best Evidence*. New York: Carroll & Graf Publishers, Inc., 1988.

Livingstone, Harrison Edward. *High Treason 2*. New York: Carroll & Graf Publishers, Inc., 1989.

————. *Killing the Truth: Deceit and Deception in the JFK Case*. New York: Carroll & Graf Publishers, Inc., 1993.

Marchetti, Victor, and John D. Marks. *The CIA and the Cult of Intelligence*. New York: Alfred A. Knopf, 1974.

Marrs, Jim. *Crossfire: The Plot That Killed Kennedy*. New York: Carroll & Graf Publishers, Inc., 1989

Matthews, Jim, Publisher. *Four Dark Days in History*. Los Angeles: Special Publications, Inc., 1963.

Meagher, Sylvia. *Accessories After the Fact*. New York: Vintage Books, 1992.

Menninger, Bonar. *Mortal Error: The Shot That Killed JFK*. New York: St. Martin's Press, 1992.

Moore, Jim. *Conspiracy of One*. Fort Worth, TX: The Summit Group, 1991.

Myers, Dale. *With Malice: Lee Harvey Oswald and the Murder of Officer J.D. Tippit*. Milford, MI: Oak Cliff Press, 1998.

Newman, John M. *JFK and Vietnam: Deception, Intrigue and the Struggle for Power*. New York: Warner Books, 1992.

North, Mark. *Act of Treason: The Role of J. Edgar Hoover in the Assassination of President Kennedy*. New York: Carroll & Graf Publishers, Inc., 1991.

O'Neill, Tip, with William Novak. *Man of the House: The Life and Political Memoirs of Speaker Tip O'Neill*. New York: St. Martin's Press, 1987.

Osborne, Burl. *The Day JFK Died—Thirty Years Later*. Kansas City, MO: Andrews and McMeel, 1993.

Parmet, Herbert S. *JFK: The Presidency of John F. Kennedy*. New York: Penguin Books, 1984.

Posner, Gerald. *Case Closed: Lee Harvey Oswald and the Assassination of JFK*. New York: Random House, 1993.

Prados, John. *Presidents' Secret Wars: CIA and Pentagon Covert Operations Since World War II*. New York: William Morrow and Company, Inc., 1986.

Russell, Dick. *The Man Who Knew Too Much*. New York: Carroll & Graf Publishers, Inc., 1992.

Savage, Gary. *First Day Evidence*. Monroe, LA: The Shoppe Press, 1993.

Scheim, David S. *The Mafia Killed President Kennedy*. London: Virgin Publishing, Ltd., 1992.

Smith, Matthew. *JFK: The Second Plot*. Edinburgh: Mainstream Publishing, Ltd., 1992.

Summers, Anthony. *Conspiracy: The Definitive Book on the JFK Assassination*. New York: Paragon House, 1989.

———. *Official and Confidential: The Secret Life of J. Edgar Hoover*. London: Victor Gollancz, 1993.

The Saturday Evening Post. December 2, 1967.

The Warren Commission Report. Washington, D.C.: Government Printing Office, 1964.

Trask, Richard. *Pictures of the Pain. Photography and the Assassination of President Kennedy*. Danvers, MA: Yeoman Press, 1994.

Valentine, Douglas. *The Phoenix Program*. New York: Avon books, 1990.

Vankin, Jonathan. *Conspiracies, Cover-Ups and Crimes*. New York: Dell Publishing, 1992.

Weberman, Alan J., and Michael Canfield. *Coup D' Etat in America: The CIA and the Assassination of John F. Kennedy*. San Francisco: Quick American Archives, 1992.

Weisberg, Harold. *Never Again.* New York: Carroll & Graf Publishers, Inc., 1995.

Vincent Foster

Adams, James Ring. "The Obstructionists." *American Spectator,* April/May 1994.

Barnes, Fred. "Spinning Grief." *New Republic,* August 23, 1993.

Bernstein, Carl, and Bob Woodward. *All the President's Men.* New York: Simon & Schuster, 1974.

Boyer, Peter J. "Life After Vince." *The New Yorker*, September 11, 1995.

"Final Report of Special Committee to Investigate Whitewater Development Corporation and Related Matters." *Senate Report No. 104-280,* June 17, 1996.

Fineman, Howard, and Bob Cohn. "The Mystery of the White House Suicide." *Newsweek,* August 2, 1993.

Fiske, Robert B., Jr. "Report of the Independent Counsel in Re Vincent Foster, Jr." *Hearings,* June 30, 1994.

Geberth, Vernon J. *Practical Homicide Investigation: Tactics, Procedures, and Forensic Techniques.* Boca Raton, FL: CRC Press, 1993.

"Hearings Before the Committee on Banking, Housing and Urban Affairs on the Death of Vincent Foster." *United States Park Police Report,* July, 29, 1994.

Isikoff, Michael, and Mark Hosenball. "A Gentlemanly Lawyer Plays Political Hardball." *Newsweek,* February 19, 1996.

Jaynes, Gregory. "The Death of Hope." *Esquire,* November 1993.

Kellett, Michael. *The Murder of Vincent Foster.* Columbia, MD: CLS Publishing, 1995.

Mayer, Jane. "How Independent Is the Counsel?" *The New Yorker,* April, 1996.

Moldea, Dan E. *A Washington Tragedy: How the Death of Vincent Foster Ignited a Political Firestorm.* Washington, D.C.: Regnery Publishing, Inc., 1998.

Ruddy, Christopher. *The Strange Death of Vincent Foster: An Investigation.* New York: The Free Press, 1997.

———. *Vincent Foster: The Ruddy Investigation.* Western Journalism Center, 1995.

Stewart, James B. *Blood Sport: The President and His Adversaries.* New York: Simon & Schuster, 1996.

JonBenet Ramsey

Bardack, Ann Louise. *Vanity Fair,* September 1997.

Hodges, Andrew G. *A Mother Gone Bad.* Birmingham, AL: Village House Publisers, 1998.

Ramsey, John, and Patsy Ramsey. *The Death Of Innocence*. Nashville, TN: Thomas Nelson Publishers, 2000.

Schiller, Lawrence. *Perfect Murder, Perfect Town*. New York: HarperCollins, 1999.

"This Murder Is Ours." *Time,* January 20, 1997.

Wecht, Cyril, and Charles Bosworth, Jr. *Who Killed JonBenet Ramsey ?* New York: Penguin Group, 1998.

O. J. Simpson

Aaseng, Nathan. *The O. J. Simpson Trial: What It Shows Us About Our Legal System*. New York: Walker Publishing Company, Inc., 1996

Baker, Paul R. *Stanny, The Gilded Life of Stanford White*. New York: The Free Press, 1989.

Barbieri, Paula. *The Other Woman: My Years With O.J. Simpson*. New York: Warner Books, 1997.

Barker, Teri. *I'm Not Dancing Anymore: O. J. Simpson's Niece Speaks Her Mind*. New York: Kensington Publishing Corporation, 1998.

Bender, David. *Confessions of O. J. Simpson: A Work of Fiction*. New York: Berkley Publishing Group, 1997.

Bosco, Joseph. *A Problem of Evidence: How the Prosecution Freed O.J. Simpson*. New York: William Morrow & Company, 1996.

Branch, Edgar M., ed. *Clemens of the Call*. Berkeley, CA: University of California Press, 1969.

Bugliosi, Vincent T. *Outrage: The Five Reasons Why O. J. Simpson Got Away With Murder*. New York: Dell Publishing Company, 1997.

Butler, Paul. "Racially Based Jury Nullification: Black Power in the Criminal Justice System." *Yale Law Journal*, Volume 105, December 1995.

Carpozi, George, Jr. *The Lies of O. J. Simpson*. New York: Celeb Publishing, Inc., 1995.

Cerasini, Mark A. *O. J. Simpson: American Hero, American Tragedy*. New York: Kensington Publishing Corporation, 1994.

Clark, Marsha. *Without A Doubt*. New York: Penguin USA, 1998.

Cochran, Johnnie L., with Tim Rutten. *Journey To Justice*. New York: Ballantine Books, 1996.

Cooley, Amanda, et al. *Madam Foreman: A Rush to Judgment?* West Hollywood, CA: Dove Books, 1995.

Davis, Don. *Fallen Hero*. New York: St. Martin's Press, 1994.

Dershowitz, Alan M. *The Abuse Excuse*. Boston: Little, Brown, 1994.

"Developments in the Law: Legal Responses to Domestic Violence." *Harvard Law Review 1498,* 1993.

Duane, James Joseph. "What Message Are We Sending to Criminal Jurors When We Ask Them to 'Send a Message' with Their Verdict?" *American Journal of Criminal Law 565*, 1995.

Dunne, Dominick. *Another City, Not My Own: A Novel in the Form of a Memoir.* New York: Random House, 1998.

Eliot, Marc. *Kato Kaelin: The Whole Truth.* New York: HarperCollins, 1995.

Fuhrman, Mark. *Murder In Brentwood.* Washington, D.C.: Regnery Publishing, Inc., 1997.

Geis, Gilbert. *Crimes of the Century: From Leopold and Loeb to O. J. Simpson.* Boston: Northeastern University Press, 1998.

Hastie, Reid, et al. *Inside the Jury.* Cambridge: Harvard University Press, 1983

Hunt, Darnell M. *O. J. Simpson Facts and Fictions: News Ritual in the Construction of Reality.* New York: Cambridge University Press, 1999.

Justice, Loretta. *Trial of the Century: Obstruction of Justice: Viewpoint of a Trial Watcher.* Brookline, MA: Branden Publishing Company, 1996.

Knox, Michael, with Mike Walker. *The Private Diary of an O. J. Juror.* West Hollywood, California: Dove Books, 1995.

Lange, Tom, and Philip Vannatter, as told to Dan E. Moldea. *Evidence Dismissed: The Inside Story of the Police Investigation of O. J. Simpson.* New York: Pocket Books, 1997.

Linedecker, Clifford L. *Marcia Clark.* New York: Kensington Publishing Corporation, 1995.

Lockhart, L. L. "A Reexamination of the Effects of Race and Social Class on the Incidence of Marital Violence: A Search for More Differences." *Journal of Marriage and Family 603,* 1987.

Morrison, Tom. *Birth of a Nationhood: Gaze, Script and Spectacle in the O. J. Simpson Trial.* New York: Pantheon Books, 1997.

Pearson, Edmund. *The Trial of Lizzie Borden.* New York: Random House, 1984.

Resnick, Faye D., with Mike Walker. *Nicole Brown Simpson: The Private Diary of a Life Interrupted.* West Hollywood, CA: Dove Books, 1994.

Rice, Earle. *The O. J. Simpson Trial.* San Diego, CA: Lucent Books, 1997.

Schmalleger, Frank. *Trial of the Century: People of the State of California v. Orenthal James Simpson.* New York: Prentice Hall, 1996.

Schuetz, Janice E. *The O. J. Simpson Trials: Rhetoric, Media, and the Law.* Carbondale, IL: Southern Illinois University Press, 1999.

Shapiro, Robert L., with Larkin Warren. *The Search for Justice.* New York: Warner Books, 1996.

Shapiro, Robert. "Secrets of a Celebrity Lawyer: How O. J.'s Chief Strategist Works the Press." *Columbia Journalism Review*, Volume 33, September 1, 1994.

Simpson, O. J. *I Want to Tell You.* Boston: Little, Brown, 1995.

Spence, Gerry L. *O. J. the Last Word: The Death of Justice.* New York: St. Martin's Press, 1998.

The Family of Ron Goldman, with William and Marilyn Hoffer. *His Name Is Ron: Our Search for Justice.* New York: William Morrow and Company, 1997.

Thomas, Evan. "Day and Night." *Newsweek,* August 29, 1994.

Toobin, Jeffrey. *The Run of His Life: The People v. O. J. Simpson.* New York: Random House, 1996.

Uelmen, Gerald F. *Lessons From the Trial: The People v. O. J. Simpson.* Kansas City, MO: Andrews and McNeel, 1996.

Wecht, Cyril. *Grave Secrets: A Leading Forensic Expert Reveals the Startling Truth About O. J. Simpson.* New York: Onyx Books, 1996.

Selected Forensic Science Books and Articles

Some readers who are interested in researching forensic science may find the following material helpful.

Blaker, Alfred A. *Handbook for Scientific Photography.* Boston: Focal Press, 1989.

Bodziak, William J. *Footprint Impression Evidence.* Boca Raton, FL: CRC Press, 1990.

Cassidy, Michael J. *Footwear Identification.* Salem, OR: Lightning Powder Company, 1995.

De Forest, Peter et al. *Forensic Science—An Introduction to Criminalistics.* New York: McGraw-Hill, 1983.

Di Maio, Dominick J., and Vincent J. M. Di Maio. *Forensic Pathology.* Boca Raton, FL: CRC Press, 1989.

Di Maio, Vincent J. M. *Gunshot Wounds.* New York: Elsevier, 1985.

Dodd, B.E. "DNA Fingerprinting in Matters of Family and Crime." *Nature* 318, 1985.

Douglas, John E. et al. *Crime Classification Manual.* New York: Lexington Books, 1992.

Duckworth, John E. *Forensic Photography.* Springfield, IL: Charles C. Thomas, 1983.

Eckert, William G., and Stuart H. James. *Interpretation of Bloodstain Evidence at Crime Scenes.* New York: Elsevier, 1989.

Farley, Mark A., and James J. Harrington. *Forensic DNA Technology.* Boca Raton, FL: CRC Press, 1990.

Field, Annita T. *Fingerprint Handbook.* Springfield, IL: Charles C. Thomas, 1959.

Fisher, Barry. *Techniques of Crime Scene Investigation.* Boca Raton, FL: CRC Press, 1992.

Gaensslen, R., and Henry C. Lee. *Forensic Science: An Introduction to Criminalistics.* New York: McGraw-Hill, 1983.

Geberth, Vernon J. *Practical Homicide Investigation.* Boca Raton, FL: CRC Press, 1996.

Gerber, Samuel M., ed. *Chemistry and Crime*. Washington, D.C.: American Chemical Society, 1983.

Giannelli, Paul C., and Edward J. Imwinkelried. *Scientific Evidence*. Charlottesville, VA: The Michie Company, 1993.

Gill, P., et al. "Forensic Application of DNA 'Fingerprints.'" *Nature 318,* 1985.

Hilton, Ordway. *Scientific Examination of Questioned Documents*. Boca Raton, FL: CRC Press, 1982.

Jeffreys, A. J. "Raising the Dead and Buried." *Nature 312*, 1984.

Jeffreys, A. J., et al. "Hypervariable 'Minisatellite' Regions in Human DNA." *Nature 314,* 1985.

———, "Individual-Specific 'Fingerprints' of Human DNA." *Nature 314,* 1985.

Kind, Stuart, and Michael Overman. *Science Against Crime*. London: Aldus Books, 1972.

Kirk, P. L. "The Ontogeny of Criminalistics." *Journal of Criminal Law, Criminology and Police Science*. Volume 54, 1963.

Kirk, P. L., and L. W. Bradford. *The Crime Laboratory: Organization and Operation*. Springfield, IL: Charles C. Thomas, 1965.

Lee, Henry C. *Crime Scene Investigation*. Taiwan, ROC: Central Police University Press, 1994.

———, "Forensic Science—Where Scientific Methods Are Used to Fight Crime." *Connecticut Journal of Science Education*. Volume 18, 1980.

Lee, Henry C., et al. *Physical Evidence*. Enfield, CT: Magnani & McCormick, Inc., 1995.

Lee, Henry C., and Robert E. Gaensslen, eds. *Advances in Fingerprint Technology*. Boca Raton, FL: CRC Press, 1991.

———, *Advances in Forensic Science*. New York: Elsevier, 1990.

MacDonell, Herbert L. *Bloodstain Patterns*. Corning, NY: Laboratory of Forensic Science, 1993.

Maehly, A., and R. L. Williams. *Forensic Science Progress*. Berlin: Springer-Verlag, 1988.

Marriner, Brian. *On Death's Bloody Trail*. New York: St. Martin's Press, 1991.

McDonald, Peter. *Tire Imprint Evidence*. Boca Raton, FL: CRC Press, 1989.

Noon, Randall. *Introduction to Forensic Engineering*. Boca Raton, FL: CRC Press, 1992.

Osterburgh, James W. *The Crime Laboratory: Case Studies of Scientific Criminal Investigations*. New York: Clark Boardman, 1982.

Osterburgh, James W., and Richard H. Ward. *Criminal Investigation*. Cincinnati, OH: Anderson Publishing Company, 1996.

Perry, W. L., et al. "The Autodegradation of Deoxyribonucleic Acid (DNA) in Human Rib Bone and Its Relationship to the Time Interval Since Death." *Journal of Forensic Science 33,* 1988.

Peterson, J. L. *Forensic Science.* New York: AMS, 1975.

Redsicker, David R. *The Practical Methodology of Forensic Photography.* New York: Elsevier, 1991.

Reichenbach, H. *The Rise of Scientific Philosophy.* Berkeley, CA: University of California Press, 1951.

Saferstein, Richard. *Criminalistics: An Introduction to Forensic Science.* Paramus, NJ: Prentice Hall, 1990.

————, *Forensic Science Handbook.* Paramus, NJ: Regents/Prentice Hall, 1993.

Serrill, M. S. "Forensic Sciences: Overburdened, Underutilized." *Police Magazine,* January 1979.

Thorwald, Jurgen. *Crime and Science: The New Frontier in Criminology,* trans. Richard and Clara Winston. New York: Harcourt, Brace & World, 1967.

Wecht, Cyril H. *Forensic Sciences.* New York: Matthew Bender, 1983.

————, *U.S. Medicolegal Autopsy Laws.* Arlington, VA: Information Resources Press, 1989.

Willard, H. F. "The Genomics of Long Tandem Arrays of Satellite DNA in the Human Genome." *Genome 31,* 1989.

Wood, D. J. "Commentary on the Law-Science Relationship in the Admissibility of Scientific Evidence." *Idea.* Volume 18, 1976.

Zonderman, Jon. *Beyond the Crime Lab* New York: John Wiley & Sons, 1990.

Zuckerman, A. A. S. *The Principles of Criminal Evidence.* Oxford: Clarendon Press, 1989.

<u>Newspapers</u>

As each story broke, some or all of the following newspapers featured the crime. It is not within the scope of this book to include every related news article about each of its seven crime stories. However, if the reader is inclined to research additional information, these newspapres are good sources.

Atlanta Journal & Constitution, Boston Globe, Boston Herald, Boulder (CO) Weekly, Chicago Sun-Times, Chicago Tribune, Cincinnati Enquirer, Daily Camera (CO), Dallas Morning News, Denver Post, Detroit Free Press, Hartford Courant, Houston Chronicle, Indianapolis Star, Knight Ridder Newspapers, Miami Herald, Minneapolis Star Tribune, New York Daily News, New York Post, New York Times, Orange County Register, Philadelphia Inquirer, Providence Journal-Bulletin, Rocky Mountain News (CO), Star-Ledger (NJ), St. Louis Post-Dispatch, USA Today, Wall Street Journal, Washington Post, Washington Times, Waterbury Republican-American (CT).